Praise for this book...

Taking New Paths *is an essential read for anyone seeking to gain a balanced understanding of why people question religious belief. Drawn from a wide variety of faith experiences, this book documents the common experiences of those who find that long held "truths" may indeed not be grounded in fact. It provides insight into why someone would come to that conclusion. How does one cope with it? What replaces one's beliefs? Do they indeed need replacement?* Taking News Paths *begins answering those questions.*
 —Isaac Carmignani, former Jehovah's Witness

Current Pew research shows that American religious practice and identification has dropped drastically in the last decade, and for those brave enough to walk away, this book serves as a manual for deconstruction and deconversion. It's a roadmap to a new kind of religious redemption... freedom FROM religion. The stories are candid, heartfelt and inspirational, and they create a new community to which the "nones" and "dones" are invited to belong.
 —Dr. Terri Daniel, Educator, Hospice Chaplain, Founder, The Conference on Death, Grief and Belief

Matheson's collection of essays is a must read for anyone experiencing a religious faith crisis, especially for those who were once the most committed. As a former true-believing Mormon, I immediately connected with the stories of Casey Corbridge and Brady. Both share compelling stories of pain, loss, and bewilderment that so often accompany those who find themselves in the maelstrom of losing the faith. Fortunately, the reader will also discover that the storm does pass with time, and a fresh journey of hope and renewal awaits.
 —David Hubble, former Mormon

This is a wonderful collection of escape stories! It shows that learning to think for yourself—to rebel from ideological mind control—is not only courageous. It is beautiful.
 —Dan Barker, Founder and Co-Chair of the Freedom From Religion Foundation

Taking New Paths
Stories of Leaving Religion

An Anthology

DOUG MATHESON

Copyright 2023 Doug Matheson

ISBN# 978-1-941052-68-6 Trade Paper
ISBN# 978-1-941052-69-3 eBook
Library of Congress Control Number:
2023943693

This is a collection of individual stories
from writers expressing their personal experiences.

All rights reserved.
No part of this book may be reproduced or
transmitted in any form or by any means,
electronic or mechanical, including photocopying,
recording or by any information storage and retrieval
system without written permission from the publisher.

Cover Design: Antelope Design

Published by

pronghornpress.org

This book is dedicated to all those who have experienced, are experiencing, or will experience the deep internal confusion of re-evaluating the traditions and beliefs they grew up with, and the sense of loneliness that too often goes with that process. May you take some courage in knowing that you are not at all alone; you can grow past that feeling. And if you are one of those who nearly immediately found the intellectual freedom to question and freely explore, to be meaningful and joy-giving, may you still help others who might more slowly find that it does get better.

Table of Contents

Preface..11

Introduction...13

Chapter 1   Leaving Islam....................................17
Background: Sunni Muslim

Chapter 2   My Deconversion..............................27
Background: Evangelical Baptist

Chapter 3   My Exodus to Ex-mormonism..................33
Background: Latter Day Saint

Chapter 4   Leaving Catholicism and Christianity.......49
Background: Catholic

Chapter 5   Evidence 54
Background: Ultra-Orthodox Jew

Chapter 6   My Journey of Life...............................88
Background: Hindu

Chapter 7   My Roots, My Journey, My Present.........93
Background: Seventh-Day Adventist

Chapter 8   From Mind Control to Freely Thinking.....131
Background: Jehovah's Witness

Chapter 9   My Tapestry of Change........................149
Background: Shia Muslim

Chapter 10 Who Am I?...157
Background: Maronite Christian

Chapter 11 Precarious Faith..................................168
Background: Buddhist

Chapter 12 Two Changes Before a Final Exit..............186
Background: Latter Day Saint

Chapter 13 Comparing and Questioning.....................211
Background: Hindu & Sikh

Chapter 14 From Shattered Pieces to
            Freedom and Inner Peace........................217
Background: Seventh-Day Adventist

Chapter 15 My Journey as a Muslim Apostate.............238
Background: Sunni Muslim

Chapter 16 Out of Watchtower................................245
Background: Jehovah's Witness

Chapter 17 A Turbulent Journey from Judaism
            and Orthodoxy......................................252
Background: Modern Orthodox Jew

Chapter 18 My Anthology of Influences
            and Choices Re-Affirmed..........................275
Background: Christian Scientist

Afterword..289
Acknowledgments...291

Taking New Paths
Stories of Leaving Religion

An Anthology

Taking New Paths *Stories of Leaving Religion*

Preface

WHY THIS BOOK?
First, this book is not written for strong believers with the hope of convincing them to change. It is intended to help those who are living through the fog of re-evaluation, and are feeling alone. Today, as the numbers of people who find themselves midstream in this state of affairs significantly increases, many are seeking guidance and it can be appreciated when coming from others who share their struggle.

Changing religious identity can, and does, go in many directions. I've known Christians who became Muslim, Hindus who became Christian, and Buddhists who became Evangelical—we can all imagine the many possibilities—but this is not a book about changing religions but rather about leaving them behind and following a new path.

It is easy to see how outside observers may underestimate the degree of disorientation or even trauma that can go with abandoning the entirety of one's previous beliefs, understanding of life, sense of self, and social network. Many of these writers spent years feeling lost and isolated, confused, and not understood. Their stories may help others avoid feeling alone in their search as they find themselves

Preface

ignored by old friends and family, and paralyzed by not knowing how to seek a new path, new connections. While some of these contributors felt a need to use a pseudonym, this in no way lessens the value of their experiences.

Several points discussed in Enstedt, Larsson, and Mantsinen's *Handbook on Leaving Religion* (2019) explain that leaving involves more personally powerful factors than dogma. It involves "core identities," forming "new selves," "an overhaul of one's previous conception of self, a re-creation of one's way of being in the world." It can be a "crash," a "pulverization of my fortress," and because of this "it is rarely smooth." This earthshaking remake is not trivial or remotely easy. For anyone feeling an acute sense of need for professional help in this matter, you might consider The Secular Therapy Project; seculartherapy.org.

Amidst the wide-ranging variety of religious backgrounds, the length of the re-evaluative process, and age at the point of writing (some in their twenties extending to one man in his nineties) also vary greatly. And besides a good number of Americans, this book also includes stories of re-evaluation and change in people from Bangladesh, Canada, India, Iran, Lebanon, Singapore, South Africa, and the United Kingdom.

Within these varied religious and cultural backgrounds, each struggle is unique, with those shared here merely revealing similarities in the search for a personal truth. Hopefully, some journeys may provide meaningful connections to what readers may be experiencing.

You will find that most of these authors have either mentioned, mid-chapter, various books that they found helpful, or at the end of their chapter provided a short list of books that they found to be perhaps disturbingly thought provoking, or simply helpful.

This book may also encourage those who remain in their faith to become cognizant of the risks that have historically gone with strong, unmoderated beliefs, and lead them to self-monitor so as to avoid those risks becoming realities in their own lives.

These personal stories of sincere struggle may also increase the public understanding of people who no longer claim any faith, and decrease the fears and suspicions toward such people. Being able to hear their stories is certainly one important way of coming to understand us.

Taking New Paths *Stories of Leaving Religion*

Introduction

IN COLLECTING these stories I have found too many personal narratives of change to include them all in this first volume. By way of introducing some of the thoughts of people reflecting on this process, I am sharing here snippets from several stories not included.

One gentleman, writing in his eighties, shared this crystal-clear memory from his first decade of life:

"My family was a member of the First Baptist Church, and we were very active participants in our church community. My first test of faith and reason was during a drive around the countryside after church one Sunday when I was about nine years old. My buddy's church was having a fair that weekend to raise money. I suggested we go to the fair, but my folks said it was a sin to gamble and drink and that we shouldn't go and be tempted by God. Sinning was the pathway to Hell. This blunt response startled me.

"My buddy was a Catholic and I said, 'Jim's not going to Hell.'"

"My Mom said, 'Oh, yes, I am afraid he is. You see, all Catholics are going to Hell, because they have not accepted the Lord Jesus Christ as their savior.'

Introduction

"'Jim was baptized as a baby,' I said.

"'But that doesn't count. He didn't make that decision himself.'

"I thought, hmm, he didn't make a decision to be in that family either, nor did I make a decision to be in my family. We just are. What makes my parents' views right and his parents' views wrong? His parents love him just as much as my parents love me. That question lingered for years and forged a wedge of doubt."

A woman shared that, from an unusually early age, her motto was "Question everything." As she matured, she added "Do no harm, but take no shit." She admits to sensing an urgency, "because life is too short for prolonged mistakes, years lost."

Facing that she can be "raw and blunt, because why waste time and beat around the bush?" she tells of hearing some friends from backgrounds of strong faith describe abuse they had endured, and then being very bugged "that some of them were still deeply involved to the point of raising their children that way, even after such horrible experiences."

Pointing to a very different problem, she calls religion the "peddler's disease" because it's like "an earworm that, in a sense, can whisper in one's mind when one is in their loneliest or most desperate hour."

Evaluating her motives, she notes that, "I volunteer in my free time not for a so-called afterlife in heaven, but because I can and want to help people, and feel useful." Recognizing that some are amazed at her willingness to critique religion, she observes that, "There was a time when people were killed for speaking out against the churches and religions of the world. People still are killed in other countries." Looking back at historical context, she states simply, "Religion has taken millions of lives."

Another person shared a more politicized view that today's combination of Christianity and capitalism which have come to strike her as very incongruous because of the "unrealistic economic ideals for everyone to attain, and unsustainable extraction, use, and pollution of natural resources. Mother Earth is weeping, weeping, weeping," she concludes.

For her there is a further contradiction in "all this heavy militarization of the world by the 'Superpowers' as the United States proclaims itself to be. From what I hear from Christians, Jesus is the true

Taking New Paths *Stories of Leaving Religion*

Super Power. So why would a country like the U.S. with a government that claims to be representative of a 'Christian' country—there's no hiding it—go military-obsessed around the world, establishing some eight hundred bases, spending the largest percentage of U.S. taxpayer money on military proliferation?"

She goes on:

"What in the world does spirituality, and religion specifically, have to do with military might? I think of the military as devoid of spirituality, blind to the disastrous actions and consequences. Spiritually bankrupt. Stuck in the primal brain of fear. Destructive power with no saving grace. I cannot buy into any religion, organization, or belief, that is arrogant, violent, greedy, and duplicitous."

These isolated personal statements give the reader little life-context in which to begin to understand the writer's experiences and reasoning. It is my expectation that the chapters that fill this book will do that.

Taking New Paths *Stories of Leaving Religion*

1
Leaving Islam
Zainab

MY JOURNEY to leaving Islam began on the morning of September 11, 2001. Turning on the TV in my apartment in the Bronx that morning, walking to the hospital and experiencing the eerie silence of humans intently listening, news broadcasts repeatedly flashing images of carnage, and experiencing with all of New York City and the world the aftermath of what would become the single most important day in our lifetimes, so far, left me reeling.

I had last been on top of the World Trade Center building on the night of my twenty-fifth birthday the year before; I had first encountered the city in the subway network that pulsed with an ocean of humanity underneath those structures. I was gutted. I loved the city for what it meant to the world, and the more I learned about the perpetrators, the more conflicted I became about what it meant to be Muslim anymore.

Leaving Islam

If Muslims were celebrating and defending this tragedy, if my parents and their friends were beginning to embrace conspiracy theories in order to avoid self-examination, if this event was becoming a litmus test for identity in the Muslim world, then I would have to decide if I accepted such action being taken in my name. If I were going to call myself a Muslim anymore, I would have to do so in full support of the 9/11 attackers and their worldview. It was not enough, in my mind to try to explain it away by saying, this is not Islam.

The problem was, I had no idea what their worldview was. Just as it was for the majority of the world, my confrontation with radical Islamist theology started on that day and would eventually lead me through cleaving even closer to my faith before I would leave the fold for good.

I was born into a Muslim family and when I was four years old I was whisked away to the United Arab Emirates where I would experience my formative years. In addition to the regular subjects in school, all students also took Islamic Studies. Early Arabia was an alive place to me, where Prophet Muhammad grew up an orphan, raised by his grandfather and his wet nurse. I fasted and prayed and even believed in a God who watched my every move and angels who recorded my sins and good deeds. Islam tied me to family back home who sacrificed for Eid Ul Adha and gave our portion to the poor; it embedded itself in my sensory environment as the call to prayer five times a day.

I proudly fasted my first full day when I was seven years old, and throughout my early years prayed and read the Quran, reciting it aloud and memorizing large portions of it. I knew to cover my hair, perform the wudu, and pray in the proper way. I was taught that menstruation made me dirty and so I never touched the Quran during those times.

As a teenager, I learned to enact the expectations of my parents while struggling internally to emerge as my own self. Externally this split manifested in a different set of values from my parents, which I knew to keep hidden.

As a young Muslim woman I was unable to be fully myself in front of my parents without risking their disapproval or even condemnation. I did not have the words yet to describe what I was experiencing, and the lack of a safe space and supportive community drove the isolation deeper.

Taking New Paths *Stories of Leaving Religion*

For example, in my young mind, being a Muslim meant there was no room for questioning the rules that treated women as less than men. Only when I left home and encountered other perspectives did I even start to formulate the questions.

When I moved to the US for my training is also when I began to feel more comfortable in expressing my opinions without censoring myself for the first time in my life. That is when I started the necessary adulthood stage of questioning my own values.

I knew I was the Muslim child of Muslim parents, but I had never considered what I was outside of that construct, not until I was twenty-five years old and driven to it by the events of 9/11. This is when I began the process of confronting my own personal internal struggle with a part of my identity I had always believed was rock solid.

I would interact with other young Muslims in the west, also struggling to make sense of what had happened on that day. We would try to answer the question: was this sanctioned in our religion? And if it was, what were we supposed to do about it? In order to understand the religion was I born into I read widely from many sources, trying to find the truth embedded within the very framework of my beliefs as a person.

I needed to know where I stood on this question, as I was starting to have a family of my own, and we were raising them Muslim. I wore hijab for a while but never quite comfortably. I prayed and fasted, attending mosque and *halaqa* (Quran study), reading and interpreting Quranic scripture, listening to powerful preachers at the annual Islamic Society of North America conferences, immersing myself in Islam in a way I had never experienced in the Middle East.

I was living in the Midwest by the time retaliation in the form of war rained down in the search for fake WMDs and a dictator in a ditch. I anxiously watched targeted strikes on TV and the absurdity of an embed neurosurgeon reporting from Iraq while the U.S. government hunted for Saddam and the WMDs.

Meanwhile, the images would only fuel the transformation of Islam into a spreading Wahhabi monolith, recruiting Muslim youth from Asia, Africa, America, and Europe to the cause of defending the *Ummah (community)*.

I slowly became aware that Islam had become a geopolitical force while also being a source of identity for one billion people. Most disturbingly, the story of "jihad," or religious struggle, something I had never confronted before in my experience of it, was becoming central to its narrative.

Let me explain what I mean by that. In addition to the usual religious norms of belief, prayer, charity, pilgrimage, and fasting, which to me had always denoted the four walls and content of this religion, suddenly there was added jihad, or "internal struggle." This nascent idea that Islam was under attack and must be defended took root, galvanizing even moderate Muslims and reducing the tolerance for debate.

From where I stood, it appeared to be an absurdist mind trick: Islamists had succeeded in convincing Muslims around the world that their religion needed to be protected, and they had done it by destroying the World Trade Centers in Manhattan.

The years following this event, with the ill-conceived wars and violence against the people of Afghanistan and Iraq while rewarding the Saudi Arabian regime, would raise the stakes even higher: the narrative of the Muslim *Ummah* would become one of resistance against the American Empire. Criticizing Islam under these circumstances would take on more far reaching and dangerous connotations than ever before, inviting social and even legal consequences.

Questioning my beliefs would become more personally, and eventually more publicly, hazardous as my entire family would slowly adopt hijab, embracing the Muslim identity while losing their ties to Bengali culture and heritage. In time they would even come to reject the parts of Bengali culture that originated in Hindu rituals.

The Wahhabization of Bangladesh has occurred in my lifetime and has effectively driven a wedge between me and my extended family. The daytime massacre by machete of the Bengali-American secular blogger, Avijit Roy as he left a book fair in Dhaka, left me unable to feel safe anymore in the country of my birth. That this crime could not be prosecuted without inflaming Muslim sentiment left me with the realization that protesting such extra-judicial killing would involve taking on greater risk than I had expected.

In this way I have endured the consequences of questioning the religion that I had been born into and believed in for most of my life. I have become aware of Islam being used as a tool, both to advance the narrative of Muslims gaining their place at the table on

Taking New Paths *Stories of Leaving Religion*

the geopolitical stage, a positive outcome, while also being used to take away the freedoms of millions of women. Dissidents of Islam are treated like political prisoners, and yet Islam enjoys the protections offered to other non-political religions.

Take the example of Raif Badawi, creator of a website called Free Saudi Liberals, and arrested in 2012 on charges of "insulting Islam through electronic channels," which parts of this essay may qualify for such a crime as well. He is still imprisoned, awaiting the completion of ten years in prison in addition to a thousand lashes.

He endured fifty lashes on January 9, 2015, and the second flogging is yet to be scheduled given his failing health. He is thirty-five years old and has watched the world forget him while his wife and three children continue to live for the day he is released. This idea of "insult" as equal to injury is a dangerous orientalist sleight-of-hand at the heart of this term called Blasphemy. And it is used very effectively by those with bottomless financial means of immunity, like the Saudis, to commit human rights crimes while sitting on the UN Human Rights Council.

Blasphemy is not a real crime, and all blasphemy laws deserve to be rusticated to the dustbin heap of history. Instead, they are being used more frequently to silence Muslims and non-Muslims alike and terrorize individuals to remain quiet in the face of atrocities.

This increasingly popular charge of blasphemy has been wielded in many different instances leading to mob violence and murder in the name of Allah. Blasphemy laws exist in sixty-nine countries and are increasingly being used to target individuals for lynching or imprisonment.

In many cases the killers are celebrated as heroes for preserving the honor of Islam, and the presence of Blasphemy Laws allow them to escape prosecution. If the victim survives the attack, they are not only denied their measure of justice, but also black-balled as blasphemers deserving of death.

In yet another absurdist twist, Hindu extremists would adopt the same mob-fueled tactics against Indian Muslims by accusing them of disrespecting Hinduism by eating beef or marrying Hindu women, in what has become labeled "cow protection" and "love jihad" respectively. Terrible ideas, once found to be useful, lose their provenance and spread like spores released far and wide, falling on accidentally rich soil. In this case the Bharatiya Janata Party, which remains in power based on its long-standing persecution of Muslims in India, using the same playbook without irony, is exactly where this road logically leads.

The word Islamophobia has also become more prevalent and has now become indistinguishable from the rights of Muslims to protection from persecution. As a word, a phobia denotes an irrational fear, while irrational fear of a religion, i.e., Islamophobia, is conflated with the more dangerous Muslim-phobia, or irrational fear of Muslims.

It has now come to conflate any criticism of Islam with hatred towards Muslims. This has also occurred just over the Jordan River to the word Anti-Semitism as when it is conflated with legitimate criticism of Israel's policies towards the Palestinian people.

By using fear of persecution as a rallying cry, Muslim leaders are able to unite the majority of Muslims in opposition to any and all non-Muslims entities—whether Israel, Hinduism, or the American Empire, merely on the basis of identity.

Questioning Islam under these circumstances is to commit an act of treason, and questioning Islamic theocracy, whether Saudi or Iranian, is a crime punishable by death. The assassination of the journalist Jamal Khashoggi by agents of the Saudi government in the Saudi consulate in Turkey in 2018 serves as a chilling reminder of the reach and extra-judicial power of geopolitical Islam.

The geopolitical process that led us here had already started in the 1970s with the increasing Wahhabization of the Middle East and South Asian Muslim nations, including my own. It had been occurring, for example, under the surface through donations of oil money to fund madrassas in poor countries.

By the early 2000s, political Islam had reached a maturation point in many of these countries, where Islamically affiliated political parties had previously been a minor part of a larger, more secular coalition, but now had made significant political gains across the spectrum. This appeal of belonging to and identifying with a unifying set of social values led to a renewed sense of political purpose amongst the Muslim diaspora in the United States as well. And so, while I was going through my own personal crisis of faith, Islam would find its political voice in the heartland of America.

Encountering Islam as a set of human ideas in relationship to

Taking New Paths *Stories of Leaving Religion*

all human ideas, understanding the evolution of ideas over time, the necessity of religious thinking for an early primitive people to find meaning in their existence, began to take root for me.

I finally had access to books like Reza Aslan's *No God But God,* an excellently written historical account of the early years of Islam. While reading it and other books like it, I realized that once placed into language, which read more like secular descriptions of people from history who were encountering their own special set of circumstances the best they could, the stories of Islam became for me what they are—human stories encoded in scriptural garb compiled over hundreds of years, no more mystical or powerful than Greek mythology. Necessary, yes. Prescriptive and functional in a modern secular world, no.

Certainly, there were lessons for humanity, as there are in any literary, religious, or spiritual tradition, but I was growing wary of the ascendency of the more fundamentalist branches of Islam to geopolitical power in the twenty-first century.

I could not reconcile my own growing understanding of human rights with the application of Sharia principles to the present, day-to-day functioning of Muslims. Public beheading and hand amputations are enshrined in Sharia Law and nowhere have I found a legitimate condemnation of this practice.

I would think this alone would disqualify an Islamic Theocracy as a legitimate geopolitical force on the world stage. But no, Saudi Arabia gained enough votes to sit on the Human Rights Council from 2017-2019 despite this track record. That the right of women to drive a car continues to be an ongoing debate is the tragic consequence of trying to reconcile seventh century values with twenty-first century modern life.

More recently, the reaction to the beheading of Samuel Paty has been met with condemnation of France for its heavy-handed stance towards extremists, thousands of Muslims taking to the streets in support of the beheading of a French school teacher for showing cartoons in a class on free speech. The concept of blasphemy is medieval at best, and the realization that the last frontier of free speech would be in Voltaire's France, is ironic. That vast swathes of Muslims can condemn the French in defense of such a barbaric act, is to me unthinkable as a rational human being.

Leaving Islam

For those who wonder, Muhammad was a man, and collective outrage when confronted with his image should be a subject of self-exploration for Muslims. Where did this idea come from? Why are we being led to this particular line in the sand? Unless Muslims ask themselves these questions, we will continue to see an expansion of this tolerance of intolerance, greater authoritarian overreach, and ultimately the rise of the far right and the seeds of the next World War.

Reactionaries begetting reactionaries, while outrage at the insult of religion is used as a trump card to gain the upper hand. I began to realize that we, as Muslims asking for a seat at the table, are responsible for what is done in our names, and unless we are willing to address these hypocrisies that undermine the fabric of stability that is necessary for multicultural societies to thrive, we are willfully ignoring our duty as global citizens who value the duniya (world) as much as we value the akhira (afterlife).

However, as I have attested to, asking questions of Islam is forbidden, and this particular mental block is one that I felt compelled to write about in the aftermath of yet another Islamic terrorist attack, this time closer to home in 2015 in San Bernardino, California. As a mother and pediatrician, the image of a woman with a six-month-old child, leaving her in the care of her grandmother the morning she and her husband planned to shoot up their own colleagues at the Inland Regional Center, a place where disabled children go for therapy, was for me the final shoe drop.

I was pulled into immediate identification with the shooter, particularly the young mother, Tashfeen Malik. I realized that just as I had identified with the 9/11 attackers, finding similarities with the background and experiences of Muslim boys and girls I went to school with in the UAE, I was now confronted with a much more personal link.

She was a woman I would have sat next to, spoken to, and tried to find common ground with. I even might have seen her baby as their doctor. I simply could not reconcile her image with that of a person responsible for the deadliest terrorist attack to occur in the U.S. since 9/11.

As a doctor and healer, I must ask, what are the experiences and ideas that bring one down such a path? Not just from a preventative

Taking New Paths *Stories of Leaving Religion*

standpoint, but from a place of understanding the internal shifts in psyche that must occur for a mother to face certain death so calmly. Is it possible to dissociate so completely from reality by believing so strongly in an afterlife?

These thoughts led me to do something I had never dared to do before: I wrote a Facebook post and came out as ex-Muslim to my family and friends and the world in one fell swoop. I described the inner mental landscape of trying to balance being a moderate Muslim in a reality where the extremists were co-opting the identity, and it was met immediately with outrage.

The initial volume of complaints triggered Facebook's algorithm and the post was removed until it was reviewed, found to be benign and re-instated a day later.

When I wrote that Facebook post, it was for me a moment of clarity in which I tried to describe "the wall," which seemed to stand between what I can only call my pre and post conversion consciousnesses. In a moment of rare vehemence, I wrote an essay on this topic, more as a thinking exercise, of trying to confront the truth.

That is what went viral. I was mortified but also overwhelmed. Many people wrote to me thanking me for speaking what they could not say, many wrote to me fearing for my safety, and many, frankly, wished me death for being an apostate.

What I was trying to describe is what Sam Harris calls "Waking Up." My believing self was in a dream, it feels like, one which I was completely unaware of the downstream consequences of my beliefs.

For example, I realized in that moment the danger that exists in the belief that life should be lived with a focus on the afterlife. I realized it had been this deadly laser-like focus on the afterlife that had caused this mother to abandon her only child in this world because she believed so completely in the existence of that afterife. And that she would happily do so, using the most deadly and violent means possible, was abhorrent to me. I couldn't mask it; it hit me deep. That I would have any values in common with such a woman shook me to my core.

I'll never forget that day, that crazy feeling of my words connecting with people so powerfully. I said a thing that seemed very dangerous at the time; That moderate Muslims had a choice to make,

Leaving Islam

to overcome their fear of blasphemy. If we were to behave responsibly, we had to be able to criticize the parts of our religion that no longer spoke to us and have the ability to modernize it.

What followed after that viral post meanders through loss, both personal and professional, a cost, both psychological and physical, but through it all I've come to be even more humble and grateful for the opportunity to have even the slice of life that I was able to get back. I envy young ex-Muslims, wishing I had unfettered my mind sooner than age forty.

In my head I no longer live with an awareness of a condition called "afterlife." There are no seventy-two virgins or rivers of milk and honey. These are the pornographic fantasies of nomadic mercenaries high on the same belief of divine intercession that colored every religion from the period.

All members of a modern society have an interest in ensuring that all religious ideas remain open to criticism and that the right to practice a religion is protected as much as the right to leave it. The animosity towards ex-Muslims keeps alive this idea of apostasy, a medieval concept bearing no modern judicial counterpart, and yet it is wielded as a tool to persecute dissenters and progressives alike.

I will end this essay by noting that I bear no ill will towards Muslims, and only seek to normalize critical thought about the religion and its ideas. That those ideas have real world consequences is what I have tried to demonstrate, through the lens of my own experience. Islam is now a geopolitical force as much as it is a religion, and as such the ideas embedded in it affect the future of every one in eight individuals on this planet. It was my personal choice to leave the religion. It is not my intent in writing this essay to persuade anyone to do the same, as these are personal decisions with far-reaching consequences.

Suggested Reading:
The Atheist Muslim, by Ali A. Rizvi

Taking New Paths *Stories of Leaving Religion*

2

My Deconversion
William Pate

I'VE OFTEN JOKED that I was born a Baptist because I was actually born in the Baptist hospital in Louisville, Kentucky. My family had a deep church background on both sides, but we didn't attend church throughout my childhood except for special events like Christmas and Easter plays. I think my dad just wasn't into it, so hadn't attended church much in his adult life.

My mom, supposedly, was "propositioned" by more than one deacon at the church she grew up in, and so decided church was not the place for her. Despite our non-churchgoing ways, I was keenly aware of God and faith throughout my childhood. Part of it was a little of that southern cultural Christianity, with the talk of the "Good Lord" and prayer coming out of every mouth, no matter how profane the rest of the time. But my mom's parents were very devout in their own way.

My Deconversion

I never heard my grandmom swear, and rarely my granddad. Their faith in God was the cornerstone of their lives, just not church attendance. My mom was the product of that upbringing, mixed with a '60s and '70s rebellion and selfishness, giving her a faith that seemed to come and go as needed, while still being culturally acceptable and somewhat a foundation in life.

When I reached the age of eleven or twelve, the magical "age of accountability," my mom suddenly decided that her kids' eternal destination was more important than her checkered history with the church, and we started attending the closest church to our house: the local Southern Baptist church.

Within a year, I had been convinced that I was destined for the same Hell as the worst serial killers and child abusers, and decided I wanted to be saved. I went forward at the "invitation" at the end of the Sunday morning service and was baptized in the evening service the same day.

I remember walking around the grocery store that afternoon feeling like I was walking on air. Within a couple of weeks, I had convinced all my neighborhood friends that becoming a Christian was the best thing in the world and had them all going to church as well.

I was a Christian's Christian. From the moment I walked down the aisle when I was thirteen, I poured my all into my faith. To be fair, I was a teenager and did teenager things. I was far from perfect, but the overarching theme of my life was church and Jesus.

Being a reasonably talented musician, I played in various worship groups from about the age of fourteen.

I taught Sunday School and other classes not long after I finished high school. I was in a Christian band that played youth groups and summer camps. I went to Bible college. I moved across the Atlantic to be a youth pastor. I started a Christian study resources business. I completed a BA degree in Christian Studies and was studying for the MA. My dream was to be either a church planter or a Bible college professor and I was working academically toward those goals when the wheels began to come off of my faith.

Taking New Paths *Stories of Leaving Religion*

I had always had a little bit of a rebellious streak running through my faith, probably because I felt there needed to be a reason for believing something other than church tradition or doctrine that wasn't based on the Bible. For example, despite my Southern Baptist affiliation and training, I simply didn't believe drinking alcohol was inherently wrong. I didn't believe "Republican" and "Christian" were synonymous.

I believed in asking questions. I believed that we grew and matured in our faith when we asked difficult questions rather than when we blindly accepted. I believed the God of the Bible was the "Ultimate Truth" and it was our job to dig beyond the easy answers in order to find out the truth, and I had absolute faith that, no matter how far we dug, what we would find would be Him as the result of our digging.

I wasn't immune to adversity, either. When my pregnant wife and I were planning our move to the UK for my first paid church job, we found out that the baby had major health issues, probably wouldn't survive the pregnancy, and definitely wouldn't survive after birth.

Despite this overwhelming news, we completed our move and found ourselves a mere twenty minutes from a children's hospital with a specialist unit dedicated to just the right subject. Also, thanks to my wife's citizenship and a letter from my new employer, we were covered by the health system for free.

Our son was born two months after we arrived, spent three weeks in intensive care, and survived. Since then, he has had more time in hospital than I can remember, innumerable surgeries including an organ transplant, and will be on medication for the rest of his life. He will turn seventeen next year.

All this was seen to be nothing short of answered prayer. Life was undeniably hard, but our faith sustained us and gave meaning to the suffering...until it didn't. I included this story for the simple fact that, as hard as it may be to imagine, this suffering absolutely did not cause me to question God or my faith in Him. It was our story, and we were proud to tell it.

But come to a place of questioning and doubt we did, and not in a way I would ever have expected. Imagine my surprise when a textbook for a biblical interpretation (hermeneutics) class—in an MA degree program at a devout evangelical college—told me the difficult

My Deconversion

truth that the Bible was not reliable. Obviously, it didn't say that in so many words, and that was not the intended take-away.

But what was I supposed to think when, for example, I found out that many people believe that much of the work attributed to the apostle Paul in the New Testament (in other words, most of the New Testament) was actually written by unknown others who simply used his name to lend weight to their words?

What was I to do with the argument for a long-lost "Q document," which was essentially source material for the Gospel writers? I mean, if at least two or three of those guys were physically present during Jesus' ministry and the others were getting their facts directly from eyewitnesses, why would they need a source document for their first-hand experience?

What was I to do with the fact that there are NO original writings still in existence that became the Bible, that the earliest documents we do have disagree with each other, and that no one, for hundreds of years after the time of Jesus, seemed to have been able to agree with what was authoritative and what was not? If the Bible was supposed to be The Word of God, these were serious problems.

So, I started going through the various options of biblical interpretation and church practice. I moved from being in the biblical inerrancy and infallibility camp (believing that the Bible is the perfect Word of God, without the possibility of error), to the progressive Christianity neighborhood of believing that the Bible isn't perfect but still gives us a great insight into God and what we should believe and do, to a very stark realization indeed: *the Bible is untrue.*

Not only is it untrue, it has been used, abused, edited, and rewritten over the centuries to control people and to reinforce itself and the structure of the Church it has given birth to.

In terms of my deconversion story, my loss of faith in the Bible is my loss of FAITH. I tried to maintain a faith in some hazy notion of a vaguely Bible-shaped God that could still be real even if the Bible wasn't a great representation of Him, but I just couldn't keep a hold on it.

The Bible is the basis of authority for the Christian faith, and if Christianity is to be believed, it must have a foundation. If the Bible is the foundation of Christianity, it has no firm basis for belief

Taking New Paths *Stories of Leaving Religion*

because the Bible is untrue. For me, the whole faith experience simply crumbled, ironically, like the proverbial house built on sand.

Unlike a standard Christian "testimony," there wasn't a sudden moment of decision for my deconversion. I can tell you the date, time, and place I decided to become a Christian, but not so for my apostasy. It simply melted away, slowly like mist in the morning sun. Some days I wrestled with questions, some days I didn't think about them at all.

Sometimes I contemplated meaning in life, most times I just lived. As time has gone on, the wrestling and contemplating have happened less and less. I must say, if I'm really honest, living life has been easier outside of faith.

I'm no longer running all my actions and thoughts through that filter and it's just easier. I'm not constantly "seeking God's will" and wringing my hands. I'm free to think what I actually think and not what I *should* think. I'm free to treat people according to actual real-life ethics rather than according to outdated prejudices.

So where does this all lead me to? I find myself on a different journey, yet in some ways not entirely different from my previous one. My struggling to find God's direction for my life is gone, to my great relief, but I am now left with the new struggle of being on the wrong side of forty, with a weird resume that has little application outside of the church cul-de-sac, and a degree that is nearly useless. In personal relationship terms, we live in a small community where most of the people I actually know are people I used to go to church with.

Thankfully, I haven't run into anyone at the grocery store yet, but I dread the time that I will. Also, my Facebook feed has gotten increasingly boring as I've hidden people who were filling it up with posts about all things Jesus-y that I just can't stomach any more.

Deconversion is hard. It is freeing, but it can be lonely. I am so absolutely grateful (if that is the right word to use, considering the subject) that my wife has been on the same road with me at the same time.

Also, recently I have begun to turn my vast experience in church life and my academic theological mind to helping others through

My Deconversion

the same journey I have been on, by writing a blog about deconversion, hoping that those struggling through the process will feel encouraged. In a strange way, I almost feel like I'm fulfilling my teaching and pastoring aspirations, yet working in the opposite direction.

I will be honest; sometimes I miss prayer. I miss the idea that there is purpose. I miss the assurance that someone powerful has my back. I miss being special to God. But that is all outweighed by relief. I don't have to search for God's extremely elusive "Will." I don't have to worry about not doing enough or not living up to God's expectations. I don't have to repress natural feelings or avoid certain behaviors that would otherwise be perfectly acceptable but are somehow "sinful" or don't do justice to a good God.

I feel like I have woken up out of a dream and am now operating in the real world. Deconversion is hard, but it is good, and I wouldn't go back, even if I had the choice.

Taking New Paths: Stories of Leaving Religion

3

My Exodus to Ex-mormonism
Brady

ON SEPTEMBER 16, 2018, I officially left the Mormon Church. This was a decision made in culmination of many things and because of the treatment and excommunication of a bishop who had been trying to lobby the church to prevent leaders from asking sexual questions in "worthiness interviews." His excommunication finally broke me.

But before I get into that, allow me to give you my background and story. I come from a long line of Mormons that goes back to the very beginning of the church. Both my maternal and paternal sides were converted in the first round of missionary efforts in Ireland (1840) and England (1837).

My paternal grandfather was an aide to Joseph Smith, the church's founder. He was at Carthage Jail when the founder was killed in a gunfight. Both paternal and maternal grandfathers were members

My Exodus to Ex-mormonism

of the Nauvoo Legion, the church's personal militia. My family was in the first group of Mormon Pioneers to reach Salt Lake City. From there, both sides of the family were sent to northern Arizona to settle the area for the church.

Flash forward to the late 1980s and you get to me. I was "born in the covenant," which means I was born into a Mormon family where the parents had been sealed together forever in the temple. This sealing also bonds any children that would be born to the couple. I am the fourth of six children.

Growing up in a Mormon family is very restrictive. From the beginning, we were very locked down. Television was allowed but only for certain shows and sports. We were very much encouraged to only have Mormon friends, unless we were willing to subject non-Mormon friends to church doctrine and church services.

Obviously, the dietary restrictions or "The Word of Wisdom" as it is called, were always enforced. No coffee, tea, alcohol, or tobacco are allowed. As a child, I would see people rationalize ways to get around these rules. To this day, family members of mine chew tobacco and drink teas. However, they aren't disciplined because the church is hemorrhaging members.

Church was three hours long every Sunday. It was split into three separate blocks, the first being a meeting of all members to take the sacrament. The sacrament is water and bread symbolizing the body and blood of Christ. The next meetings were classes split up by age groups. The last meeting was split by genders. I had mostly positive experiences during these meetings, other than the extreme boredom of church. It was always the same lessons, same rules, being taught in varying ways.

I was baptized at the age of eight. The doctrine states that children at the age of eight are mature enough to make an eternal commitment. I can definitively state that children at that age can barely commit to a favorite cereal, having seen my own children turn eight. I remember the water being cold. I was nervous because this was the first of many commitments one makes as a Mormon.

To be able to be baptized, one must submit to a worthiness interview. This interview was done by the bishop of the congregation. A good bishop will ask the basic questions:

Taking New Paths *Stories of Leaving Religion*

1. Do you believe that God is our Eternal Father? Do you believe that Jesus Christ is the Son of God and the Savior and Redeemer of the world?

2. Do you believe that the Church and gospel of Jesus Christ have been restored through the Prophet Joseph Smith? Do you believe that [current Church President] is a prophet of God? What does this mean to you?

3. What does it mean to you to repent? Do you feel that you have repented of your past transgressions?

4. Have you ever committed a serious crime? If so, are you now on probation or parole? Have you ever participated in an abortion? Have you ever committed a homosexual transgression?

5. You have been taught that membership in The Church of Jesus Christ of Latter-day Saints includes living gospel standards. What do you understand about the following standards? Are you willing to obey them?

a. The law of chastity, which prohibits any sexual relationship outside the bonds of a legal marriage between one man and one woman.

b. The law of tithing.

c. The Word of Wisdom.

d. The Sabbath day, including partaking of the sacrament weekly and rendering service to others.

6. When you are baptized, you covenant with God that you are willing to take upon yourself the name of Christ and keep His commandments throughout your life. Are you ready to make this covenant and strive to be faithful to it?

These questions are designed to weed out folks who would be detrimental to the church. I will comment more on these questions further along in my story.

My Exodus to Ex-mormonism

After I was baptized, I became extremely cautious. Not only could I commit sins through commission, but through omission as well. Trying to navigate through this moral minefield was extremely difficult for a young child.

I was an extremely impetuous child, so I could sin without a second thought. Something that made it worse was scripture. In *The Book of Mormon*, the "translated" scripture by Joseph Smith, it says "ye should be perfect even as I, or your Father who is in heaven is perfect." These were words supposedly spoken by Jesus. Although Mormons will deny that it literally means "be perfect" as a commandment, I took it very literally.

However, my insistence on piety was, at times, a huge impediment to my social development. That is until I attended junior high school. There I met some of my now life-long friends that are non-Mormon. They quickly accepted me for being a Mormon and lived what appeared to be their true authentic lives.

One of my friends was a Catholic Hispanic boy. I remember asking him, "Why isn't your religion looked at as harshly as mine?"

"Because you all still practice polygamy," he replied.

I snorted and responded, "Maybe back in Brigham Young times, but not now."

He looked at me. His eyes were sad with empathy as he said, "Homie, ask your parents. I guarantee it's still happening."

So, I did just that. I went home and asked my parents, point blank, whether it was true. At first my parents explained the "why" of polygamy. They said that so many of the men in the Mormon church were killed in the beginning that surviving men of importance needed to marry multiple wives so that these widows and spinsters would then be married women, and thus be safe in both getting across the plains and finally settling in new places.

I said, "Okay, that makes sense. But why did he say it's still happening?"

My parents looked at each other, straining to come up with a satisfactory response. My father started, "Well son, it technically is still happening. In the temple, your mom and I were sealed, remember? If Mom were to die, I could, if the Lord willed it, be sealed to my new wife as well."

Taking New Paths *Stories of Leaving Religion*

I was flabbergasted, "Mom, would you do the same thing if Dad died?"

My mom sighed, "No son, I am only sealed to your father."

I became a little frustrated, "How does any of that make sense? Why would Dad need a second woman? Wouldn't that take away from the love you have for Mom? For ETERNITY???"

My parents denied that there would be love lost or diminished.

It was at this moment that I first officially disagreed with the Mormon Church.

I took it in stride, my parents asking me to pray about it—that's a common Mormon tactic. My parents would take a step further and have me listen to my favorite instrumental song while thinking about the issue and then praying. How convenient that I became euphoric listening to the song and then experiencing a good feeling during and after praying. I had become Pavlov's dog.

During Junior High, I unknowingly met a gay person for the first time. Come to find out, there were quite a few of my friends who were in the closet; however, it was still taboo to speak about homosexuality. This will be a turning point for me later in life.

High school was interesting. I was a walking contradiction. In high school there is an optional class that Mormon students are socially required to take, called Seminary. I was really good at that class. I had a knack for memorization, and this served me well. I would impress the teacher and the female students.

This leads to part one of the contradiction. The law of chastity was a rule that I flirted with. I was sixteen to eighteen, and a male. Being talented in music, theater, and sports gave me a bit of an advantage over other males at school. I never fully broke it, but I got close. I always wondered why something was off limits if it felt so good.

Part two of my contradiction: I had a mouth like a sailor. I realize that to some this is a non-issue. However, growing up in a home where they wouldn't even say some of the "rougher" words in the Bible, this was a huge issue. I was pretty clever; I was always very aware of who was around. I was always looked at as the pious guy. I

My Exodus to Ex-mormonism

played the role, and it was always well received. I had leadership roles in every new church group that I aged into.

The biggest crisis of faith I had in high school was a doozy. From the age of fifteen, I had been the bass guitarist and singer in an alternative/punk band. The members of my band were adults; however, I was pretty good at what I did, so good that we received a recording contract from a label that was a subsidiary of Sony Records.

It was the most important artistic expression that I had at the time. We didn't swear in our music, it was pretty tame. Senior year of high school, we had formed a plan as a band to move to L.A. after I graduated so we could be closer to Sony Records. It was the dream that I'd had since I was a kid and picked up my first guitar. But then the Mormon Church and societal pressure reared its ugly head.

Mormon youth are encouraged to dedicate time to the church after high school graduation. At the time, if you were male, you were asked to spend two years, from ages of nineteen to twenty-one in full time missionary service away from your family and friends. It was a humongous taboo if you chose not to follow along with the norm.

I wanted to please my parents, the church leaders who had taught me, my siblings. I remember meeting with my bishop and parents. My bishop promised massive eternal blessings if I gave up my dreams. I was skeptical and spent weeks agonizing over the decision.

Finally, I called the band's leader and broke the news to him. It was terrible. I remember weeping on the phone. The response from him has stuck with me. He said, "Why are you giving up your dreams for a decision that makes you feel this bad?"

Preparing for a Mormon mission is a bit of work. The first step is the massive amount of paperwork required. They want to know everything about you— possible unresolved transgressions you have not confessed to your bishop, the missionary's and the parents' financials, and other information. At the time, it cost four hundred dollars a month to send a missionary on this service. No small feat for a family with six kids.

The second step is receiving your temple endowment and the

Taking New Paths *Stories of Leaving Religion*

Melchizedek priesthood. The Melchizedek priesthood is required for entry into the temple. Mormons believe that they have direct ability to pass down this priesthood through laying on of hands. The temple endowments are only allowed if you pass a beefed-up worthiness interview, similar to the other questions for baptism. However, one stuck out to me. "Do you support or promote any teachings, practices, or doctrine contrary to those of The Church of Jesus Christ of Latter-day Saints?" That question gave me pause because I disagreed with "Spiritual polygamy." I had to lie on that question.

The temple endowment was weird. I had attended baptisms for the dead in the temple, so I had at least been in the building. I remember being put into a jumpsuit and being anointed with oil. In my inner narrative I joked, "Am I about to be sacrificed?"

From there, you are dressed in all white with a large cloth envelope. You go through a line where they give you the name of the deceased who you are performing the endowment for and, if it is your first time through, they give you a special name that will be called during the final judgment. Years later I found out that the same name was given to male members of the church on the same day each month for about ten years.

From there you are sent to the endowment room where you are separated by gender. This wasn't too weird; it was only slightly disconcerting because the women were wearing largeish veils. I don't want to go into the whole process (all of that information is readily available on the internet). However, as I went through the ritual, I was embarrassed. I felt silly wearing Zeus type robes with an apron that looked like leaves and a semi-chef's-hat. My mind flashed a single thought: "Oh shit, am I in a cult?"

After my temple experience, I was ready to go on a mission. I had received a response, calling me to Mexico City West. As a missionary, you are not sent directly to your assignment. You are sent to a missionary training center. For me, I spent eight weeks in Provo, Utah. There I was taught to parrot Spanish phrases that were all based around teaching the gospel.

About five weeks in, I fell terribly ill. At first I thought, "Why am I so sick?" Mormons believe that through the "power of the Melchizedek priesthood" that they can summon Christ-like powers of healing.

My Exodus to Ex-mormonism

I had seven blessings performed on me from different "authority levels," the final being the President of the training center.

Nothing worked to give me reprieve. I was sent to a doctor outside of the church. After learning that I came from Arizona, the doctor sent me for a spinal tap. It resulted in a diagnosis of meningeal coccidioidomycosis, a life-long, incurable disease from a fungal spore in the dirt of the Sonoran Desert.

There was an upside after this spinal tap; I was ordered to drink caffeinated drinks. In the training center, caffeine was forbidden.

After my diagnosis, I was sent home for eight months to try to get healthy enough to return to the field. Those eight months were horrible. I was ostracized. It is quite taboo for a missionary to return early.

Most members figure an early returning missionary is ineligible to serve because they are not worthy. They create large narratives, mostly consisting of conjecture surrounding the law of chastity.

"I heard he had sex with a sister missionary in the MTC."

"Well, I heard it happened before his mission and he lied to get into the MTC."

These are things I overheard while walking through church. Even though my local leaders announced over the pulpit the reason why I was home, the rumors persisted. I lost friends through this misinformation, all because of the Mormon gossip mill.

I finally made it through eight months of hell, traveling three hours to see my doctor every other week, seven spinal taps and countless blood draws. After my doctor cleared me, I was reassigned to a mission in Northern California, still speaking Spanish. I mostly enjoyed the experience. It was difficult to learn a second language, however I managed.

Some fun recollections from my only eight months in the field: being spit on, chased off porches with machetes/guns/brooms and a lot of door slamming. Why were we being treated so poorly?

Proposition 8 was being argued in California and the Mormon church was its biggest backer. The proposition called for a pre-emptive ban on same sex marriage. I remember being confused at the hate we received. We weren't allowed on the internet except to email family. This was before smartphones, so we didn't have instant access to news and our monthly allowance did not help us afford the newspaper.

Taking New Paths *Stories of Leaving Religion*

My confusion became even more heightened when we went to the Oakland Temple one night. There were thousands of people protesting outside of the gates. To this small-town Arizona boy, this was terrifying, even though they were peaceful.

One is conditioned as a young Mormon to expect opposition. Joseph Smith was killed by an armed mob, there was a massacre at Sutter's Mill in Mormon history...the list goes on, and I was expecting to be a martyr.

There were some great things that came out of my mission. First of all, I acquired a second language that I am now able to use in my employment. I also gained a deeper love of the Mexican/Hispanic culture. I learned recipes from little *abuelitas* (grandmothers) and cooked on the grill with the men of the family.

I honestly became a part of every family I worked with. The best thing to come from my mission time—I met my wife. Not to worry; there was no fraternizing. However, I definitely pursued her after I went home. After eight months, my valley fever returned and I was honorably released.

I got employment speaking Spanish and pursued my wife. She finally came to visit and we were engaged shortly after. My family was very lukewarm towards her. The reason being that my wife is a loud, outspoken, European immigrant. Growing up, women in my family were supposed to be submissive. They were expected to stay out of philosophical/opinionated debates.

They would speak in private later about their own opinions. It was a very 1950s vibe. My wife railed against this mindset. She caused many arguments between my older brother, my father, and me. I wholeheartedly supported her, but the night before we were married, my older brother pointed out that I could "still pull out."

We were married in the temple in Portland, Oregon, and sealed together.

We settled in the Phoenix area. A month after we were married, I was laid off. In that time, my family continued to be a tad hostile to my wife, and we decided to move to Portland. In Portland, I found a job and started schooling. I really enjoyed the community college I attended; it was an enlightening experience. After two years in Portland, a major event occurred.

I met my first openly gay man. I know, I know, I was in Portland.

My Exodus to Ex-mormonism

Seems like that would have happened earlier. However, it was a life altering event for me.

Suddenly, all the conditioning from the church, and the experiences from my mission all came into focus. Gays are not evil or disgusting. This man had a husband and I saw no difference between their relationship and my own. On that day, I started to distance myself from the church, not because of history or offense, because of love.

I didn't immediately stop attending or not drinking alcohol/coffee. I actually continued to hold positions in the church leadership for my congregation. I served as the financial and membership clerk.

I was amazed at how much the church collected in tithing. The amount we sent to Salt Lake and did not redistribute through the congregation, was shocking. As the financial clerk, I cut the "welfare" checks. The checks barely covered bills for the poorest of the congregation.

To qualify, one had to go line by line through his or her expenses with the leadership. It seemed like a church as pious as the Mormon church would be more trusting of their membership.

Realizing that the church had billions of dollars in real estate and other financial holdings made me sick. The poor be damned; they needed a slush fund of billions. My connection with the church continued to wane.

In community college, I met a professor of religion. I had never actually studied world religions before college. The only information I knew about other religions was information that I could use to rebut them and convert them. I realized how much Mormonism was created by a fourteen year old, dishonest child who became an adult conman.

I began to realize how much of the Book of Mormon was plagiarized from the Bible. I began to truly study the history of the church and was appalled. Lies, murders, massacres, and polygamy were commonplace.

This professor spoke with me about Mormonism once; he didn't push me one way or another. He encouraged us to think critically, question everything.

While attending community college, I would eat lunch at a

Taking New Paths *Stories of Leaving Religion*

little pub down the street. Growing up as a descendant of the Ulster-Scots, I learned the traditional drinking songs with Stout, Whiskey, and Poitín the main focus of the lyrics.

One day, after my classes, I went to have lunch. I was actually wearing a Guinness shirt when I walked in the pub. I sat down and the waitress asked me what I wanted to drink. In a split second, I had made my decision. "Ma'am, I have never had a drop of alcohol and today is the day to remedy that. What do you recommend?"

The waitress glanced at my shirt and said with glee, "Holy shit! This is amazing! You're getting a pint of Guinness! Do you want a sampler first?"

I had to think about it. *What if I didn't like it?* Then I said, "I'll have the pint!"

Shortly after, she returned with a perfectly poured Guinness, with a beautiful head and richly brown. She sat down across from me, waiting in anticipation.

I picked it up and sniffed the head. The smell was incredible! I lifted it to my mouth and took a large swig and held it in my mouth. The flavor was incredible. How was I kept from this delicious nectar my whole life?! I swallowed and let out an audible "ahhhh" of happiness.

My waitress's eyes widened, "You like it?"

I smiled and responded, "I love it. Set me up a tab, I'll be here for a while." I ordered a fish sandwich and continued to drink my stout. I had two stouts and began to feel something that I would "feel" at church, when I "felt" the spirit, except this was actually real. Euphoria and excitement washed over me.

The waitress returned after the second stout and asked how I was doing.

I remember giving her a hug (don't worry, I had known her for months) and saying, "How about a Jameson?"

Again she giggled and then asked, "Single or double? Do you want a beer back?"

I again had to stop and think. I'd never ordered a shot, and what the hell was a "beer back?" I expressed my ignorance and she just smiled.

"Let's get you a single and a beer back." She returned with my order. She again watched me.

I sniffed the Jameson. Something in my subconscious

My Exodus to Ex-mormonism

activated, I could feel my ancestors calling. I sipped the Jameson. It was wondrous!

My waitress again laughed. "You know it's called a shot for a reason? You're supposed to drink it all at once!"

I was confused. *Why drink such wonderful nectar in one go and not savor it?* I complied and then began sipping the beer back.

Again she laughed, "You're supposed to do the same thing with beer back!" I had a couple more shots, without the beer back.

I got up to leave and she said," Oh no, honey, you're going to have some water and here's the control to the jukebox. You have to sober up."

I didn't feel "drunk" as I now know that feeling. But I complied with her wishes. I learned many things that day. Firstly, there is a reason Jesus drank wine. Two, people in bars are actually friendly and look out for each other. Three, the Word of Wisdom was bullshit.

As I continued through my crisis of faith, I became depressed. Not only was I doubting the church, but I was losing my faith in god. I remember having racing thoughts, some of self-harm, others of crippling doubt. I was all alone.

Both sides of my family are staunchly Mormon. I felt that I couldn't talk to my wife without upsetting/disappointing her. I suffered in silence for over a year.

One day, I was perusing YouTube. I decided to look up the term "atheist Mormon." One of the videos that popped up was a video of Richard Dawkins, speaking plainly about Joseph Smith. The second was a chapter of the audio book of *God Is Not Great* by Christopher Hitchens. Needless to say, I was hooked. I went from sadness to anger.

I attended Portland State to complete my bachelor's degree. I loved my time there. The best class I completed was Nietzschean Philosophy. It made me think even more for myself.

I also joined the Freethinkers group. It was mostly made up of atheists and agnostics. Luckily for me, they had a surprise in store. Richard Dawkins had been invited to PSU to do a book signing and Q&A session. I was one of the first in line. When I finally got to him, I smiled and said, "Thank you for helping me out of Mormonism."

Taking New Paths *Stories of Leaving Religion*

He chuckled and then asked, "Seriously? You were a Mormon?"

I replied in the affirmative.

He said, "I'd like to speak with you before the main event. Would you come to the green room?"

I enthusiastically agreed. No matter what anyone says, Richard Dawkins is one of the kindest people I have encountered. He earnestly listened and sympathetically nodded when I expressed my sadness and anger. He may appear strident, but he is far from that. He asked an assistant to take notes in our meeting. He gave me a hug after and thanked me for my time.

Over the next few months, I slowly started to share thought provoking quotes and posts on Facebook. Most of them were questions about Mormon history and doctrine. During this time, I was warned that if I kept it up, I would be disciplined by the church.

Both sides of the family were angrier than a kicked hornet's nest. I had to deal with a lot of guilting and name calling. My father-in-law was the calmest out of everyone.

He tried to have good conversations with me, but other family members would leave comments like: "I am so ashamed to have you in our family," "What is wrong with you? Are you a satanist?" "You should just leave the family if you are going to leave the church."

It put a major strain on the relationship with my wife. It was my fault; I was angry and dealing with anger from all sides. She got hit with the emotional shrapnel.

As I completed my bachelor's degree, I finally resigned from my positions at the church. Earlier that year, they had banned children of same sex marriages to be baptized until they were eighteen and denounced their parents relationship. Along with my resignation, I had announced I would not be attending church until the church changed their policies on gays.

My wife had started to see my side of things, because I had begun to calm down after many fervent talks with her. Things were getting so much better. However, my proclamation threw my parents into a frenzy. They came to visit for my graduation and acted very upbeat until Sunday.

My graduation was on a Sunday so there wasn't time for church. Sitting on the back porch after my graduation, the mood took

My Exodus to Ex-mormonism

a turn. It went from light banter to annoyance, then frustration, and then righteous indignation.

Here are some highlights from the conversation: "You are spitting in the face of your great grandparents," "You are breaking up our family," and the worst thing said was "You are spiritually abusing your wife and children by your actions."

Then I saw red. I remember holding a glass of water. It ended up shattered on the ground, supposedly I threw it down as I stood up. I remember shouting, "I am ashamed that you think so little of me. I am still the same son you raised. I love my wife and kids. If you honestly believe I am abusing my family spiritually, get the fuck out of my home and never come back. You are never welcome here again!"

With that, I turned around and stormed into my house. I remember walking in to check on my toddler son napping in his crib. All of a sudden, I heard my wife shouting at my parents, defending me. She told them they should be ashamed of themselves, and that she has never felt spiritually abused. She then asked them to leave. Promptly, I heard the slamming of car doors and they departed.

My wife and I became a stronger unit because of this. Over the next year she also stopped attending church. As I worked through my year of graduate school, my parents reached out many times, and we had tense but mostly respectful conversations.

We worked into a tense agreement that if they were to come for my graduate school graduation, no religious talk would be allowed. It was a one strike rule. Luckily, they followed through.

Promptly after graduation, we moved at least six hours away from both sides of the family. This was a blessing in disguise. We were able to truly branch out on our own. My wife was able to explore her own religious proclivities without pressure from her family. I started work in the fall.

One of the first days at work, a Mormon co-worker shuffled up next to me. He said, "So, you're Mormon right?"

I replied with a big smile, "Used to be."

He wasn't able to process that so he silently slunk away.

Other than a couple of blow-ups with both sides of the family, I began to heal. I started focusing on more important things instead of my anger for Mormonism. I began to completely ignore big Mormon

Taking New Paths *Stories of Leaving Religion*

events because they no longer mattered. I turned from anger to pity. I began to pity the members who would speak out.

I was lucky to not have been excommunicated; that would have been even more devastating to my family. However, this is where it all comes full circle. I had been contented for two years, not worrying about Mormonism, but then I heard about Sam Young.

Sam Young was a member of the church who had previously served as a Mormon bishop. He started collecting stories of grooming and abuse behind doors during child worthiness interviews for baptism. The stories of these monsters are atrocious.

Clergy can be called at random from the congregation to serve over hundreds of people. They are supposed to give marriage advice, rudimentary counseling, and interviewing of members for worthiness. These men are not background checked. They are called through the "power of discernment," meaning the spirit speaks through the leader tasked with finding a replacement.

Sam had been doing public displays in front of the main church office building because the church would not respond to his concerns. He went on a twenty-three day hunger strike and demonstration in front of the building. In the end, he was called in for a disciplinary meeting and excommunicated. The man wanted to protect children from predators and they excommunicated him for it. I remember watching him read the excommunication letter live.

I had an immediate visceral reaction—I wept. I remembered all the pain, loneliness, and anger I had experienced. I looked at my wife, tears streaming down my face and said, "It's time to fully resign my membership."

She was crying too with a look of fear. If I resigned, it would break our temple sealing. Although we weren't believers, we still lived in fear. She finally nodded and said, "I can't. It'll kill my parents. But I respect you and your decision."

Immediately thereafter I sent my letter through a free Utah excommunication lawyer.

Now that I am almost four years past this decision, I don't regret it at all. I have learned how to channel anger, listen to concerns without becoming upset or offended, and assert boundaries. I have learned compassion and acceptance of folks different from me. I can

My Exodus to Ex-mormonism

have philosophical debates and find common ground. There is a light at the end of the tunnel, even though it has taken years to get through it.

You can make it through. If you seek to love and understand, it will go even easier.

Taking New Paths: Stories of Leaving Religion

4
Leaving Catholicism and Other Forms of Christianity
Elizabeth

I GREW UP in a small town and did not experience much diversity, in any sense, during my first eighteen years of life. I am twenty-nine now and left the church when I was approximately twenty years old. There are many reasons why I stopped believing in god, and why I started to look down on Christianity, which may be best explained chronologically.

I was raised by a Catholic father and a protestant mother. My mother "converted" to Catholicism before getting married to my father because it was "what you are supposed to do." She received first

Leaving Catholicism and Other Forms of Christianity

communion and was confirmed into the church, just as I was. I was baptized when I was two months old, received my first communion at eight, and was confirmed at age fourteen.

When I received communion and was confirmed I had very little understanding of the world, my own religion, other religions, and of myself. I am still learning about all of these things and will always be until the day I die.

Once I reached high school, I became really interested in traveling the world, globalization, world poverty, religions that aren't well represented in the U.S., neglected tropical diseases, and in general, how other people on this planet live. I remember googling pictures of other countries.

I was disheartened to see that the first pictures when I googled "Mogadishu," the capital of Somalia, came up with images of large riots, dead people being dragged through the streets with ropes around their necks, and images of people with large weapons. I quickly realized a lot of this world didn't live like I do as an American.

When I left for college, I was faced with several hardships. Sexual abuse, being a victim of bullying, my parents divorcing, more sexual abuse, suffering from severe anxiety and anorexia, and the unexpected death of a friend. I remember screaming out to god, begging for help, and feeling as though I was never heard. I had family constantly telling me that if I prayed more, if I went to church more, then I would be happier and that would fix my problems.

I know that this was not a fair thing to say to someone struggling with PTSD, but I remembered that religion does bring comfort to many and so I kept trying to reach out to god. My religion did not bring me; comfort. It brought me shame and confusion and the feeling of hopelessness. I never felt that I was answered and felt that all progress I have made in life was due to my own hard work and perseverance.

My religion brought me fear. I was taught as a Catholic that though god was all loving, he should be feared. It seemed that although god created you in his image, could forgive your most horrible sins if

Taking New Paths *Stories of Leaving Religion*

you repented, and loved you more than you could ever comprehend. God also had absolutely no problem sending you to hell so that you could burn for all eternity.

I went to confession. I told the priest about how I called my friend's brother "stupid," how I pushed the cat off my lap, how I lied to my parents about cleaning my room. I said the Hail Mary's and Our Father's. I was scared. I didn't feel loved. I felt controlled. I felt obligated, restricted, and as though I was always walking on thin ice.

Learning and using the scientific method has been a big part of my reason for leaving religion. It was a major focus in my education in the biological sciences that I was encouraged to use outside of class. I feel the need for things of high importance to have credibility, proof, and reproducible results.

It's hard to say prayers are answered when those praying in Texas live in a developed world full of things, from simple all the way to excessive luxuries. But those in areas of sub-Saharan Africa, who pray just as much, do not have access to basic human needs.

It's hard to say, "God has a reason for everything" when you consider there are hospitals full of children with horrible forms of cancer that will take their lives, or why so many women on this planet are oppressed, sexually abused, and raped.

When you consider the number of children who die every year from malaria or for the horrific non-sensible amounts of violence seen in nearly every single nation on this planet, how are you supposed to believe this holy benevolent force is watching over you and protecting you? We simply lack proof of this "wonderful deity."

When topics such as violence, injustice, disease, etc. are brought up, I don't think it's fair to say "things happen for a reason" or try to blame it on the devil. How the devil works has never been explained clearly enough for us to know if something bad is his doing. It almost feels as though god allows the devil to do these things. At least, I've never heard of god trying to stop the devil doing all this harm on earth.

I know that religion is supposed to be a faith, and that you follow it blindly, without legitimate proof. But how can Christians say that Muslims are wrong (or vice versa)? Most Christians I know who feel this way know very little about Islam.

I know that behaviors like this poorly represent what

Leaving Catholicism and Other Forms of Christianity

Christianity is supposed to be like, but the overwhelming sense of "we are right and you are wrong" has destroyed "faith" and has become a divisive way to frame an "us versus them" dynamic that only caters to the ego and does nothing to validate one's faith.

In 2015, when I was twenty-two, I learned about modern day Satanism. I was taking an English course at my university and the theme was religion. We read books like *Life of Pi* and, though the class was not meant to be preachy, many of my classmates boasted about Christianity and how involved they were at their local church.

We were required to post on a class blog and when I had to write about religion, I decided to write about Satanism. I knew no one else would and I was sure no one would know that Satanism is probably not at all what they think it is.

I enjoy current Satanism as lead by the Satanic Temple (rather than LaVeyan Satanism as led by the Church of Satan that rose to fame in the 1960s by Anton LaVey). The Satanic Temple protests against making the U.S. a Christian nation and fights for religious pluralism and diversity. In reality, they fight for what the founding fathers fought for, except the Satanic Temple wears more leather and eyeliner.

I am twenty-seven now. I still enjoy cathedrals and certain religious ceremonies. I enjoy the history, the architecture, and the traditions—things I feel that most humans enjoy because it's simply a unique part of human culture.

I don't consider myself religious now, but I consider myself spiritual, even though that is now the most cliché thing to say. I like to believe that there is some type of unseen energy in this world that we can't quite explain. That maybe good things will happen if we do good things and focus on positive outcomes.

I would love to believe in an afterlife, but I have never been faced with any type of proof for one. Maybe one day I will find some sort of evidence, but I think it's also very reasonable to hypothesize that when we die, we simply die. I have spent most of my life feeling negative and cynical and sometimes I just want to feel hope and connection.

I know that hope and connection is why many stay devoted to

Taking New Paths *Stories of Leaving Religion*

their religion, but because I couldn't stay with mine, I made my own beliefs that are open for change and different interpretations.

For many years now, I have felt particularly connected with Buddhism because it does not have a god. I am fine with Buddha being a teacher that followers look up to. Buddhism does not instill fear into its constituents, nor does it try to tell you that everyone else is wrong and going to suffer in the afterlife.

If religion makes other people happier and nicer people, then I am happy for them. Religion did not make me happy, and I feel freer without it.

I do believe I would have reached this same conclusion had I not experienced all the trauma in my early twenties as I had already been questioning my beliefs for years. I feel that, at least in America, Christianity has become a divisive religion that in many ways creates more problems.

I enjoy things like Satanism that don't try to crush Christianity but plays devil's advocate to groups that try to undermine people of minority religions in the U.S. and fight for religious equality. I am not a Satanist, and I still read books about Buddhism but do not consider myself a Buddhist.

I think it's a shame that though I lead my life happily, I have a master's degree in biological sciences, I do volunteer work, I try to lead a respectful and peaceful life, I am still told my soul is destined to burn in hell, simply because I do not believe in god. The more I learn about this world the more I cannot fathom the possibility of an all-loving deity.

Would I ever change my beliefs if I were given concrete proof? Yes, I will always do my best to follow a path of truth and evidence, even if it means admitting I was wrong.

5
Evidence
Lauren Stoss

*All names changed
to protect the innocent, the guilty, and everything in between.*

THREE YEARS AFTER leaving my ultra-orthodox Jewish community I wrote: *It's difficult to explain why leaving is hard, why years later I'm still leaving. Why, in fact, I did not leave earlier? Why I would be sad to leave a life I was not happy to be in?*

Leaving a life, a world, a thing I have always been is not a day's work, or a week's, or a year's. How do you grieve for something when it isn't gone, when the one who is gone is you?

Taking New Paths *Stories of Leaving Religion*

The assembly room in our elementary school had a big enough stage for the whole first grade. We were standing there, all together, singing *Ma Tovu Ohalecha Yakov*, the first song in our new *siddurim*, our prayer books, which we would use every day to *daven*, to say nice things about Hashem and ask him for things. Hashem loves prayers from children especially, our teacher said so. The tears of children open the gates of the heavens.

I was so grown up! I would have my own *siddur*! The letters were big and bold, easy to read. We came up, one by one, to the front of the stage, and our school principal would give us our blue fabric hardcover *siddur*.

I stood on the stage, looking out at the audience of mommies and Babbies and Bubbies. All the other girls in my class were on stage with me. My mommy and Babby were there, too. I knew I was cute in my paper crown, that I would make everyone smile. Everyone said how cute I was, and they all liked to touch my red curly hair and say things like, "Wow look at this..." "...she's Annie," "...she's like Raggedy Ann," "...she's like Pipi Longstocking," "...she's like Anne of Green Gables," "...look how cute." I wanted them to see me get my *siddur*, my time to be the special one on stage. I liked making the grown-ups smile.

Holding my *siddur* close to my chest, singing the words of the morning prayer, a thought floated into my mind...*Just because you're davening, doesn't mean someone is listening....* I knew that was bad, very bad, very wrong. I looked at my classmates, in their patent leather shoes and construction paper crowns, and I knew none of them had ever thought that, not ever. I knew no one's mommy had ever thought that. Certainly, my teacher, who was mouthing the words to the song at the bottom of the stage, and pointing with an insisting finger to her smile, reminding us to smile, would never have thought that. My stomach felt funny.

I smiled and sang *Ma Tovu Ohalecha Yakov*, with the rest of my class. *Good, cute girls* daven *nicely and make their mommies smile.*

I don't remember deciding not to think that anymore. I do remember being really excited about my new *siddur*—it's probably still in my parents' house somewhere. It's an *aveirah*, a sin, to throw out a holy book, or anything with the name of Hashem written in it. If

Evidence

you want to get rid of it, the Torah commands you to bury it deep in the ground.

Did it truly happen this way? With every access, my memories are rewritten. I know this. I know about mistaken eyewitnesses, faulty human minds, and yet I cannot stop myself from looking at them, again and again. I rewrite them and rewrite them, with every review. What of the truth remains? I look and look but I cannot see clearly.

My most vivid memory of Niagara Falls is not of the Falls or the Maid of the Mist, but of the border. My mother told me when we were close to the great falls that I would see our border with Canada. I felt a rush of excitement. I did not remember ever seeing an international border before. Looking around, I searched for signs of the big line on the ground, the space, the crack in the earth... whatever it was the map meant with those lines. What did I think would be there? I can't even imagine it now. *Something.*

What I did see was a metal plate with writing on it that said "America/Canada." My mother positioned me in front of it to take a photo. She said this was the border, and all the other visiting people were standing, feet spread out, one in each country. I looked around. There was no difference between what was Canada and what was America. There were big, beautiful waterfalls, and people, and everything and everyone looked the same. The Falls crashed and roared and mist came up all around them on both sides, in both countries. They didn't seem to know they were supposed to be different. Not like us, we knew we were different, the chosen ones, Hashem's special people, *the light unto the nations.*

The grown-ups made this up, I thought. *It's all made up. There aren't any lines. The map is make-believe, it's a hopscotch board drawn in chalk. It's not real.* Everyone had decided on the rules of the game together, rules I didn't know.

I smiled, posed for photos, and did not share these thoughts. They were unclear, more a sense than an idea. Like the mist, I could feel them but could not touch them. It wasn't about religion, of course, except that it was. Doubt is a seed. It grows.

Taking New Paths *Stories of Leaving Religion*

I've seen many borders since then, between states and countries and contested political areas. I've seen the Berlin Wall remnants and the peace wall in Belfast and the guard towers in Hebron. They all left an impression, but Niagara's was the deepest. I want to go back in time and take that little girl by the hand, and tell her about natural borders and man-made borders and nationalism and ideology and tell her no, you're not crazy.

The grown-ups made this up. They made everything up.

The women's section in our *shul*, like many ultra-orthodox *shuls*, was in a balcony above the men, upstairs, where we could look down through curtains at the men as they prayed, but they could not see us. Looking upon a woman, hearing her voice, may distract them from their prayers. What would distract us was less relevant, of course. We were always less relevant.

"That's not what it means, girls. What it means is you are more special." I can still hear my teachers say over and over again, *"Kol kevudah bas melech penimah. All the honor of the princess is inside."* Be inside, quiet, modest. Our great biblical Matriarch, Sarah, the wife of Avraham, stayed in her tent. It says it in the Torah: *Sarah B'Ohel,* Sarah stayed in her tent. That means it is the role, the privilege, of the woman to be inside the home, her true domain, and she should not speak in public. When women speak too much, like the first woman, Chava, we cause men to do sin.

As a small child I wasn't expected to participate in the three-to-five hour Rosh Hashanah service, or the six-to-eight-hour Yom Kippur service, but when I passed Bat Mitzvah age at twelve I could no longer get away with reading books and playing hopscotch with the other kids in front of the *shul* instead of praying, and I took my place amongst the atoning adults.

That season of services in autumn filled me with dread every year, a dread that was compounded by the twenty-five-hour fast on Yom Kippur, a day I hated with a resentful but silent passion. The commandments not to eat or drink were bad enough, but the rule against brushing my teeth made me self-conscious and irritable. The last thing I wanted to do was talk to people when my breath smelled.

Evidence

During my many hours in *shul* I calculated, like a complicated math problem, how long it was taking the *chazan* to sing the prayers on the page, how many pages were left, and how long that meant we would be here, sitting down and then standing up again. I counted other women's shoes. I peeked through the curtain of the women's balcony and looked down at the men's section and counted black hats. I counted tiles. I read the English translation of the prayers. "We have sinned, we have sinned, we have sinned..." we chanted, beating our hearts with our right fists, our sins always collective. I read some of the juicier sins "improper thoughts, lewdness" and wondered if anyone in our *shul* had actually done one of them this year. I sort of hoped they had.

Mostly, though, I packed to move to Hawaii. Why Hawaii I'm not sure, but it was always Hawaii. I sat with my *machzor* open in front of me, my eyes passing over the words, sometimes even saying them, as I pictured packing, buying bathing suits and sandals and little umbrellas to put in drinks. The more detailed, the better. I pictured the airport, getting on the plane, knowing I was going to Hawaii. The knowing was the best part, and then I would return to the beginning, and start packing again. I could entertain myself for hours moving to Hawaii.

I went to Hawaii a few years ago. It was a lovely vacation, with beaches and volcanoes, but it was just a vacation. As it turns out, it was never Hawaii I was dreaming of. It was the plane.

Why couldn't I just be like everyone else? The other kids behaved, did what they were supposed to do, *davened* nicely. Why did I have to be so different? What was wrong with me?

"You were around three, maybe younger," so goes a story my mother tells, "and you were sucking your thumb in the backseat, and you said to me, 'Mommy, why did Hashem make cows? Why didn't he just make milk in the bottle?'"

I never could leave well enough alone. Everything is a question, always was. I can't just listen to a song and ignore the lyrics, dance to the beat. I want to know what it means, what everything *means*.

Taking New Paths *Stories of Leaving Religion*

When I was young, my parents would listen to The Beatles, and Simon and Garfunkel, Carol King and Billy Joel. Before I discovered the radio in high school, I used to listen to their music, which was English music, not kosher music, and therefore mildly scandalous. The Satan, my teacher told us once, could speak to our souls through goyish music. I was playing one of my favorite songs, Billy Joel's *Only The Good Die Young* in my room one day when I was a preteen, and my dad poked his head in the door.

"You know," he said, "that's not gospel music, right?"

"Gospel," I knew, was a kind of music black people sang in churches about Jesus, which was a Christian thing about a cross and had something to do with the Spanish Inquisition. The details of this were not clear to me. I thought it was obvious that this was not gospel, since I was not in a church, which was not permitted—it would be *Avodah Zara*, the worshipping of false idols, to go into a church. I must have looked confused.

"I mean, we don't believe in it. In what he's saying," he said.

"Oh!" I said. "Yeah I know that. I just like the music."

"Okay," he said. He lingered a moment, as if the conversation was not quite finished, and then left.

I knew Billy Joel said some bad things, like that only good people died young, when good people were supposed to be rewarded with long life, and bad people punished. Or the rewards and punishments would be given out in *Olam Habah*, The World to Come.

But Billy Joel also sang about that: "They say there's a heaven for those who will wait/Some say it's better but I say it ain't/I'd rather laugh with the sinners than cry with the saints/The sinners are much more fun." These were my favorite lyrics, and I agreed with him that sinners seemed more fun, and also that "they built you a temple and locked you away," which made me feel like someone was reading my mind. I liked that he said these things.

I wasn't too sure that only the good died young, though. I was reading some books about the Civil War and it seemed like lots of young soldiers died, just about my sister's age, sixteen. They died whether they were fighting on the side of keeping slaves or the side of freeing slaves. It seemed like good and bad people sometimes died young. Maybe Billy Joel didn't really get it. So far my teachers didn't get it either, or they would just say Hashem knows better than us.

Evidence

It was not much longer before my friends taught me to use the radio, and we found *NSYNC, and Eminem and Missy Elliot and Pink. These were more exciting things to listen to, clearly not meant for parents' ears, and I forgot about Billy Joel and the questions of what is and isn't the gospel of crime and punishment.

I heard *Only The Good Die Young* recently. It's not quite the song I thought it was when I was eleven. It's not a song about questioning religious beliefs and death. It's a song about a guy trying to talk a Catholic girl into having sex with him. "Come out, Virginia," he sings, "Don't let me wait. You Catholic girls start much too late... I might as well be the one."

As a teenager, I had never interacted in any personal way with a boy. The lives of boys and girls were entirely separated in our world. I had been in girls-only education since kindergarten. I never went to camp with a boy, had a friend who was a boy, even did any extracurricular activities with a boy. These lyrics had meant nothing to me, the unsubtle wink of the song I missed entirely.

No wonder, my father had hesitated. He was right to be worried about the song, about my ideas, but wrong about which ones. The Satan, the boogeyman of rebellion and change, can indeed speak to you through music, through books, through the ideas of the world. These ideas can threaten the walls so carefully built to keep the world out. The real dangers, though, the questions and the doubts, are not the barbarians at the gate. They come from within.

Was I truly the only one who had such thoughts? I know now that I wasn't. Why couldn't I have found someone to tell? Perhaps I really am making it up. Maybe if I had told them the truth it would have been okay? Why didn't I?

Midvar sheker tirchak, I learned. *Never tell a lie.*

My first memory of breaking a *halacha* and lying about it was roll-on deodorant. I had undoubtedly broken some rules before, especially regarding *davening*, an activity I always found interminably dull, or regarding television, which I often saw at my friend's' houses.

Taking New Paths *Stories of Leaving Religion*

The deodorant incident, however, feels like a different kind of rule breaking, its own category of offense.

It was summer, likely July, because it was early in my camp session, an eight-week marathon in sleepaway camp, an experience I had loved as a little girl. As one of the youngest kids in camp for a few years in a row, I enjoyed being the darling, and the center of attention, but also not scrutinized and bothered by parental figures. The adults in the camp thought I was cute, but they didn't care too much about my behavior as long as I didn't do anything disruptive.

Once I approached puberty, though, everything changed. Suddenly camp was as scrutinizing as school, perhaps more so. Our clothing was inspected with a gimlet eye by the camp Rebbetzin, the rabbi's wife. Our cubbies were examined, and goyish books or music confiscated. If I skipped out of *davening* to laze around outside the *shul* and play games with other campers, we were shushed and swatted back inside.

My bunkmates and I were all at the age, that edge-of-a-knife age where bras and periods have come for some but not all, the age of pimples and hair growing and suddenly not being allowed to speak to our male cousins. Deodorant was a new concept but we were catching on quickly. No one wanted to be the stinky girl in the bunk.

If you were lucky, you had older sisters to help you out. Most of the girls used Secret or similarly girlish deodorants, which made them smell powdery or flowery. My sister used a clear gel deodorant, and I followed her lead in all things puberty related. I tried her kind, which had the word "sport" on it, smelled vaguely like an air-conditioned room, and was clearly not made for eleven year old girls, or perhaps girls of any age. I loved it immediately. No more white streaks, no powder, and it really worked. Plus, I smelled like my seventeen year old sister, a smell I associated with sophistication, rebellion, and a devil–may-care attitude, which I was attempting unsuccessfully to cultivate.

Shabbos, of course, was another story, as it was for everything. Starting at sundown on Friday and ending "when three stars are visible in the night sky," or about an hour after sundown on Saturday, Shabbos, our Sabbath, was the axis on which our world turned. Shabbos was the day of rest, when Hashem rested at the creation of the world, and therefore work was forbidden. My mother would start cooking

Evidence

for Shabbos on Wednesday, and she would continue cooking on Thursday and Friday. Cooking was *muktzah*, forbidden on *Shabbos*, and therefore it all needed to be done in advance. What was *muktzah* was a bit confusing, because the ancient rules of *Shabbos* said things like "don't light a fire," and our sages then decided how those rules applied in our modern lives. Electricity, for example, was *muktzah* because it was like fire, or maybe it was fire, it wasn't clear to me. Destroying things was forbidden, which is why we were not allowed to tear toilet paper, and had to cut up rolls in advance.

If we saw a small child touch a light switch or a toy with batteries, we would gasp theatrically and say "no! It's *muktzah*!" Of course, Hashem isn't cruel and wouldn't blame a small child for touching something, this was more for *chinuch* purposes, to teach and train the child how to serve Hashem. You needed to learn early that *muktzah* was not to be touched on *Shabbos*.

The rules of *muktzah* were detailed and complicated, and often hard to comprehend. A pen was *muktzah*, and forbidden to pick up. This was not because it was actually *muktzah* to touch a pen, but because it was *muktzah* to create new things, including by writing, and if you were to touch the pen you might come to write. My teachers called this a *geder*, or a gate around the law, to protect us from actually breaking the law. It seemed like most Shabbos rules were gates created by our sages to protect us. I often wondered who decided what would be a geder. It was something called *Daas Torah*, and I knew this was passed down to us through our great leaders. Those leaders' writings were then discussed by other leaders and then they explained to us how to apply the rules to our lives.

Roll-on deodorant was *muktzah*, even though deodorant probably didn't exist in ancient times, because smearing things was working, somehow. The workaround for this, and there was always a workaround, was spray deodorant, which was not smearing. Every nice *frum* (observant) girl had both spray and roll-on deodorant. I tried a spray, but it always seemed to spray behind me, all over my clothes, or into my hair. This would require repeated sprays, which meant the smell was so strong, it would have come into the room several feet ahead of me.

I found it all quite confusing and decided to just keep using the clear roll-on deodorant Shabbos morning, since it was in my own

Taking New Paths *Stories of Leaving Religion*

room, no one could see me, and if Hashem was watching, it seemed truly ridiculous that he would care about this. Surely, I figured, the master of the universe has something better to do than worry about my armpits. If I was sinning, it seemed such a small sin that I couldn't imagine it would count against me too much. Considering how often I bit my tongue and wasn't *chutzpadik* when I wanted to be, Hashem could weigh my scale of *mitzvos* and *aveiros* out and the *mitzvos*, the good deeds, would win, for sure. I used the clear roll on deodorant, smearing away happily, without an ounce of guilt.

Summer camp, however, brought a new challenge: I didn't have my own room, and everyone could see. I brought the spray, intending to use it for Shabbos, but of course I didn't want to take my shirt off, which was just not done. My bunkmates and I, in our new bras, would change our clothes without ever revealing our skin, due to a powerful and heady combination of puberty-driven shame and modesty messaging. We would, with inventive Cirque du Soleil contortions, remove our bras and put our new shirts on one sleeve at a time under the soiled shirt, facing the wall so no accidental viewing might occur. My bunkmates all stuck their hands with the deodorant spray bottle under their shirts, and sprayed their armpits with their shirts already on. My lack of coordination was already an issue with the spray bottle even when I was stark naked. This task had become unimaginably difficult, and so I gave up and decided to apply the same solution I did at home: I used my "weekday" deodorant. I took up changing in the bathroom stall, in order to apply it without anyone looking and seeing my *aveirah*.

The exact details around how I was spotted are hazy now, but I was found out. Not by a counselor or a staff member, by a bunkmate. "You know you're not allowed to use that kind of deodorant on Shabbos," she said, assured that her counsel was welcome. The only explanation for this kind of outright sin was that I must not know the *halacha*. I would be grateful, surely, for her assistance in correcting me.

I don't remember my exact thoughts at this time. But I remember clearly what I said. "Oh, my father lets me," I told her, calmly and with equal assuredness. "It's our *minhag*," our family custom

She was silent, flummoxed. But she knew she wasn't wrong, she knew that, but she couldn't be more right than my father, who

Evidence

obviously knew our *minhag* better than she did. The division between *minhag* and *halacha* was a bit murky. *Minhag* could be the difference between waiting five hours or six hours after eating meat to have dairy, or exactly how long below your elbows your sleeves were supposed to be. It was possible that I was right, maybe it was my *minhag*, and she let it go without further questions.

    I don't remember planning this in any way, but in retrospect this was a fascinating lie. I knew I was lying, but I could have said, "Oh, I didn't know! Thanks for telling me!" This would have absolved me, and it was the answer she was expecting. The sheer chutzpah of it astounds me now. The bald-faced subterfuge of it. That I got away with it at all.

    This is my first memory of such a lie, a lie that isn't just a lie but a tale spun out, an obfuscation, a manipulation. It's the first one I remember, but there were so many others they blur together. Every ripped piece of toilet paper, every *davening* mouthed, every biblical lesson ignored while I dreamt of *Lord of the Rings*, every silent resentment, every active or passive resistance, each *aaseh* and *lo'saaseh* (positive and negative commandments) done and not done, it all added up to a castle in the sand, a life built of lies. The fear of being found out was constant.

    What if I had said "I don't want to use spray deodorant, so I don't. I don't really care about *muktzah*." What would have happened? Surely I would be sent away, everything I enjoyed would be taken from me. Everyone would look at me like I had *tzaraas*, leprosy, the biblical plague on sinners. If I said it, then it would be real. In my room alone at home it was between me and Hashem, so it wasn't real, because Hashem probably wasn't real. Right? I was not ready for it to be real. I did not choose this *derech,* the way. I took the course available to me, the well-worn path, the only clear direction.

    Those words,"I don't really care about this," were not said. If you had doubts, you kept them to yourself. In fact, no one else seemed to have any doubts. It was only me, but perhaps my doubts were not as well hidden as I thought.

Taking New Paths *Stories of Leaving Religion*

My mother was called into a meeting once with a middle school teacher, Morah Friedman, an older woman who seemed jolly at first but had the kind of watchful eye our older teachers sometimes had. My mother returned from this meeting, angry, and stated that Morah Friedman had said, "Your daughter has no interest in any religious studies," and my heart nearly stopped. I was discovered. I was found out.

"She's a crazy old lady," I told my mother. "I don't know what she is talking about." My mother looked at me closely, and after a few moments discussed something else, and never brought it up again.

How convincing can I have been? Morah Friedman saw through me, apparently easily. Was I really as good a liar as I remember?

This was after the deodorant incident, but before the day in class when an earnest student asked why the Torah doesn't talk more about women. "Girls who ask questions like that," our *Chumash* (Bible) teacher replied, "are trying to cause problems." Perhaps I had not yet learned which questions were trying to cause problems.

These days I am a terrible liar. My face shows all of my emotions. It's a wonder to me I ever managed to lie successfully. I wonder, too, about my young bunkmate, looking at my roll-on deodorant, who heard my lie: did she know it was a lie? She took the course available to her, the well worn path, the only clear direction; She believed that this was the *derech*. Everyone believes this: our path is the path, and we are all on it together. A lie in service of Hashem was not a lie, for Hashem was the Truth. *Midvar sheker tirchak*, never tell a lie, unless you have to, for Hashem, for your family, unless it is a righteous lie.

How can I explain how big the Holocaust was in my world? How I can't remember a time when I didn't know about it? How can I understand my own mind when its foundations were formed in the ghetto and in Auschwitz, in Ravensbruck, in slave labor camps and in hiding? What is the world when this is the story you must understand? Can I truly blame them for saying the world is not safe, when they were right? Can I fault them for their terror, for their blame, for their anger? What could have taken its place? What clay formed me, if not the clay of our fear and rage, bottled and bursting?

Evidence

"No one understands the mind of Hashem," the rabbi who was our *Chumash* teacher in high school said, "but we can look at what happened with this tsunami, and we can be amazed at how Hashem punishes the Muslims for what they are doing to us. I can't say that's the reason it happened, of course! Terrible thing. But in every generation, there is an Amalek, girls. And you know what the Torah says about Amalek. They should be wiped out. Obviously, we don't wish suffering on anyone, but it can't be a coincidence that the Indonesians are Muslims because there are no coincidences in Hashem's world."

In the bible, the Israelites are commanded by God to kill the nation of Amalek, and to wipe them out. Referencing Amalek can be metaphorical or literal to mean enemies that must be destroyed completely. The Muslims wanted us to die, we had been told, all of us; the suicide bombings in Israel proved it. The Nazis had wanted us to die, too, very recently.

The Nazis had been the Amalek of the last generation, our great biblical enemy, and my teachers told us, there is a new Amalek with every generation, trying to destroy us. "We can't say for sure it's the Muslims this time, since we never know who Amalek is, but it's possible. It's possible Amalek is only a metaphor, but it's also possible it's a real thing, like the Nazis were real. The whole world let the Nazis kill us and they all secretly wanted us to die."

Every girl in my class was the grandchild of Holocaust survivors, including me. We knew, we had learned, that the world wanted us to die, had always wanted us to die, and, unless they were one of the few precious Righteous Among the Nations, they would laugh while we were shot into pits. We had escaped the Nazis, just us few, and we were to have our revenge on them by not forgetting and never trusting and being faithful servants to Hashem. It was the Jews becoming unfaithful to Hashem, becoming assimilated and losing their faith, which made the Holocaust happen in the first place, just like our unfaithfulness had caused our exile from our Temple centuries ago. The world was secretly obsessed with us, because we were the Chosen, and if we didn't show Hashem we were good, the next Holocaust would be coming soon.

The rabbi said more things, but I was thinking about the map

Taking New Paths *Stories of Leaving Religion*

of the Indian Ocean I had seen in the *New York Times* that morning. I was sitting in my favorite spot, in the back corner of the room, between my three favorite friends, attempting to keep my thoughts to myself. The Indian Ocean was a place I had never considered until this week, when it was suddenly in the news.

It was 2004, and there had been an earthquake in the ocean, and then a tsunami, and very suddenly thousands of people had been swept away into the sea. The final numbers of dead had not yet come in, but the estimates were well over 100,000 people, and whole villages had just disappeared. Humanitarian aid efforts were underway. I read about it in the paper, and looked at maps of the area. It was hard to imagine what it could be like to have my whole family be swept away into the ocean, and have nothing left.

Our family got the news from the *New York Times*. We did not have a TV, and we did not get the *Yated* or the *Hamodia*, the *frum* papers. We did get the *Flatbush Jewish Journal*, the local *frum* weekly, which would appear on our doorstep. The *frum* papers had ads for the businesses near our house, and for matchmaking services and kosher-for-Passover hotels. You could find notices to hire someone in Jerusalem to pray for you at the Western Wall for forty days, to help you find a husband. They were in full color, and were considered very kosher: they would print no photos of women. My parents rolled their eyes when these papers were mentioned, or politely didn't roll their eyes in front of company. Many of our neighbors believed secular news was forbidden, *frum*, but my parents thought that was silly. Those people, my teachers and counselors who said secular news and books are *frum* and Muslims were Amalek, were crazy extremists, but we were normal, they told me. I did not question this assessment.

In the classroom, I carefully considered my morning reading about the tsunami, and made a list of what I knew. I knew that the country Indonesia was far away, that it was big, and that there were a lot of Muslims living there. I also knew they were a different kind of Muslim than the kind my rabbi meant. Or maybe they were the same kind, they just looked different. It wasn't clear to me from the articles in the paper and I wasn't sure how to find this out. They looked like Indian people, not like Arab people, and Arabs were the kind of Muslims the rabbi meant, or at least I thought they were, but I wasn't

Evidence

sure. Did that matter? Did the rabbi care how they looked? I didn't know any Indian people or Arab people or Indonesian people, and I doubted the rabbi did either. Since it was Hashem's job to know everything, it seemed like he shouldn't get confused about which Muslims they were.

Hashem rewarded good behavior and punished bad behavior, even for the goyim, so he should only drown bad people, but sometimes he did things we didn't understand. Sometimes bad things happened to good people and no one knew why and not even the rabbis knew, so maybe that's what happened to the Indonesians. I thought the Indonesians probably didn't care much about us, no matter what the rabbi said about them being Muslims who wanted us to die, because they had their own problems. I had never thought about them until that week; why would they think of me? It seemed to me that they were just living every day, like we were, but probably poorer and in a hotter place.

The rabbi, I could tell, didn't read the *New York Times*. He seemed to think he knew a lot about Indonesian people, but I doubted it. I secretly thought even though he was in charge of me, he was stupid. Why blame the Indonesians for what the Palestinians did? I was pretty sure when he said "Muslims" he meant Palestinians. Palestinians lived in Israel and hated us and wanted us to die, which is why they blew us up all the time. Just a few years before the tsunami, there was an attack on the World Trade Center, by a different group of Muslims, but our teachers were clear that it was all connected. The *New York Times* was less clear on this point, and I found it all very confusing. I didn't know who to ask, or what kind of book to read at the library that would address this question, because I wasn't really sure what the question was.

After 9/11, we freshman girls had been given lectures about the Muslims and how they prayed five times a day and we only prayed three times a day. The Muslims were also excelling at modesty, this very rabbi had told us, maybe even overdoing it, but that's better than underdoing it. Underdoing it displeased Hashem, and the Muslim women were pleasing Hashem, which made us look bad.

I understood this to mean that Hashem might let them win a sort of spiritual war, unless Hashem loved us enough to save us. We could earn his love by being more modest, praying more and also

Taking New Paths *Stories of Leaving Religion*

saying the blessing for every type of food that we put in our mouths. We should carry a book of psalms at all times and say them every day. Modesty, however, was by far the most important, our ultimate weapon and our great weakness as girls. At a school assembly we were each handed a pamphlet featuring a large glossy color photo of a bus blowing up on a street in Jerusalem, and superimposed over the inferno was an image of a gas can pouring onto the fire, with the word "IMMODESTY" printed on it.

Modesty meant collarbones covered at all times, elbows covered. Modesty meant skirts four inches below the knee, ideally, though an inch or two would suffice for those who had not yet attained that level of holiness. When buying a new skirt, our teachers said, we should sit down in the dressing room before purchasing it, to be sure it didn't ride up above our knee in a seated position. A skirt should not have a slit in it, which would be like a "blinking light," calling the eyes of the yeshiva boys to places they shouldn't be looking. A skirt should also not be too long, so as to attract attention.

The main idea was to not attract attention, which is why we were warned not to wear "clacky shoes," or shoes that made loud noises on the pavement when we walked. Wearing the color red attracted attention, as did having long flowing hair not suitably contained, eating an ice cream cone in public, or speaking or laughing loudly in the street. Modesty wasn't just about clothing, they told us. It is a way of being. Modesty was both our great role and our great challenge as a *bas Yisroel*, a daughter of Israel, and the equivalent great role and challenge for the boys was to study Torah and not be distracted by us. If we fulfilled our roles we would merit being saved from the Muslims and all the other nations around the world who all hated us and wanted us to die, and then the Messiah, Mashiach, would come and we would be out of our long exile.

Still, I thought in the classroom that day, it didn't make sense, because if Hashem cared so much about our little detailed actions, our every tiny prayer and blessing, our elbows and knees, well, then he shouldn't make mistakes. If, as the rabbi implied, the Indonesian adults were evil for hating us, punishing Indonesian children by killing them in a tsunami for things Indonesian adults were doing, well, that just seemed stupid and careless of Hashem. And if he's being careless and we might get tsunamied for someone else's crimes at any time,

Evidence

why bother being *frum* at all? I might as well just have fun, wear open-necked shirts and short sleeves, and watch movies on Shabbos.

Also, I decided finally, what if I didn't want Indonesians or Muslims to die. even if they did hate me? I didn't think if someone hated me that was a good reason for Hashem to drown them. If Hashem killed everyone who hated someone, we would all be dead anyway. I hated the rabbi teaching my class, hated him more than any Muslims or Indonesians. I hoped no tsunami was coming for me. Maybe we are Amalek, I thought to myself, suddenly. How would we know?

It's easy now to say, they are crazy, they are so paranoid, how can they live like this, how can they believe these things, how can they be so ignorant, but I was once one of them. Was I crazy? Was I paranoid and ignorant? Where is the dividing line between them and me? Did it appear in a moment, when I first turned on a light on Shabbos? Did I draw the dividing line, or was it always there for me to find?

When I was nineteen years old, I attended the wedding of a classmate, and bumped into one of my high school teachers there.

I don't remember which classmate's wedding this was, as there were so many, sometimes two in a week. It was during a period of time when most of my former class was getting married, after all of us returned from our year of study in religious seminary in Jerusalem. A young woman, known to us as a "single girl" until she married, would ideally be married as soon as possible once she returned. She had only a few years before her expiration date started to sting, and people would begin to whisper about what must be wrong with her. Was she too fat? Were her parents divorced, or maybe one of her siblings was Off the *Derech*, no longer religious? Whatever it was, she had better find someone before she reached her mid-twenties, when her options would become limited. Everyone knew all the good boys would be married by then. Every girl I knew lived in terror of becoming an old maid due to the shortage of "good boys," what was colloquially known as the "*shidduch* crisis."

In our senior year in high school, we had a class called Family

Taking New Paths *Stories of Leaving Religion*

Living, when our principal explained to us how to date properly. Our dates, boys we didn't know and had never met, would be vetted by our parents, arranged and investigated before we went out. We should have a reason before we said no to another date, she explained. Love grows, you don't know if you love someone right away. That feeling that is in goyish movies and magazines is infatuation, which isn't real love. Real love is shared values, which grows through building a *bayis ne'eman b'yisroel*, a home of faith in our Jewish community. That happens after years and years of being married, and therefore dating is for seeing if someone is basically on the same page as you, and if there is a good reason not to see him again. Good reasons included not being on the same "level" religiously, or wanting a different kind of home—for example, does he want to have internet or TV in his home? She acknowledged that if you find him repulsive, this would be a good reason to say no, but if you simply find him unattractive, well, this wasn't a good reason, because as you get to know people you find them more beautiful. Over time, she told us, a mole on the face can start to seem so small you won't notice it. You have to just wait it out.

Five dates, my friend told me, was about the point at which you are sure you're probably going to get engaged. I'm not saying you have to, just that if it gets that far you probably will, she said. I never got five dates in with any man I dated in the eight years I was *shidduch* dating.

Our principal did not cover a lot of very relevant information in Family Living. She did not talk about *niddah*, or about Family Purity, *taharas hamishphacha*, the laws around menstruation and the *mikvah*, the ritual bath. When we high school girls were to get married, hopefully in about two years for the lucky ones, these laws would completely govern our sexual experiences. This was not discussed, and would not be discussed, except in special bridal classes, or in hushed tones with two of us girls sharing bits of stolen information.

"You're not allowed to touch your husband until you get in the mikvah," we would whisper to each other, "you know, after your period. You're *tameh* (ritually impure) until then." I did not know details, but I knew this was the reason my parents, and all my friends' parents, slept in separate beds. Married life seemed distant and frightening.

Evidence

In the first year after seminary, I went to many weddings. They were something of a chore at times, but I also enjoyed them. At three hundred to six hundred guests on average, weddings were essential to our communal life. My classmates would be there, and we would catch up, our lives only just beginning to veer off in different directions.

At the wedding in question, I was wearing a sort of suit, not my usual wedding outfit, a sleeveless black dress with the "shell" underneath, an extra shirt that would cover my arms and my neck up to my collarbone. I don't remember why I wasn't wearing that. Black was what most of the women wore to weddings. Black was slimming, black was forgiving. Black was modest.

I saw my former teacher, Mrs. French, out in the hallway of the event. It had been some time since I had seen her. She had been known by the students for her inspiring lectures, expounding on how we should all have a close relationship with Hashem, and take joy in our faith. "If you dance with your children in the kitchen," she had said, "none of them will go off the *derech*" I greeted her warmly, and she did the same. I thought nothing of it.

Several days later I was in the kitchen peeling apples for Shabbos when the phone rang. I picked it up, and it was Mrs. French. "I'm calling because I love you, and I noticed your collarbone was showing at the wedding, and I thought someone should tell you," she said.

"Well, I appreciate that you mean well," I said, "but I'm not in high school anymore and I get to decide what I want to wear."

It was not unheard of for older women to approach younger ones in the supermarket or at events and comment on their insufficient modesty. I had heard of it before. In high school, my button-down shirts had all been custom fitted with an extra button at the neck, a "modesty button," that our teachers, including Mrs. French, policed with diligence. I had once been sent home for wearing a shirt that was "too tight." We were not to wear clothing that "distracted the boys from their Torah learning."

Mrs. French said something and then hung up. I called all

Taking New Paths *Stories of Leaving Religion*

my friends to tell them and we gossiped about who did she think she is. It was humorous, and while I thought it was an overstep and inappropriate, I didn't think too much of it.

It wasn't too long before I received a letter in the mail. Mrs. French had written four pages to me on loose-leaf paper, her looping handwriting tightly packed together with barely a paragraph break. She prefaced the letter by saying this was not a *tznius* (modesty) speech, and "NO *MUSSAR!*" meaning no words of rebuke.

In the letter, Mrs. French explained that she never calls a student the way she had called me, because it's pushy and it doesn't "work" anyway, and it's what's inside that matters. She has had students who even wear "sleeveless, tight dresses, slits in their skirts, no haircovering, even pants," and she never comments. Why would I call you, then? the letter asks. She comes to the conclusion that it is my special gift, the gift of *emes*, honesty, that moved her to call me. You are so straight forward, she says in the letter, so honest and clear about what you think, and you're so not into acting like something you're not. You're so real and it inspired me to be real with you. She pointed out that even in our phone conversation I had been "blunt and to the point…Almost everyone is full of fluff and into appearances, but not you!" She said in closing that in spite of the awkwardness, she was glad we spoke because it was an open and honest exchange, and asked me to please not be upset with her. "When you see me around next time," she wrote, "please do come over and give me one of your famous twinkly smiles and a big shiny 'hello!' And if you do, I will gleefully grin right back."

Emes. Me. Full of secrets and lies, I was always interested in the question of *emes*.

Over fifteen years later, this letter sits in front of me, and I still don't know what to make of it.

I cannot dismiss them all as fools, or crazy, or automatons. That would be the easy way out, the coward's way out. I can't let them off the hook that way. I can't let myself off the hook that way. The harder, truer thing is this letter, the meaning well, the manipulation, the "fluff" and the closest we can come to being honest with each other. This bittersweet letter that never lets me forget. I kept the letter because it keeps me honest, really honest. Not blunt or straightforward, not the kind of honesty she meant in the letter, but a different kind. The

Evidence

kind of honesty that knows that context always matters, and that two different things can be true at the same time.

Can people be good to us and hurt us at the same time? Is it love if it hurts? What if they don't know any better? What about seeing things from their perspective? Do I have the right to be angry at them, or to expect something different?

I remember clearly the first time I knew, truly knew, that I did not believe. I had arrived in Jerusalem to study for a year in religious seminary. Or, I was supposed to be studying in religious seminary. With the first taste of freedom away from my parents and my high school, my lack of belief in the foundations of our religion became impossible to ignore. The evening I arrived at the seminary at the edge of Jerusalem, I sat sobbing on the cold white stone stairs outside the dorm, suddenly, terrifyingly aware of the truth of my own mind: I was not a believer. I was an *apikores*, an apostate, a heretic, the most hated creature of all, worse than any other kind of sinner. The ground cracked open before me and I almost fell in.

I did not slowly remove each brick in the wall of my faith and examine it, checking it for veracity and stability. It was the foundation that was cracked, and I knew it, and there was no coming back from this knowledge. For several years following this realization, I attempted to paper over this crack, ignore it, build something lighter on top of it, but I could never forget what I knew: I was an *apikores*. I did not believe. Perhaps, though it's hard to say for sure, I had never believed.

That year, for the holy fast of Yom Kippur, I stayed in a cousin's house in East Jerusalem. I woke up in the middle of the night, hungry and thirsty, went to the kitchen, and popped a green grape in my mouth. When the grape split and I tasted its juice, I suddenly realized it was Yom Kippur, the most important fast of our calendar, the chance at atonement. In that moment I could not deny what I felt: I did not care. I swallowed the grape.

My life that year in Israel was a life on pause. When I told my parents about my doubts, they sent me to a special missionary school

Taking New Paths *Stories of Leaving Religion*

for secular Jewish women seekers, to teach them why they should join ultra-orthodox Judaism, why it is inspirational and true and the best possible way to live. I attended a few of the classes. The lectures fell flat, as I sat in the audience, acutely aware that I did not, *could not* believe this story. I skipped all the other classes, wandering the streets of Jerusalem for months. I sat for hours in cafes reading moody novels about doomed love. I bought a pair of jeans and wore them, but I had no other ideas for what rebellions I could exercise as an *apikores*. No one was watching me for the first time in my life, and I didn't even have the desire to get into any trouble. *Apikorsim* were supposed to be depraved and hedonistic, with lives full of sex, drugs, and rock and roll, but I felt pretty much the same as before. There was nothing in particular that I wanted. Everyone I knew was religious. What else was there to be? How else could I be?

When I returned to the U.S. I put aside my jeans and tried to become acceptable. I wore modest clothing, skirts over my knees, sleeves past my elbows, and went on *shidduch* dates. Over time, I would try to believe. I read religious books and for a while I adhered to the many rules of *Shabbos*, and a group of friends and I met every Friday night after *Shabbos* dinner to learn Proverbs together.

When did I stop trying? I don't remember. The details grow hazy now, and time runs together. Nothing worked, and I could not believe, but I also could not let myself consider this reality. My Friday nights would consist of our family *Shabbos* dinner around the table with the white table cloth, after my father said the blessings over wine and bread, and then I would pretend to say Grace After Meals, to *bentch*, mumbling the words and counting the minutes until the charade could be up. Then I would help clean off the table and go to my room, where I blocked the door and set up my mini DVD player to watch *Sex and The City*, or *Queer as Folk*. Often I would watch until 3:00 or 4:00 a.m., always with my heart in my throat, waiting to get caught.

I never was.

I did not feel guilty for breaking the rules. If there was no god, and our nitpicky rules-based way of life was all founded on a lie.

Evidence

What was I doing wrong to feel guilty about? Instead, I felt outside of myself and apart from everyone, adrift. Lost in my lies and alone on my island of doubt.

I continued to go on *shidduch* dates. When I went with my worried mother to see matchmakers, I told them I wanted a nice *frum* boy who was a bit "modern," who would like to have internet in the house. I knew marriage was inevitable, to not get married was to become an *alta kaker*, an old maid, a pointless and pathetic person with no place or purpose in our world, but I could not quite picture it.

I sat across from man after man in hotel lobbies and coffee shops and restaurants and I could not picture it. I would sit there, as if I was two women on these dates, one who was interested and considered these prospects real options, and wanted to get to know the young man, and another who was totally shocked anyone was actually considering this. They can't really think I'm going to do this.

I couldn't tell which woman, which me, was real.

What if I woke up next to him and didn't want to be there? What if we had two or three or four kids and eight years later I realized I was not happy, had never been happy, and didn't know whose life I was living? This seemed a distinct possibility, given that I wasn't certain even then whose life I was living now.

For eight years I *shidduch* dated, and said no, and no, and no again. I found reasons, always that he was too this, or not enough that, didn't quite fit. Not that it was me. Never me. Not that I was the one who didn't fit, that there was a crack in my story.

I grew to hate my deceptions, sputtering my lies and gritting my teeth. With each passing day, I felt myself dissolving into smaller and smaller pieces. The future was a black hole. I looked at myself in the mirror and felt nothing. Everything was nothing.

What does it do to us, to keep a secret? What happens when we lie, when we hide, when we live someone else's life? What happens if we do it for years? How do we find what's underneath, when the lie becomes the life?

Taking New Paths *Stories of Leaving Religion*

The leaving was slow, and then sudden. It took years, and then it took days. The creeping hopelessness of my life, the smallness and sadness of it, was starting to feel like a heavy blanket over me, and I was suffocating under it. The walls of my loneliness had threatened to close in on me, and I ran as far as I could imagine, and then I kept running. Moving out and then moving away, the cloak of my false faith fell away nearly instantaneously.

"Why didn't you tell us," they asked me. "You did it at the wrong time, the wrong way, too quickly, you made it all about you, so inconsiderate, so selfish."

Once I stopped lying, the relief was water in the desert, and I could not hide again. I was free, and the fire of my freedom consumed all that I had left behind.

What happens when we truly leave, as completely as we can? What happens to the life we leave behind? What do we owe each other? What suffering do I cause to escape my own? Are they right about me? I cannot see it clearly.

I have paraphrased some messages here, but the spirit of the original texts is intact.

I should say to start off that I'm not proud of all of my behavior in this story. I poked the bear to watch it roar. I'm not ashamed of myself, either, as I recognize why I did what I did, and I have compassion for myself, but I wouldn't recommend this:

I got engaged in the summer of 2019. I had been out of touch with most of my high school friends for several years since leaving the *frum* community, and had never filled them in on the details of my Off-the-*Derech*,-*apikores* life: my atheism, my move to another state, my struggles with my family, and ultimately dating and falling in love with a woman. The ocean between us felt so big, the bridge building required so labor-intensive, that I mostly focused on surviving this intense transition, and did not invest time in explaining these foreign concepts to anyone who I believed wouldn't understand them.

As the others gave birth to their second and third children, and moved to the *frum* neighborhoods and cities of Lakewood, Monsey,

Evidence

and the Five Towns, I'd worn jeans, developed a love of hiking, tried dating apps, and went to Burning Man. Though there were a few painful divides, with most friends it wasn't an acrimonious separation, a shunning; it was instead a loss of relatability, a gentle but real divorce of lives and interests. What was there for us to talk about?

My engagement brought back all the memories of every *vort*, the ultra-orthodox engagement parties I had ever attended; all the friends from high school with whom I had squealed over engagement bracelets and rings, all the times I had sent around breathless messages "Shani is engaged! *Mazal Tov*!" I was excited and felt a strong desire to tell my high school friends about my engagement.

The first *frum* person I shared my news with was a beloved, very devout cousin, Rivky. We were on our way back from Burning Man, where I had gotten engaged as the sun rose over the desert. When my cell reception came back, I got a voicemail from Rivky, whose wedding was taking place in a few short weeks. My whole family was going to be there, most of whom I had not seen since I wore skirts and kept *Shabbos* a lifetime ago. I had been invited and was planning to attend, though I had not been to a *frum* wedding in nearly a decade.

This was a special wedding, as my cousin had been an "older single," well into her thirties, and, as the whispers went, she was "*nebach* (pathetic) not skinny." Though she was generous, warm, and told the funniest stories of anyone I knew, she struggled to find a *shidduch* in a system where you can never be too thin. In her *shul*, the rav announced at the pulpit that everyone should *daven* for Rivky to find a match. Unbidden, cousins would approach her at Bar Mitzvahs and holidays to suggest gastric bypass surgery. For years the family had murmured about what would happen with Rivky, will she find a *shidduch, nebach*? To others she was defined by her single status, her life waiting to begin. And now she was engaged. I was really happy for her and wanted to dance at her wedding, though I was nervous about seeing my family.

"I don't know if I will be invited," I had told a family member, when she asked if I would be at the wedding., "I mean, I am the gay cousin so…"

"Oh please," she said dismissively, "that's not how our family is. Rivky would never do that; she doesn't think that way. I don't know why you would say something like that."

Taking New Paths *Stories of Leaving Religion*

It's not us, it's you.

When I returned Rivky's voicemail I told her I was engaged, too. "*Mazal Tov*," she said, and then hesitatingly asked me not to tell anyone at her wedding, so as not to embarrass my parents, who she believed wouldn't want anyone to know, and not to make her wedding into "your coming out party." Looking over at my fiancée, covered in dust and dirt from our week in the desert, her beloved eyes meeting mine, I knew the only answer I could give. I informed her that I loved her and if she didn't want me to come to her wedding, I wouldn't, but I wouldn't lie about myself or my life. "I won't stand on a table and announce it," I told her, "but I won't hide either."

She asked me not to come.

You shouldn't be angry at her, I told myself. How long has she been waiting for this? Think about how hard these years of *shidduchim* have been for her. How can you expect her to take this, of all moments, to stand up to everyone? You know how hard that is. Don't be selfish. Don't make this into a big deal.

It's not us, it's you.

"The problem isn't that you're gay," a family member told me. "It's how you handled everything. Why can't you respect us? Why do you have to shove everything in our faces?"

It's not us, it's you.

"The community is much better about LGBTQ issues than it used to be!" a *frum* friend assured me, telling me she knows of a gay couple, and that some rabbis are now telling parents not to throw their gay kids out of the house.

It's not us, it's you.

My desire to tell my *frum* friends about my engagement confused me, but it was undeniable, so I decided to do it. I sent a picture of my future wife and myself to a few old friends and said I was engaged. I received lovely messages of congratulations in response. I had been friends with these people for a reason, I remembered.

My friend Esther, a warm, sweet, enthusiastic, and sincerely religious woman I had known since kindergarten, was very excited for my good news. She had not known I was in a same sex relationship, and she immediately called me with many questions like, "who does the dishes," "who asked who out," and gave me list of every movie she had ever seen that had lesbians in it. Another friend I knew from *shul*

Evidence

jokingly suggested we put it in the weekly *shul* announcement email. This made me laugh, and I said I wished I could.

Esther, in her bubbly excitement, suggested she could post an engagement announcement in our high school class WhatsApp group. I didn't even know there was such a group. A good percentage of my high school class was by then up to their fourth child and living in Lakewood, a *frum* town known for its piety. It was nearly fifteen years since I had seen most of these women. I assumed Esther was kidding, just like my other friend.

She wasn't. "I mean it!" she told me.

I found this to be a ridiculous, hilarious idea. I wanted to see it happen. I knew the epic *frum* meltdown could be impressive. I should have said no, but I didn't. I wanted to see it.

She added me to the group.

I had been very involved in Esther's wedding years earlier. We had danced and laughed and cried and promised to be friends forever. I can't say for sure that that is what she was thinking about, three kids, a house and a whole different life later, but it's what I was thinking about. She giggled as if she was pulling a cute prank, but didn't seem to understand the gravity of what she was suggesting. I told her, "this could blow up you know…" and she waved me off.

"I think we should announce it in the traditional way!" she said, composing an announcement that was nearly identical to the usual ones: "*Mazal Tov*! Miriam Weiss is engaged to Moshe Stern!" except of course she inserted our names. At first glance, nothing unusual.

I sent her some pictures to post with it and watched it unfold. I really thought she wouldn't do it in the end. But she did. She posted the announcement with a photo of the two of us, in our hiking clothes atop a mountain vista. We stood far from the camera, and my wife is half a foot taller than me, and she has short hair. The *Mazal Tovs* came rushing in. Lots of exclamation points and excitement. What a relief. An old single was engaged! One less *alta kaker*.

"See!" she said. "Nothing happened! People are just happy for you."

It's not us, it's you.

"It's because they think she's a man," I told her.

"No…really? You think so? She doesn't look like… I guess maybe since it's far away…"

Taking New Paths *Stories of Leaving Religion*

I told her we should post a picture of the two of us at our anniversary, in dresses and lipstick. She was laughing when we decided this. She posted it "*Mazal Tov*, Lauren! We love you!" I was doubling down.

Someone wrote *Mazal Tov* and immediately deleted it. Several other women wrote *Mazal Tov* and "you look so happy!"; A total of five or so responses from the eighty in the group. No one else said anything. The women who did respond were, as I remember, almost all the most liberal-minded ones, or friends of mine in high school. Otherwise there was silence. I was surprised, and paradoxically both pleased and disappointed. My feelings confused me. I didn't care about these women. What did it even matter?

The next day the first message was, "Good morning. Does anyone have Rabbi Weiss's number?"

Rabbi Weiss was our high school principal. This message came in at 5:45am. It came from a former friend of mine, Miriam. She had not been a very close friend, but I had really liked her in high school and in the years after. A small group of my friends would get together at her house on *Shabbos* on occasion. She was especially known for being soft-spoken and calm, gentle and sweet. I had expected this, but I didn't expect it from her. At 6:11 am she posted the following message:

> "*Hi my sweet friends. You all know me and know that I am a kindhearted person. But I feel compelled to speak up. I am speaking with* Daas Torah. *I say this with love for all of you. But while Hashem says we must accept all* yidden, *all Jews, we can't condone or tolerate anything that is an* aveirah. *We cannot allow lifestyle choices that are against* Halacha. *All* Mazal Tovs *should and must be retracted. I love you Lauren, and I wish you all the best, but I cannot be okay with this. Sending you all my love.*"

I felt paradoxically proud of quiet, demure Miriam for finding her voice. It was a disorienting emotion.

I said nothing. A few women defended my marriage strongly, with the comments that "the Torah only speaks about men lying with

Evidence

each other!" "I don't want to be in this chat if we are judging each other" and a call to civility: "Lauren is so sweet and we remember her. Lauren I'm sure you understand where Miriam is coming from! We should try to keep these things from dividing us."

Someone posted a photo of a salad recipe, and I commented that that looked good. I thought this was very clever.

When I spoke to Esther, she was crying hysterically. She had been getting several private messages from women in the chat, telling her she should be ashamed of herself for posting such a message. She was horrified. And then, as you may expect, Rabbi Weiss had called her that morning. Presumably, he had been notified by Miriam of the events in the chat. Esther had not spoken to him in over a decade.

She recounted the conversation to me. He was bellowing, berating, blustering at her. How could she do this? She must take it down immediately. She had to delete the message.

She told him she would have to consult *Daas Torah* before doing any such thing.

"I AM DAAS TORAH!" He'd shouted. She calmly stated that she does not have a relationship with him, but she does have her own rav and she would ask him. He grumbled agreement and questioned her: Where did she live now? Where did she go to *shul*? He said *yiddishkeit* (ultra-orthodox Judaism) is about doing what's right, not what's nice. He said to her that she should be careful about what she does here.

I saw the threat immediately: *Be careful. Your children go to school here. Your nieces and nephews need to get* shidduchim *here. Be careful.*

She was laughing about his behavior even through her tears. I told her she was really brave to stand up to him, and she cried. She said she felt now that she had to ask her rav what to do. Go ahead and ask, I told her. I understood.

She asked, and her rav told her to delete the engagement announcement. She called me back crying even harder. "I can't do it! WhatsApp won't let you delete messages after twenty-four hours. Also I can't bring myself to do it! How could I do that?"

I felt terrible. They didn't come after me—I was free of their clutches. But I should have known they would come for her.

"I didn't know it was so bad!" She said through her tears, "I didn't

Taking New Paths *Stories of Leaving Religion*

know this is how they treat people, that this is how they treated you, really I didn't."

I believed her.

"I just wanted to do something nice for you! I just wanted to show you I love you!" she said.

"Maybe you can issue a retraction!" I suggested. Like *The New York Times* does when they make a mistake. Say you were wrong to post it."

"I can't write something like that!" She was weeping on the phone. "How could I write something so mean like that?"

"Oh I'll do it," I told her. I felt guilty for getting her involved. I felt amused and validated, yes, this is how they treat us, the outsiders, but I was also a little sad and angry on her behalf. Esther was clearly shocked, betrayed and angst-ridden. The effect of this had hit her much harder than me. I had wanted the evidence, and I had it now, and this was its price.

"I can't ask you to do that…"

"No big deal! I got it! It will be easy! And I will make it clear it's Rabbi Weiss's fault, too," I said.

That is how I ended up writing a retraction of my own engagement announcement. At this point I felt I was in some kind of absurdist comedy.

I helped her write a retraction. It said "I'm so sorry to have created a *Teheram*. I was contacted by Rabbi Weiss and I always strive to stick to *Daas Torah*.... I asked my own rav who said that would be best from a *halachic* perspective to delete the post, however the time limit already expired. So I apologize and will kindly ask for people to delete the message personally. However, I love Lauren and intend no harm to her. She knows I'm writing this message. Going forward I will consult *Daas Torah* more carefully. And will strive to uphold the standards that many on this chat hold."

The rest of the chat was clearly relieved by this and applauded her response. They praised Miriam effusively for being kind and generous with her forgiveness and magnanimity in response to Esther's message. Esther told me she got several private messages praising her for being brave enough to post the retraction. A woman who had defended me left the group, telling me privately that she had stayed for

Evidence

one day extra "in case there is bashing." I didn't expect any bashing, and there wasn't. Everyone was relieved civility had returned.

I contacted the women who had publicly stood up to the others in private messages, thanking them and wishing them well. One, who had been a very *frum* girl in high school, told me she wasn't what I probably thought she was, that she had changed. I told her we all have.

Miriam contacted me privately as well. In a voice note, she told me that she still thought of me as a friend and surely I can understand where she is coming from. I told her that while I have many happy memories of her, "telling people publicly not to celebrate with me at the happiest time of my life isn't an act of friendship, and you know that." She said something polite in return. That's the last I heard from her.

This incident became a good story for me to tell. "I didn't know *mazal tovs* are retractable!" my secular friends would laugh. It was funny, and I wasn't exactly hurt by it—this cruelty from women I barely know paled in comparison to years of rejection by people who knew me well, who were supposed to love me. It didn't sit comfortably with me, though. I knew it wasn't right. I did it for the validation. I wanted to see them act that way. I wanted them to act the way I knew they felt.

Years of self-doubt plagued me, their voices in my head "maybe I was wrong, maybe I could have stayed *frum* and not lost so much, maybe people are nicer now..." and I wanted to see them prove me wrong. I wanted to know it was *them, not me*.

It's an ugly reality, the search for evidence. It never really resolves: what evidence could be enough? What receipts do I want? The validation needs to come from within. It needed to be okay for me to be angry at Rivky for disinviting me from her wedding and for not being brave enough to fight for me. It needed to be okay for me to detach myself from our relationship, and yet, still, to love her. I do love her. No threatening rabbi could give me that permission—I needed to give it to myself.

This story has repercussions, and my actions here have

Taking New Paths *Stories of Leaving Religion*

consequences. Esther was hurt, badly. Her beliefs about her world, and her treatment within it, were damaged. Maybe you could see that as a positive, a win for the Off-the-*Derech* cause, but it also caused her pain. I can't see pain for my friend as a positive, no matter the cause. I'm not Miriam.

I worried about a secondary consequence, too. Approximately eighty women in the group, statistically, meant there had to be women in the group who are lesbians or bisexuals. Maybe some whose parents and siblings will come out to them as queer, or who already have. And one day, in the not-too-distant future, their kids. It weighed heavily on me that they had witnessed this public discussion of whether my marriage is a sin, and what this may cause them to believe about the life they could expect to have as a queer person.

This public rejection was a snapshot, a moment. In reality, I am happy with my life and my choices, and am surrounded by supportive people. I didn't want them to think this is all they can expect. I didn't want to push them towards "reparative therapy," which some in the *frum* world continue to practice, even though it has been outlawed. I didn't anticipate that consequence when I decided to play around and bother the *frummies*, but it crashed back down on me.

It took a long time for me to address that concern. Two years later I wrote this message:

"Hi fellow grads,

I've been thinking about what happened a couple of years ago with my lesbian engagement announcement in this group. I have only one regret—that I didn't say what was on my mind at the time, that I didn't reach out.

I know some of the women in this group who were reading the argument that came out of that announcement are, statistically speaking, gay, lesbian or bisexual. I know some of your parents, siblings, cousins are. Someday you may find out your kids are.

I want you to know that if you want to talk to someone about this, someone safe who won't tell any *frum* people, feel free to call me. I also want you to know that while those responses we saw here are common, there were also some loving responses and that it's changing, it's getting better, and you're not alone.

We knew each other when we were young, and our lives have

Evidence

changed, and now we are unrecognizable to each other. But know this: I will not judge you for your questions, and I won't ask you to do anything. I'm here if you want to talk.

Thanks to (the moderator) Leah for allowing me to be in the group. I'm going to leave now but please feel free to contact me."

I added my contact info at the end. And then I exited the group.

Esther and I are still friendly, though not close. She's a true believer and those differences continue to stand in the way. A shared history is a beautiful thing, though, and a valuable one. I apologized for not stopping her, and she apologized for not understanding how hard things have been for me, and we expressed our affection. She really meant well. It amazed me that she truly didn't see how this would go. There is so much we don't see, cannot see, don't want to see. There is so much I did not see, for so long.

I don't have this story wrapped in a nice bow, a clear lesson. Like the people in it, it's a complicated story. My need for evidence bothers me, and I wish I hadn't done these things. But maybe that's a lie, a kind of self-delusion because even now, as I write this, I am sharing this story. Perhaps this writing is a continuation of the search for evidence.

Maybe the search for evidence is a good thing, and what I should be doing. Lay it all out, piece by piece, all the joy and pain and beauty and sadness, all of the ways we love each other, all of the ways we hurt each other, all of the times we speak up and all of the times we stay silent, our surroundings and our secret thoughts, our histories and our heresies, all of our shared and private suffering, lay it out, side by side, gaze at it, and trust my eyes to see.

It's all here. I can see it now.

Additional Resources:

The Book of Separation by Tova Mirvis
Uncovered: How I Left Hasidic Life and Finally Came Home by Leah Lax

Taking New Paths *Stories of Leaving Religion*

Hidden Heretics by Ayala Fader
Hush by Aishes Chayil AKA Judy Brown
Disobedience, a novel by Naomi Alderman
Trauma and Recovery by Dr. Judith Herman
Take Back Your Life! Recovering from Cults and Abusive Relationships by Janja Lalich and Madeleine Tobias

My Journey of Life

6
My Journey of Life
Ashoka Gautam

HELLO WORLD. I hail from West Bengal state in northeast India. I was born and brought up in Kolkata (Calcutta). Being born in a Hindu upper caste (Aryan descendant) family, I had privileges: our own house in a posh area of the city, English medium school, private tuition, and exposure to global media.

All the above privileges helped me to gain an education that satiated as well as encouraged my inquisitive mind to go into science and technology, which needs lab work, field work, using technical and mental tools that most Indians cannot afford. Although I recognize these now, during my formative years I was not aware of all of these privileges. At that time our state was under a Revisionist Left Front rule, although the Union Government of India had already taken a Neoliberal path since 1991.

Taking New Paths *Stories of Leaving Religion*

In my childhood, my father, himself a devout Hindu, tried to teach me the rituals and practices he followed. My grandfather, who was a Left Liberal Hindu unlike my father, stopped that indoctrination and guided my father to encourage my inquisitive bend of mind.

My father, although himself religious, understood the value of education and bought books of general knowledge, primary science, as well as Aesop's fables, and Panchatantra fables (Indian moral stories). Along with these, almost every evening Hindu religious books were read, preached by elders of our family (we Indians often live in big undivided families).

In my young mind, the Hindu teachings and moral teachings clashed when I faced bullying in school. Hindu mythology taught us violent repercussions, revenge, while the fables (I later came to know they were based on Buddhist, indigenous atheistic philosophies) taught us wisdom, ending violence, seeking justice.

Another thing happened during the same time: Due to my father's acts of initiating me into religious rituals, I started believing in spirits, ghosts, and became afraid of the dark. That is when my grandfather guided my father in the wiser path.

Within a few years of school—studying about light, darkness, and the rotation of Earth—my fear of dark decreased but somewhere the basic survival instinct taught me to be careful in the dark, without fearing anything supernatural. (Rats, pests, poisonous snakes, violent humans, etc. are enough to worry about; no need for the supernatural.)

Meanwhile, at school, the bullying continued for a few more years, till my best friends and I confronted the bullies and without much violence showed them reason. Around that time, in history I came across Siddharth Gautam (Buddha) and his teachings of wisdom, truth, peaceful congregations. I learned about the Four Noble Truths, Eight Fold Path of Buddhism, and started practicing that lifestyle as much as possible.

During my childhood when my father tried teaching me Hindu rituals, he also taught me meditation. Although he himself chants during meditation, I figured out silent meditation is better for the mind. That lifestyle helped me overcome the bullying and improve in studies with less stress distracting.

My Journey of Life

Somewhere down the line, I became an agnostic. Just when this good change was happening, my grandfather passed away followed by my aunt and uncle (my father's sister and brother respectively) within a few years.

I, an agnostic, already knew gods are imaginary. During all those memorial ceremonies I first understood the business of religions, seeing the family deciding these things firsthand.

Parallel to those in the family, our country's Secularism faced huge losses since the 1992 demolition of Babri mosque (an archaeological site apart from a mosque) and retaliatory violence in 1993.

Both Hindu and Muslim believers killed each other, police and paramilitary forces had to shoot fellow Indians; the country again started dividing along religious lines the same way it had before Partition in 1947.

The contemporary Neoliberal Union Government of India kept hiding the divisions for their own political gains. But in 2002, religious conflict between Hindus and Muslims happened in Gujarat. This time the media kept the division in the news till people of India brought a Hindu nationalist government in 2014 to build a Hindu nation and end Secularism.

Personally, from 2000, I became obsessed with getting a career in engineering (a trend in India for youngsters back then). But a new challenge in the form of schizophrenia attacked my mother. Her hysterias and depression put immense pressure on my father and me in those crucial years.

On top of that, my devout Hindu father would not take my mother to a doctor for treatment as he did not believe it as a disease. He finally accepted the scientific truth around the time my college entrance examinations were near.

My adolescent years were so dreadful that I developed trauma from those experiences, avoided dating, concentrated only on career to get away from that life.

In my obsession of passing entrance examinations and getting a high paying job, I strayed from my path of Buddhist philosophy/ value system. I graduated from college with a Bachelor of Technology

Taking New Paths *Stories of Leaving Religion*

in Civil Engineering in 2009. After working for two years (reading various books like *Brief History of Time, Holy Blood Holy Grail, the Dhammapada*, etc) I found my way back to reasoning and values.

I even contemplated becoming a Buddhist after I tried and failed badly getting into a relationship.

Meanwhile, at home Mother's schizophrenia has been brought under control by medication.

But after failing at that relationship and an entrance examination for a Masters, I fell into depression. From 2011 to 2014, I was depressed, and no amount of Buddhism helped as I found out about the misogyny, the current established religion's ritualistic ways straying from its core teachings.

From 2015, I became an atheist, as all these years I have been reading various books like *The World As I See It* by Albert Einstein, *Srikanto Trilogy* by Saratchandra Chattopadhyay, books on Buddhist and Taoist philosophies, books on sociology, as well as our departmental books describing how things work.

Apart from all these teachings, while working in sites, I noticed the stark inequalities within the Indian people. The main cause behind these inequalities was religions, and even more than that the caste apartheid. Casteism is a form of social hierarchies created by the Brahmins (clergy class and direct descendants of Aryan migrants from Eastern Europe) who kept themselves as the highest caste and placed all other Indians under them.

When working outside our state, I saw the divides, the untouchability, and the resulting inequality firsthand. In India, this caste apartheid is causing losses of billions of dollars every year as children of so-called low caste parents can never choose the professions of higher caste people, get the necessary education, or even get water from the same well or reservoir.

Needless to say, although inter-caste marriages are not illegal, honor killings are done to inter caste couples in rural, suburban, and sometimes urban India. All these injustices are done as per religious teachings stipulated in Hindu religious texts. As the people here still consider religion over Constitutional law, the country is fragmented into religions, castes, and subcastes.

Politicians, corporations, British colonizers in the past, local money lenders, authorities and people in power are taking advantage of these divisions to exploit natural resources as well as the people of our country. As a result, the ecology and society, now with pandemic, face economic collapse.

Those years of work experience—seeing India up close—made me move farther away from religious ways of life. The more scientific temperament, reasoning, and values grew in me, the more I noticed the decaying ecology and the imminent danger it poses to humankind.

Since 2012, I wanted to do something for Nature as I knew about Climate Change back then. In 2017, while at a work site, I saw a dying river, dead soil, people leaving their villages due to dying livelihoods.

That's when I decided to change the track of my career and get into Sustainable Engineering, Eco friendly Architecture, Sustainable Habitat Planning. Currently, I am preparing for that kind of job in the near future.

I realized that without social change, none of these ecological changes can be brought. So, apart from my professional work, in my social work and lifestyle choices, too, I am working for Climate Action where gender equality and ethnic equality are paramount to bring Climate Justice. We are building a united, inclusive India, fit for 2050 so that the next generations don't have to face crises like we have.

I hope that the pathway of my life experience, my explorations and re-evaluation, might be useful to others. I hope that the evidence-based problem solving central to engineering and science can help my country—and humanity broadly—face the challenges of our times and find solutions.

And last, but not the least, I must thank those teachers at school and others who encouraged thinking, questioning, held discussions on relevant topics, explained the history, the cultural significance of various practices that we have today. Without their guidance I could not have broken free of a religious way of life, coming as I did from a religious family, while enjoying privileges owing to the position that that religion had placed me in.

Taking New Paths *Stories of Leaving Religion*

7
My Roots, My Journey, My Present
Doug Matheson

MY FIRST MEMORY of a public event was the assassination of President Kennedy. I was almost seven, and although we were living in the southern British Columbia town of Kelowna then, the talk on the radio in our kitchen/dining room was non-stop. Part of what really made it stand out in my mind then was that my dad, a good hard-working man whom I loved and looked up to, principal of the Adventist first-through-twelfth-grade-grade church-school there, said "Good; America will be better off."

As I listened to my mom and dad discuss this event, and answer questions from my brothers (one seven years older than me, the other five years older), I quickly came to understand that this man, the President of the country where all four of us kids had been born,

My Roots, My Journey, My Present

was a "Catholic," and that that particular religion, different than the "Seventh-day Adventists" that we were, was somehow quite bad.

My preschool years, and my then current year in first grade, had been happy, busy, and carefree. We lived in a modest house, but it had a couple acres of space for fruit trees, and cactus. Spring and summer could find me and my sister (only a year and a half older than me) eating ripe, dark-burgundy Bing cherries, and, much later in the season, tree-ripe peaches, juice dripping off our elbows, while sitting in the branches of the trees. The cactus? Let's just say that my mom had to use tweezers to get all the cactus spines out of my rear-end because I insisted on tobogganing down the hill toward the community pond before the snow was deep enough.

In the midst of that carefree childhood, my only prior knowledge of religious differences was very limited. We shared a somewhat long driveway with our neighbors whose two boys, Greg and "little Doug," were my best non-sibling playmates. (Enjoy the humor of me, at ages four to seven, being called "big" Doug because little Doug was two years younger) Their dad was an Anglican Minister, and I knew that they were somehow different than Adventist, but it was all good.

I also knew that we went to church on Sabbath, Saturday, and that apparently most people went to church on Sunday. In preparation for Sabbath School (just like Sunday School) each week, we kids learned our 'memory verses'; there we sang *Jesus Loves The Little Children, Brighten the Corner Where You Are*, and many more, and listened to stories and lessons. At home we had family worship, especially on Friday evening to welcome the Sabbath, and we thanked God for and asked blessing upon each meal.

In my mind, clearly God was real and good, and Adam and Eve, and Noah, and Jesus were real characters in great and real stories. The stories did include instances where if you were not on the side of 'right,' God could seem pretty strong handed. (Goliath; the Philistines; Jezebel; the kids who teased the prophet Elisha; etc.)

That someone in some "other" church in our modern world was therefore automatically bad enough for it to be better for the country if they were dead, was still a bit of a surprise. I had no way to question it, though. My dad was a good man. Certainly he believed in "spare the rod, spoil the child," but he was not a drunk, not abusive, and he took good care of us. He was respected in the community.

Taking New Paths *Stories of Leaving Religion*

Of course at the time I had no idea then that Protestants in America broadly, from at least the seventeenth century into the mid-twentieth, had issues with Catholics and the Papacy; further beliefs on the Mark of the Beast and the Anti-Christ would come my way as I grew older.

I didn't puzzle over this; I accepted it as a reality, and moved on with living my busy little life. A few months later, two big things happened in our family: 1. my little brother was born, (of course making me happy to not be the youngest anymore, and understandably briefly making my sister sad because she now had one more brother… and no sister); and 2. my parents decided to accept a call from the church to become missionaries in India.

Before that school year was even over, our family became seven of the only eight passengers on a WWII vintage freighter called the Java Mail, headed from Seattle to Calcutta (spelled as then). Our route was arched via Alaska, Japan, etc., and our primary cargo was dynamite.

On our stop in Manila, after waiting for a while outside the harbor, we were radioed to weather the incoming Typhoon Winnie outside of the protections of the harbor. Our skipper was experienced and after moving to somewhat deeper water, he put down the two fore-anchors, and kept us always pointed into the wind by keeping the propeller slowly turning and using the rudder.

I remember the sound of the wind in the wires, and the horizontal rain as the typhoon passed over that night, and we slowly pivoted. In the morning the fore-anchor chains were twisted, but we were safe. We could see a good number of ships inside the harbor had been washed up and turned on their sides.

My mom and dad and uncle Ernie talked about a miracle of safety. My uncle and family were missionaries in the Philippines. He had come out from the city to our ship the afternoon before, and got stranded on board when everyone suddenly realized a typhoon was bearing down. (No weather satellites in 1964.)

They discussed what might have happened if we had been inside the harbor, and either gotten washed up on our side like others, or been crashed into by one of those ships; Our dynamite would likely have blown our ship to pieces. In prayer, everyone thanked God for

My Roots, My Journey, My Present

His "protecting hand" while I pictured the many paintings I had seen of guardian angels.

And then my sister and I spent the next several days playing with our same-aged cousins and swimming in the flooded yard of the home we had come to for our brief stop in Manila.)

Several weeks later we were finally tied up to the wharves on the Hooghly River (near the Ganges) in Calcutta. The sights and sounds and smells were new and exciting. I couldn't wait to get on the steam engine train that would take us on a couple-day ride to Vincent Hill School (VHS), where my dad would be principal.

Before we left the ship, I remember watching two crows peck at the eyes of a bloated dead person as the body slowly floated by. In Calcutta, and during the days on the train, poverty, sickness, extreme inequality, apparent risk of death, and death itself, were much more obvious than in the US and Canada, even in the eyes of a kid not yet eight years old.

Religious differences, and their sheer variety, were also immediately obvious, although I didn't think deeply, or really at all, about them. I soon saw Hindu Temples and Muslim Mosques, Sikh Temples and Buddhist Shrines, and learned that there were many different denominations of Christian missionaries from many countries, all right there as well.

Our train's path ended in Dehradun, right at the bottom of the abrupt rise from the plains of the foothills of the Himalayas. The final leg of getting to our new home was a jeep ride up and up and up the switch-backed road to Mussoorie, and then a few miles around mountains to Vincent Hill School.

Although our days in Calcutta, and then the train ride to Dehradun, had quickly exposed me to 'new and different' things of all sorts, the campus family of VHS was an almost instant island of the familiar. Everyone spoke English; virtually all of the boarding school kids there were the Adventist children of Adventist missionaries scattered around India, Ceylon (now Sri Lanka), West and East Pakistan (the latter now Bangladesh), Nepal, and maybe a few others. Those kids included Brits, Aussies, Canadians, a very few Indians, and more Americans than any other group.

My elementary classroom was a good old-fashioned multigrade room. Besides Sabbath School and Church on Sabbaths,

Taking New Paths *Stories of Leaving Religion*

all students, in grades one through twelve, had at least some kind of brief Bible class as part of daily school life. I don't remember anyone grumbling; beyond accepting it, everyone expected it.

At home, we had brought our set of *Uncle Arthur's Bedtime Stories*, and the *Bible Stories* set of books. Whether at school or at home, the depth and breadth of Bible stories, and budding degrees of understanding them, continued to broaden and deepen, as did my level of belief. In my circle of hearing, no miracle was ever questioned. And among the sudden multiplicity of gods on my new horizons, everyone on that campus seemed to be equally certain that *our* God was the right one.

Some stories were a bit troubling. I remember being puzzled, but impressed, that good intentions don't count if you don't get the details right. In the case of Uzzah (II Samuel 6:1-7) reaching out his hand to steady the Ark of the Covenant, which the rough road apparently made lurch when one of the oxen pulling the cart stumbled, God struck Uzzah dead. The reason? The Ark was supposed to be carried on priests' shoulders, and not even be on an oxcart. It apparently didn't matter that Uzzah was a young man, and was not in charge of the decision to ignore the shoulder rule and put it on a cart. But I don't remember anyone puzzling out-loud about any story, or rules, or Biblical principle. I'm sure some teenagers there must have, but I wasn't in their peer group, and didn't hear their questions.

Life just actively moved forward. We played softball at recess sometimes, even in the thick monsoon fog that made the catcher yell "left field" or "right field" after the batter got a hit, for the outfielders sometimes couldn't even see the batter, let alone the ball being hit. If you were an outfielder, you just held your mitt protectively in front of your face, stood still, and listened to hear the ball hit the ground somewhere in your part of the alerted field. We also took up local games like tops, which gave us boys a good outlet for aggressive throwing with intent to injure some object, not a person.

By my second year there I had discovered that several older students, and one faculty member, had a hobby of collecting and preserving the wonderfully varied species of beetles that were

My Roots, My Journey, My Present

abundant during the summer monsoons. I took up that hobby, too, and had lot of fun with it, even if it's not typical for a nine-year-old to get out on the trail at the crack of dawn on weekend mornings. My dad paid a local carpenter, Baru, to make a nice three-drawer cabinet for my collection and I still have it, filled with beetles, more than a half century later. I was assured that God had specifically created all their bizarre shapes and ways of life.

The whole school went on an annual campout to a place called Kansrao. A far as I could tell, every person there greatly looked forward to this yearly expedition. This involved getting everyone, and who knows how much equipment, down the mountain, then on an hour's train ride, and set up at camp. I can't imagine now the overall logistics of pulling this off, and certainly admire everyone, especially the kitchen staff from top to bottom, who managed to make it possible. Our campfire songs and stories had light and funny secular parts, and warm and inspiring, and sometimes even very sober, religious parts.

My dad was given the additional responsibility and privilege of being "Ordained" as a Minister, which from my point of view primarily meant he could now be a pastor who baptized people. I thought it was cool that when I was considered old enough to make an informed decision, he could baptize me.

My mom was the school nurse, sometimes not at all busy, and sometimes very occupied with some somewhat critical cases. One of the most critical was when my then roughly two year old little brother took a tumble down a steep slope below our walkway.

That campus had a drop of about a thousand feet of elevation from the principal's house to the boys' dorm; everything except the girls' dorm/main building, and playfield, was steep hillside. I remember goofing around with some of my friends on the playfield when I heard my mom scream and call out my dad's name. I don't know who ran into the building to get my dad, because I just reflexively took off running up the back path toward home, as one of my older brothers, running faster, passed me.

My little brother had hit his head on a rock, and was unconscious. They took him in to the Mussoorie Landour Hospital,

Taking New Paths *Stories of Leaving Religion*

but the doctor, being able to see and feel the dent in the shape of the right side of his skull, which was confirmed by x-ray, said they needed to take him a day's drive away to a hospital where they had the expertise to cut out that piece of skull, reshape it, and put it back in. This they did.

You can imagine there was a lot of sincere praying done, first imploring, then thanking.

After three years at VHS, my dad was asked to become the principal of a boarding school for Indian young Adventists, way over in the skinny part of West Bengal, just north of East Pakistan (Bangladesh) and south of Bhutan. Although it meant leaving good friends, and leaving my brothers as boarding students at VHS, I was excited about another adventure, this time to a place called Falakata.

Kids make friends quickly, and a language barrier didn't get in the way. There were more than ten languages represented on that campus, with the common language among them Hindi. Within a few months I was functional, and in less than a year, fluent.

It was a great place for a pre-teen kid. My friends and I often swam in the river. With my multi-pump-action pellet gun I'd shoot doves for my friends to roast and eat. I later graduated to permission to use the .22, and shot unnumbered crows and parrots to protect school crops menaced by them, and rabid or mangy dogs to keep campus safer.

When the low-lands flooded with the monsoon rains, my friends and I would cut down four banana trees, spear them together with thin young bamboo, and go rafting and fishing; we'd play tag in a series of trees with overlapping branches. One friend liked to ride my horse, too, though most wouldn't try. Naturally, we played lots of "football" (soccer).

When classes were over, I'd go help at the school dairy, and in the rice fields... I pretty much did anything I could to avoid my homestudy schoolwork.

My poor mom. She was the school nurse, and ran a community clinic especially focused on poor women and children from our front porch, and had my pre-school brother to take care of. The last thing she needed was me being what today would probably have been labeled as hyperactive. My sister spent part of those three years in Falakata with us, and part as a boarding student back at VHS. Because she had

My Roots, My Journey, My Present

her own home-study schoolwork to do (and did it!) she was no doubt a good influence on me and helped me focus at times on getting some stuff done.

Besides being the principal, my dad took it upon himself to change much of the school's unused land to productive farmland. He was a good mechanic, and taught by leading in the repairs of farm tractors and other equipment. I learned by helping, as did several of the young farm workers and students.

At certain times of year, the big Hindu festivals and rituals took place just off the campus. I saw flesh-piercings of various types with little blood, and body weight borne by just four hooks through what looked like just deep skin. When I asked my parents about what I was seeing, they explained that it was not naturally possible, and that therefore it was Satanic. I couldn't see or hear of an alternative idea, so I believed what thus seemed obvious.

On campus, one high school aged boy suffered repeated bouts of some kind of flipping out. They would lock him in a room away from other boys, and my dad and the boys' dean, and another teacher, would go in there with him. To me, my parents seemed somewhat troubled and uncertain about what this was. They said it might be demon possession, like when Jesus cast the demons out of a man and into the herd of pigs, and it sounded like it to me.

My dad and the two other men would pray over the boy, I imagined casting the demons out in Jesus' name, and each time the boy did eventually calm down. I puzzled with why this happened a number of times, and why, when he was sometimes alone in the locked room before they went in to be with him, the demons couldn't break down the locked door.

After six years in India, we had earned a year's furlough, and it was decided that my dad would do a master's degree in education, so we headed to Walla Walla, Washington, for a year. We were all back together in one place. My older brothers were in the same church-college where my dad was a grad-student, Walla Walla College. My sister was a sophomore in the Adventist academy, my little brother was a first grader, and I mangled together doing both seventh and

Taking New Paths *Stories of Leaving Religion*

eighth grade work to catch up on the work I missed by being so easily distracted during the last three years of off-task fun in Falakata.

Doubling up my work that year was my choice. I knew we were going back to India, and I wanted to be ready to go to academy with my age peers, so at the start of that year I asked my parents if I could double up my work, explaining that I wanted to catch up.

My dad's response was like a quiet dare.

"I don't know. Can you?" he asked.

My mom then helped me approach the principal and junior high teachers at Roger's Adventist Elementary school. They agreed I could try. It's amazing what an internal switch in motivation can accomplish. Although my dad and I often butted heads, that year I was happy and proud to have him baptize me.

When my parents and younger brother headed back to India, my sister and I headed to Far Eastern Academy (FEA) in Singapore, because VHS had closed due to declining numbers of missionary families in India and other countries. Like a larger reincarnation of VHS, FEA students were all the children of Adventist missionaries, this time from many more countries, from Japan to Kenya.

Most of us lived in the dorms, and life there was quite regimented. Quiet study-hall was enforced in the evening. Lights went out by 10:00 p.m.. Rooms were regularly checked for tidiness, with rewards for those of us who kept our rooms in military bootcamp order.

Besides regular classes, we all had an official "Bible" class every day, with graded work required, just like geometry or English. Each dorm had evening worship before study-hall and we often sang the roof off with classics like *Gimme' that Old-Time Religion*, or enjoyed a subdued positive reminder with *No Man is an Island*. Our teachers and deans did pretty good jobs of not being drill sergeants about religion.

We played lots of sports, from proper basketball and flag football, to mud-flooded 'tackle' football for the fun of a giant mess. We even had a dirt-bike club (we stripped down and heavily modified street 125cc bikes, welding our own expansion chambers).

In various group sizes, from four to fifty, we camped in the tropical jungles of Malaysia. Staff attempted to provide "appropriate" social activities for couples, and non-couples, but any couple who dared a little PDA (and God-forbid private!) were of course put "on social" for some duration. Semesterly banquets were the one time we knew we could get away with holding hands in a movie. Wow! We had 'marches' instead of dances, because dancing was strictly off limits.

Many of us still did typical adolescent nonsense like getting our hands on some cigars, breaking into what we called "the nun's pool" in the neighboring Catholic hospital compound, trying to ferment our own brew, and some trying various drugs. Telling off teachers got several of us 'free-labor' a number of times.

Each semester we had a designated "Week of Prayer" with a special guest speaker. My sophomore year the second semester Week of Prayer featured Pastor Glen Coon, of *ABC's of Prayer*, and two much younger and "cool" assistant speakers. It was like a good old fashioned religious revival; everyone, including me, seemed to be profoundly and deeply moved and committed. We were assured that none of us would reach the age of thirty before Jesus would return. We didn't doubt it and many of my fellow students spent the first several weeks of that summer on a tour of witnessing and singing in Southeast Asia.

In Biology class, when the next chapter in our textbooks was Evolution, we all seemed relieved to hear our teacher say essentially this: "Here's all you need to know about evolution: It's not real. It's made-up nonsense. The people who came up with this and who teach it were and are working with the devil, and their goal is to confuse and deceive. There is no pattern to the fossil record; it's chaotic, and it's the leftovers of Noah's flood. Any questions?" We all looked around, shook our heads, and smiled with relief.

At the end of the summer before my junior year, starting our trip back to FEA, about ten of us were in a van headed from Poona (now Pune) to Bombay (now Mumbai) to catch our flight. It was predawn, but I hadn't fallen asleep like most of my friends. As the eastern sky began to brighten beautifully, a particular cloud held my attention. Its edges were silver, and it appeared to be slowly growing bigger. It seemed so like the images in books I'd literally grown up with depicting Jesus' return, starting with a cloud "no bigger than a man's hand." I watched carefully, wanting to wake a friend, but

Taking New Paths *Stories of Leaving Religion*

instead I tried to figure out my own feelings. Was I happy? Was I afraid? What did it say about me that I wasn't exactly sure? My ideal sense of timing was that I hoped Jesus would return after I'd gotten married and had a family; this was too soon, but this thought itself... was it terrible of me?

The sun then continued to rise.

As is quite typical, I grew up from a screw-off freshman to a student leader. Graduating in 1975, I knew I was heading back to Walla Walla to start college, and continue my Christian education.

The most memorable single class period of my whole freshman year was when the General Biology professor addressed evolution. He looked around at the fairly full lecture hall, with probably around a hundred students in there, and started by stating that he suspected that most of us had been told that there's no order or sequence to the fossil record, but that in fact there is.

We were nearly all from Adventist academies. As I remember it, you could have heard a pin drop. He went on to explain, and show illustrative graphs of, the orderly pattern found in the cases of both animal and plant fossils. He pointed out that it is simply dishonest to deny the sequential pattern, that it's checkable, and has been checked, in a multitude of locations. Then he went on to say though, that the order didn't have to be explained by resorting to 'evolution.' He introduced us to an organization called the Geoscience Research Institute (GRI), whose researchers had proposed the Ecological Zonation Theory, explaining that this meant that: organisms which died during Noah's flood were buried in sequence according to 1. Where they lived to begin with (thus putting some types of fish showing up in the deeper layers of sedimentary rocks; more advanced fish higher; higher still the amphibians; etc.); 2. How mobile they were in getting away from rising waters; and 3. How smart they were in finding the best places to move to. Thus reptiles are first found in layers well above the early amphibians, and the first mammals and birds in layers well above the early reptiles, with primates and finally humans in the top layers. There were many questions, and lots of explanation.

In that single class period, it seemed to me that most of us

My Roots, My Journey, My Present

had moved quickly through shock, degrees of search and hope, and relief at what right then seemed like much better-than-nothing for an explanation. The internet didn't exist then, but I began to pay more attention to articles in *National Geographic, Scientific American*, and publications from our church-run GRI.

I don't remember any teacher or my parents giving me this thought, but in the last bit of my teen years I came to believe this: Things which I believe myself, things I claim about reality, should match up fairly well with the best evidence we can find and check, and liking or disliking the evidence shouldn't and therefore couldn't play a role. Honesty, I felt, required imposing evidence on beliefs, and therefore changing the latter, and not attempting the reverse. I came to find the fossil record, and many features about it, to be both fascinating and thought-provoking.

I spent two summers working at a church-run youth camp, Big Lake, near Sisters, Oregon, the first summer as a swimming instructor and lifeguard, and the second summer as a counselor to a weekly cabin full of boys. There were endless trivial aspects to the job, but I, and I think most of the other counselors, took the element of being a spiritual mentor to our kids seriously.

The year between my sophomore and junior year of college, I took the year out to work (as a volunteer) as an assistant Dean of Boys at Milo Adventist Academy, a boarding school in southwestern Oregon. While I also regularly helped with miscellaneous school activities like intramural sports, I took a central part of my job there to also be that of a spiritual mentor.

One evening each week it was my responsibility to lead the boys' evening worship; I tried to combine both thought provoking and uplifting/encouraging themes. When the school year was over and the students all gone, on the day before I packed up my little Pinto to drive back to Walla Walla, I took a walk up a long but gentle hill to the woods behind the boys' dorm. On a notepad I'd taken with me, I wrote a brief letter to my parents, and then laid down in the shade of a tree on that warm June day, and had another very conversational prayer. I didn't really want to go back to the demands of college, and I felt very good about my year at Milo. I remember telling God that I was going to take a nap, and that it would be good if I just didn't wake up…until the great awakening of resurrection day of Jesus' return. I obviously

Taking New Paths *Stories of Leaving Religion*

wasn't actively suicidal; I think, as a very young adult, I just wanted to "end the game while I felt good about the score," and was very content to leave the rest in God's hands. (That letter home, of course, never got mailed.)

As I continued college, preparing to be a biology and physical education teacher, I chose to take quite a few more than the required religion/theology classes. I wanted to get way past the basics like righteousness by faith, to explore and solidify my understanding of the roots, and the details, of my Christian faith, and so while not getting into Biblical languages classes, I did take upper division classes like Hebrew Prophets, Eschatology, Old Testament History, and my church's story, Denominational History.

Such classes did broaden and deepen my understanding, but of course in the process you run into questions you have to try to answer. One of the theology professors, Malcolm Maxwell, had stepped up the ladder to become the academic dean. In my junior or senior year I remember asking him if I could briefly chat. I expressed that it was kind of easy to see the Old Testament as the history and hope of the Jewish people, and the New Testament as the making of a God, out of a man, after the fact. I don't remember a lot details of what he shared, but I do remember he pointed to Saul's conversion experience in becoming Paul. And I remember the feeling of being significantly reassured, and the reminder of the importance of the experience of faith.

One of the broadest questions I dealt with came from one of my best high school friends, who was going to the Adventist college in northern California. He shared with me a poem he had written on how it was not a matter of God creating man in His image, but man who had created 'god' in our own image. I joked back with Kevin that he was lucky that God was patient, or he'd have been struck by lightning. At the time it was a question I felt I had more than adequate answers for.

While cultivating a personal communication with God and a solid foundation of understanding, I also continued to puzzle about things. I'd learned a lot more about the fossil record, including mass

My Roots, My Journey, My Present

extinctions, and about plate tectonics, etc., and had come to think that the idea of Noah's flood didn't hold much water for both scientific and theological reasons. I had grown up learning that when Lucifer (Satan) had questioned God's ways, rebelled, been cast out of heaven, and then deceived Adam and Eve into rebelling, that Earth then became a "theater to the universe" where onlooking beings from other worlds could watch and evaluate whether Satan's accusations of God not being fair were right or wrong.

I'd also been taught that things were so bad in Noah's time that God decided he would make a fresh start with a few good people, Noah's family. All others, unnumbered men, women, and children, not to mention how many animals, were drowned. I came to firmly doubt that a God of good character, worthy of worship, would do that.

I slowly shared with random people who would listen, including a few teachers, and my dad, that if I was playing a high-stakes tennis match with someone, and there were spectators, and I was losing badly, so then walked over to the scoreboard and rolled things back to a fresh start, zero-zero, that no spectator there could or would conclude that I was fair.

I didn't do this kind of independent thinking with a cavalier attitude. I sincerely felt and believed that God had been misunderstood in many ways, and that it was part of an honest and sincere believer's task to work on clearing up misunderstandings of God. I felt that there were examples of this in history. In part of the Protestant reformation John Calvin had proposed and promoted the idea of predestination, an idea that everyone I knew in the late 1970s no longer accepted. But it had been a welcome new idea in the mid-1500s, because it was much better than buying your salvation from a corrupt priest, and even more so if you were too poor to do that.

Another example was humanity's perception of how God viewed slavery. For centuries Christians used scripture to justify slavery until we finally understood that a fair/just God couldn't possibly favor the enslavement of some who He made in His image by others made likewise. I knew that understanding anything was a work in progress, and felt like there was a constructive role to be played in working on our understandings of God.

I had friends who I felt were simply better at close conversations with God than I was. I had an active prayer life, but I knew I couldn't

Taking New Paths *Stories of Leaving Religion*

honestly claim, externally or internally, that "Jesus was my best friend," and I did have some friends who seemed to honestly say that. I didn't think though, that God was a one-size-fits-all cookie cutter God.

I knew my mom, for example, had a deep, simple, and profound faith, and did not tend to puzzle, question, or seek to improve understanding. I felt that God was probably fine with that, but that he also wasn't insecure or threatened by me, and various others, who did puzzle, who sought to grow in depth and breadth of understanding, and who therefore questioned some things that the tradition around us had passed down. In fact, I suspected God appreciated sincere seeking, puzzling and questioning, which could clear up historical misunderstandings of him.

The summer before my senior year I took a job called *colporteuring*, which was selling health and religious books for the Adventist church. Adventists are sometimes confused with Mormons and/or Jehovah's Witnesses because they all emphasize "your body is the temple of God," and thus no smoking, no alcohol, and for the strict not even any caffeine. Most Adventists are vegetarians, and those who aren't, follow biblical distinctions between clean and unclean meats.

Since I knew that there was a very large population of east Indians in and around Vancouver, B.C., and felt that my still-functional Hindi could be a natural bridge, I focused on that community. I had many great conversations...but after a full month of trying, hadn't sold a single book. The church colporteur managers had been trying to convince me to move after the first two weeks of no sales, and now I was ready to listen.

Prayer seemed to confirm this. They sent me to Kamloops, where I quickly started moving the books carrying messages I believed in. In addition, my little Pinto and I served as daily transportation to three young Nigerian men who were also calporteuring there that summer. It all ended well.

I graduated in 1980, and was still shopping around for a job when I was asked if I would go teach in a small Adventist college in Beirut, Lebanon. It wouldn't pay much, but the combination of science and phys ed was perfect, and I loved the idea of the adventure.

My Roots, My Journey, My Present

I prayed about it, talked with my parents, enthusiastically said yes, and headed to Beirut.

In the spring of 1981, we had an unplanned six-week break from school because fighting had broken out in and around the city. The majority of students there were locals, some Adventists and some not. But we also had many boarding students from Egypt, Syria, and Iran, among others, and they couldn't just disappear into local neighborhoods. Most of the fighting wasn't right in our area. On some nights we could, from rooftops at a safe distance, watch tracer bullet firefights, occasional magnesium flares lighting up multi-block areas of the city, and artillery shellings.

More than once I drove past shelled-out buildings, and on one such trip experienced the momentary intense fear caused by sniper fire. We weren't hit, and in hindsight I think they were intentionally just scaring the crap out of us; it pretty much worked because we knew people were being killed not just in firefights, but by seemingly random snipers, too. And if one of the church's printing press workers had been home when his apartment took an artillery shell, he and his family would have been among the dead.

Our boarding students, with no classes to attend, needed something to do. The college President, Don Eichner, asked me to organize regular campus recreation for the students who were stuck on campus. In various arrangements of teams, we played a ton of volleyball. It is a very strange thing to get used to; playing, shouting encouragement, teasing, etc., to the background sounds of machine guns and artillery where people were killing, and dying, just a few miles away.

Some days there was no fighting. At one point after a few consecutive days of no fighting, two of my local students showed up on campus and asked if I wanted to come to an empty little valley and try out some of their weaponry. It sounded like fun to me, so I got to empty a couple magazines each from an M16, a Belgian FAL, and an AK47, and throw a hand grenade. (My ears rang for several days!)

On the drive back to campus I asked a number of questions about who had been fighting whom in these recent weeks. They gave me answers that sometimes seemed simple enough, but sometimes seemed convoluted. Our discussion continued as we sat on a roadside wall back on campus. The various militias all had a religious affiliation.

Taking New Paths *Stories of Leaving Religion*

Different alliances held for varied lengths of time. I pressed for more clarity on the role of religion. I guess I shouldn't have been surprised, but with the Adventist heritage of conscientious objectors and non-combatants I came from, I was surprised at first that religion played a central role in ongoing fights.

Alone that evening, I puzzled a bit about it. Here, in this modern era, people were still not only dying for, they were also killing for *their* God. And I had long-since seen that even when groups don't kill over it, they busily compete in converting 'others' to their beliefs, in their God, and their book(s). I was in the middle of pondering the irony of enemy groups all being so sure that their God, their book, their people, were the right ones, when it dawned on me that I, too, was confident that my God, my book, my people were the right ones. While I wasn't busy killing over it, I still couldn't deny the reality that I was participating in that first fundamental step, a step I would then ponder for years.

When I got back to the U.S. I started my masters at the University of Oregon. Other than the winter quarter of my senior year in college, when I did my student practice-teaching in a public high school near Walla Walla, I had never set foot in a non-Adventist school. Academically I thrived, as before, but socially I was always conscious of the advice we had heard since high school: "Be ye not unequally yoked together with non-believers." Here I was, surrounded by many more thousands of fellow-students than ever before, but, although I functioned well in group projects and discussions, I felt very alone.

I then taught for two years at an Adventist junior high in Torrance, a suburb of Los Angeles. I finished my masters in the summer of 1984, and headed to a new job teaching in the Adventist academy at Canadian Union College, between Calgary and Edmonton, in Alberta.

Even though we were a private Christian school, the provincial educational authorities there required that all school's curricula include a substantial, and time documented, teaching of evolution. We weren't allowed to give it the two-minute treatment that I had received in academy. So I somewhat deeply exposed my students to the fossil record, and to the mechanism of natural selection. And then I explained that as Christian believers, in the church, we believed that natural selection could account for what we called "micro-evolution," like the minor changes like coloration within a species, but not "macro-

My Roots, My Journey, My Present

evolution," the complete process from bacteria, to invertebrates, to jawless fish and on up through fish, amphibians, reptiles, birds, mammals, to, and including, humans. With regard to the fossil record, I explained the "Ecological Zonation Theory" proposed and taught by scientists in the Adventist church, and subscribed to in variation by many generally fundamentalist or evangelical Christian denominations. I explained that the fossil sequence could be explained by the three factors of where the organisms lived, how mobile they were, and how intelligent they were, when Noah's flood wiped them out.

A tall, thin, Australian exchange student raised his hand. "Is that the best we can offer?" he asked.

"Well," I started, "I'm very aware that it's not a perfect explanation, but yes, as far as I've been able to find, it is the best we have to offer."

"Come on Matheson," he replied, "imagine that some dogs, or pigs, or tigers, or crows, etc., had died and been buried in some watery sediments a year, or a decade, or a century, or more, before this flood happened. Why don't we find any bird or mammal fossils down there among the early fish? And not even among many layers above that, until we find all the birds and mammals starting?"

I could only reply, "You've asked a really good question, and one to which I don't think we have a good answer."

I had mentioned, but hadn't explained in much detail, the mass extinctions, so they didn't ask any questions there. But I still struggled internally with the fact that five separate times in the fossil layers, suddenly many millions of species until then extant, disappeared, never to be seen again. What is more remarkable is that after the mass extinction, in the fossil layers immediately above the worst of the extinction, life forms are found to have quite quickly re-diversified. And this happened after each of the mass extinctions.

How could Noah's flood account for that? And what do we do with the simple fact that there are more species specialized to some parasitic niche than free-living? We picture the Garden of Eden as perfect, not even any carnivores, certainly not any parasites. Did God temporarily grant the devil creative powers, and he made parasites? Or did major aspects of evolution happen in this narrow field?

Other ingenious and sometimes desperate attempts to explain

Taking New Paths *Stories of Leaving Religion*

the evidence had been made. One of the most creative I'd ever heard proposed that the flood did indeed create a relatively chaotic scatter of dead stuff like one would expect. But then the devil and his angels saw an opportunity to deceive future generations of man into thinking that there was a pattern which showed a sequence of evolutionary change, so they got right into the messy mud of the flood aftermath and arranged the carcasses, to then end up with orderly fossil changes.

My students recognized that we can't prove or disprove that explanation; with a smile we could simply acknowledge that it is "possible." However, the difference though between "possible" and "probable/logical" was important. It was possible that I was nothing more than a worm off in space with a vivid imagination; I imagined my life, my work, even my thinking this through. It was also possible that anyone considering this thought is the worm off in space with the vivid imagination; imagining his/her family and life, and thinking this. It seemed clearly better, to me, to get over what's possible, and begin to really look at what's probable and logical.

Interestingly, my admission to my students that our Ecological Zonation Theory attempt to explain the fossil record wasn't perfect, and had obvious shortcomings, got me an invitation to a conversation with the principal. He wasn't angry, and was understanding, but simply wanted to remind me that these students were sixteen and seventeen, and were perhaps "not ready for this."

Knowing that the college science department chair, Bruce Butler, taught a college course called "Issues in Science and Religion," I talked this through with him. Having had diverse science majors and theology majors in his class, ranging from twenty to forty years old, his final observation was, "With time, they only get less and less ready to deal with difficult stuff like this."

In my second year there, a weekend seminar for science and theology faculty and students was held by Dr. Robert Brown, then chairman of the Geoscience Research Institute. During a Q&A after one of the sessions a faculty member asked: "Is there any kind of evidence, in any quantity, which would make you recognize that evolution is real?" It was pin-drop quiet for several seconds. Then Dr.

My Roots, My Journey, My Present

Brown slowly shook his head and said, "No, my faith is too strong for that." The room filled with reassured "Amens."

I wasn't at all sure that his response represented honest science, and I knew I didn't buy the flood story anymore, but without settling on some form of theistic evolution, I put this kettle on the back burner of my mental stove.

I found it troubling that the very accusation I had heard leveled at evolutionists—that they form their conclusions ahead of time and selectively look for or create data that support their theories—seemed to be true of my then fellow conservatives.

I would simply continue to gather information, ask more questions, and search for other perhaps plausible explanations; somehow I was still confident that God was there, and was good.

While teaching there I had my first experience with being published. The Adventist church worldwide put out quarterly Sabbath School study guides aimed at various age groups, and I was asked if I would write a selection exploring the Gospel Commission (Matthew 28:16-20; "Go ye unto all the world, baptizing...") for the young adult quarterly. In my piece I asked my fellow young adults to explore the "why" behind the commission.

I made the argument that if God was infinitely insightful, and fair and loving, that he wouldn't condemn to hell some villagers somewhere who never accepted Jesus because they'd never even heard of him, or because the missionaries who did get there were power-hungry, ego-and ethno-centric, manipulative, and generally seemed to be bad people, whose Jesus the villagers then rejected. I argued that God wouldn't make an eternal judgment that depended on a coincidence, i.e. having heard of Jesus, or at least perceiving that Jesus was essentially good. I argued that if God could read the heart and mind, he could assess the honesty of character of any villager, or any of us, based on how we respond to whatever light we did get. I then suggested that in Jesus' life he paid a ton of attention to the quality of life experienced by the suffering and the poor, and he did practical things to improve that quality of life, without insisting on them dropping whatever they believed, and accepting him as God.

I got married between my second and third year there, and after my third year we moved to Loma Linda, California, where there was a major Adventist community and university where my wife

Taking New Paths *Stories of Leaving Religion*

could finish nursing school. I chose to take a break from teaching, and did one year of construction work, happily learning how to build, and one year in science research, experiencing where the rubber meets the road in exploratory science.

On Sabbaths there I regularly attended an extended and wide-ranging discussion led by Graham Maxwell (a brother of Malcolm at Walla Walla; both sons of the famous Adventist 'Uncle Arthur' Maxwell). I liked his open explorations, and frequent themes like Jesus having said "I call you no longer my servants; I call you my friends," (John 15:15) and his own oft-repeated quote that "God is not harsh, vengeful, unforgiving, and severe." I felt that Graham Maxwell was a leader in clearing up misunderstandings of God.

While still in Loma Linda, my wife and I were asked if we would consider going to Rwanda, with me coordinating our church's public health work (my master's from the University of Oregon having been in Health Education). I felt this was a perfect opportunity to work to elevate the practical quality of life of the too often suffering poor people in outback Africa, without being caught up in typical evangelism, which I felt was unnecessary.

So, with my wife in the early stage of pregnancy, we headed to France for me to learn French before going on to Rwanda. My wife's mother-tongue was French, so I had homework help, and learning went well. Our big event there was the birth of our daughter in the fall of 1990. I remember holding her in church one Sabbath as we sang a song with a verse whose words were: "This child can face uncertain days, because he lives." I believed, I felt, that.

At the end of January, 1991, we flew to Rwanda. We knew that Rwanda was mid-stride in making transitions to a multi-party democracy, and that therefore there were occasional localized conflicts, but the news and projections indicated general progress and stability. When we got there, we found a beautiful country, and wonderful and welcoming people. I busied myself with my work, including an unexpected aspect of it, that of managing five scattered very rural clinics with inpatient capacities from four to thirty-five beds.

My parents were able to visit us for a couple months around the time that our baby girl turned one. That visit became all the more special in hindsight when about a year later my sister called, telling me that Dad had died. He had lived a good life, and while at seventy-

My Roots, My Journey, My Present

five it wasn't really long, it's also was not a life cut short. I knew he wouldn't have wanted a long decline into disability.

When our girl was about two and a half, in the spring of 1993 we welcomed her little brother, our son, born in the home of a good Belgian doctor and his midwife wife. Life was good.

Even though I was not a preacher/ordained minister, I was periodically asked to speak to various Adventist congregations, some with a physical church, some with no more than a designated open space in a field or around a large shade tree. I usually spoke on a theme which included a different look at suffering. To illiterate and poor peasants, suffering was just part of life, and they mostly talked about it being from God, as either direct punishment or to help teach some life lesson.

I presented the illustration of a friend I knew in India who had been blind since the age of four. He suffered this permanent loss, not because he, or his parents, had sinned or done wrong, but because his parents were very poor, and uniformed. They had not known that foods with vitamin A (or its precursor pigment) were necessary, and that if nearly completely left out, this deficiency would cause blindness. Had they known that papayas, or carrots, or mangos would meet this need, and that brown rice was better than white, he would not have become blind. My point was that God would prefer to minimize suffering, and that we can help with that by learning all we can, thus preventing avoidable suffering.

I always did this speaking through a translator into the local Kinyarwanda. Usually my translator was a coworker whom I knew well and trusted. I talked afterward with one I knew best, and asked about whether or not this idea of suffering seemed to make sense to rural people whose lives had a lot of it. He said that he thought it did in their heads, but he was honest enough to note that he didn't think it would affect what they felt in their guts about their daily lives. I had to agree.

I think it was in mid to late 1993 that I needed to make a trip to one of the two largest of the clinics I managed. Our car needed some work right then, so I caught a lift to Kigali's big taxi/bus station, and climbed into a rapidly filling *matatu* (taxi-van; inevitably packed full) heading a couple hours to Rwankeri up north. I had almost always driven my own way around the country, so being a passenger left me

Taking New Paths *Stories of Leaving Religion*

not needing to pay attention to everything on the road. Not being able to speak the local language and chat with fellow passengers, I was really alone with my thoughts.

I remember watching the beautiful scenery while pondering that these people, just like everyone throughout history, and like me, subscribed to ideas about God that made sense in their lives. Calvin had come up with predestination, and others liked it, because it got past corrupt priests; later people rejected predestination. Early people had justified and taken advantage of slavery; later people condemned it. I realized that I, in order to not throw the baby out with the bathwater, had continued to modify things about God to make them more acceptable, at least to me. I couldn't go back from this realization.

The flood did indeed not make sense, on so many levels. The God who would 'sic' she-bears on a whole bunch of kids for teasing a prophet, strike a man dead for trying to keep the Ark of the Covenant from toppling down to the ground (despite his good intentions), lead "His people" and destroy entire city's inhabitants (men, women, and children), outline an okay way to sell your daughter into slavery, or decree that gays should be killed, our understandings of that God needed modifying. But that, it now seemed inevitably obvious, was what the evolution of religions was about: We make our gods on our idealized or acceptable terms.

I had read, skeptically at first, a lot of archaeology over the years, and now had to face what in summary I could picture: that when our early ancestors developed self-awareness, and a caveman saw his brother's eyes fade to the blank stare of death after being gored on a hunt, and saw the same thing happen in his toddling daughter's eyes from just a couple days of watery crapping, that he came not only to fear death in a sense beyond what animals do, and that he and his clan created stories of what might be possible, what might happen, after death…stories which reduced fear and added hope, thus being a helpful coping mechanism for dealing with their very hazard-filled life.

Besides this self-aware fearing of death, and the unsurprising way of coping with it, our early ancestors also had a seemingly never-ending set of puzzlers that they could not understand. What makes the river rise seasonally when it hasn't rained in months on our horizons? What occasionally makes the moon go blood-colored and then quickly

My Roots, My Journey, My Present

come back to normal? What is that rare strange fuzzy light with the long tail in the night sky? What makes the very regular tides of the ocean? What causes different sicknesses? What is the sun? What causes thunder, and what causes lightning, and even wind? What are these images I see in my eyes sometimes when I sleep? And what do they mean? By far the most likely "explanations" which people in those primitive circumstances could, and did, come up with were spirit-world explanations. Naturally, these would have been passed down in oral histories, and their collection of spirits became part of their clan's identity.

It was no surprise that as hunter-gathering ways gave way to the agriculture and to living in communities, that as labor specialized and society stratified, these spirit-world explanations solidified into increasingly formalized religions, with symbols and rituals and a priest class to rule that domain. Through this came the variety of gods, and faiths, varying with location and time.

I knew I couldn't go back and "unrealize" how humanity has made our gods. I didn't then even like where I'd arrived, but liking it or not, I was even more sure, was not the point. A number of kettles were now off the back burner of my mental stove; they had slow-cooked for years. Besides all the modern gods and religions that I had seen up close in my life, and the many that I hadn't, there were who knows how many ancient ones from western Greek, Roman, Germanic, and Scandinavian, to Incan, Mayan, Aztec, and Iroquois, to Chinese, Japanese, Australian Aboriginal, and various Pacific islander, to Egyptian, Ghanaian, and Malagasy, to Persian, to...where does the list end? Simple logic says they can't all be right. And although some adherents of each, at the right time and place in history, would claim that theirs was right and all others wrong, the mere fact of that claim from multiple contradicting perspectives made it as clearly an error from all as it did from one.

I kept my thoughts to myself; no one else there would have wanted to hear them. I could still work with focus and satisfaction trying to make a practical difference in the quality of life of poor, suffering, people. I still whole-heartedly bought into the broad idea of treating others as you'd like to be treated. And I could be an involved dad of two wonderful little people, who were both my delight, and something more. Since if I couldn't count on the supernatural to make

Taking New Paths *Stories of Leaving Religion*

my kids able to "face uncertain days," that would be my responsibility, and to do it as best I could.

Less than a year later, in the evening of the first Wednesday of April, 1994, we got word that Rwandan President Habyarimana's plane had been shot down on approach to the airport. It wasn't the first political killing in our time there, but we knew this had the most potential for trouble. That trouble erupted, seemingly everywhere at once, including on our little dirt road, before dawn Thursday morning. Machine gun fire from within thirty yards can wake you in a hurry; we got our kids and ourselves nearly instantly into our almost windowless hallway, and waited.

We then essentially lived in a hallway, on a mattress on the floor and under a sturdy table. Before the phones went dead, my oldest brother had called. I assured him, as I did my wife, that foreigners were not targets; neither side wanted to be blamed for any such deaths. All we had to do was avoid crossfire; but what was happening to local Tutsis, and any perceived sympathizers, was becoming obvious.

On Sunday we, along with a number of fellow-Adventist foreign families, joined a large evacuation convoy to drive to Burundi, the country to our south. Our son was just a baby, and wouldn't remember any of the horrific scenes, but a good number of times we made sure that our daughter ducked down to avoid them. It was obvious to her that our routine lives had turned upside, and she didn't question our instructions to duck down immediately if we told her to. By the time tropical nightfall was rapidly descending, we were out of Rwanda.

On Monday morning a U.S. Marine jet flew in to Bujumbura to take us all to Nairobi, Kenya. On boarding the jet we were seated in one of the long rows that ran the length of each side of the plane, and handed ear plugs. With almost no further delay we were off the ground and climbing steeply. After two or three minutes of steady altitude gain, I squeezed my wife's knee; "We're out," I nearly shouted right into her ear, and then involuntarily exhaled. She nodded, her eyes watery. There were no windows, but I could picture so well the land below. I knew a lot of people who weren't out, and really had nowhere to go.

We spent a week in Nairobi, waiting, and watching news on TV. At the end of that week church administrators decided that the storm in Rwanda wasn't blowing over, so it was time to repatriate everyone. Several days later church authorities informed us that the evacuated employees were being asked to participate in a debriefing/group therapy session in Virginia.

It was good to see those colleagues again, even if after only a relatively short separation. Some had worked in different parts of Rwanda, had gotten out by different means, and had experienced very different levels of closeness to horror.

Among the things that stick in my memory from those meetings were some rather tough experiences that a few had gone through. One couple from our university campus there, recounted watching with a Tutsi from inside their house as a mob of machete-wielding teenagers chased two Tutsi young ladies toward their house. They knew that if they opened the door to rescue those two, they and the third Tutsi inside their house would probably all be butchered. In that moment they decided to keep the one already hidden in their house safe; they didn't open the door, and they had to listen to the final screams of two young women mixed with sounds of machetes hacking into flesh and hitting bone until silence fell and the mob left.

Another thing that sticks in my mind is how many times someone in our group of evacuees thanked god for answering prayer and seeing them safely out. I remember trying gently to remind us that many other desperate prayers had gone and were continuing to go unanswered; a genocide was unfolding. I tried to suggest that there was nothing wrong with simply being grateful to have survived, but that crediting god for it was in a peculiar way egotistical. Were we somehow more special than Rwandans in this god's eyes?

I kept most of my questions and doubts to myself; they were unwelcome and perhaps not even constructive in the context of people trying to get back on their emotional feet. It was becoming increasingly clear that it is human nature to believe what each of us happens to want (or need) to believe.

I told my wife that I no longer wanted to work for the church. She accepted that with no trouble, and didn't really ask questions. Perhaps she knew there was stuff she'd rather not know.

Taking New Paths *Stories of Leaving Religion*

We set about trying to find a place that felt safe to raise our kids, and ultimately settled down in the fairly small town of Klamath Falls, in southern Oregon, where I started teaching in a public school.

I taught and coached, my wife took up nursing again, our kids grew, and we added our second daughter to our family in the summer of 1998, with the older two welcoming her excitedly. I was flying by the seat of my pants in terms of how to raise kids without indoctrinating them, in any direction. I didn't want to be personally dishonest with them, but I couldn't hit kids with all the hoops I had slowly worked my way through. I tried to find age-appropriate ways to encourage them to question things, to compare stuff, to see if things contradicted, notice when things did or didn't make sense, to look stuff up if possible, and to bounce questions and thoughts off me as often as they wanted.

My wife still wanted to attend church and Sabbath School, so I didn't object. My questions or comments weren't welcome in any adult discussion group, so I just accompanied the kids to their class. It gave me the perfect opportunity to be able to insightfully help them debrief with follow-up questions afterward. We sometimes looked up and compared stuff together.

My oldest brother and I, in a couple years' worth of frequent and regular phone conversations, slowly, cautiously at first, discovered we had completely independently walked very similar intellectual paths. We hadn't been close as kids, and this discovery brought us much closer.

I lived a decade plus with the approach of live-and-let-live; you could be Jewish, Muslim, Catholic, Adventist, Buddhist, Hindu, Mormon, Lutheran…it didn't matter. I didn't bother anybody with my doubts or assessments on life, and I didn't question theirs. In general, this was a fairly lonely time, though. I missed fellowship and discussion. Personally, my longing for broader interactions was reduced because I was a busy and involved dad, a teacher and coach, and so had enjoyable interactions and discussions.

I also actively studied new areas like astronomy, doing two summers of research fellowship, read more actively than ever, and joined the local tennis club, and started a local group of FreeThinkers, thoroughly enjoying deep monthly discussions. In hindsight, I didn't set out to find new venues where degrees of fellowship and discussion

My Roots, My Journey, My Present

were possible and likely, but almost stumbled into elements of interaction which really helped reduce my feeling loneliness when I had left what had surrounded me most of my life.

Watching the American response to 9/11 began to make me reassess my live-and-let-live approach. When we couldn't quickly track down and kill Osama bin-Laden in the mountains of Afghanistan, and President George W. Bush began to drum up political support for invading Iraq, several things were fairly clear to a careful observer: George Bush sincerely believed that his god was the right one, that he was a tool in that god's hands, and that he perceived communication directly from this god. He used the notion of "God Bless America," implying that this god is on America's side, to drum up support for war. The old-fashioned "For God and Country" worked quite well. Support for invading Iraq rose among those on the religious right; the secular left tended to be pointing to the same questions our allies in places like Germany and Canada were asking.

As I watched this, I realized that bin-Laden, too, was confident that his god was the right one, that he was a tool in that god's hands, and that he perceived communication directly from this god. He, too, sought support and recruits, and rallied his fighters with, "For God and Cause" if not country.

As history played out before my eyes, I first saw the risk that strong faith tends to predispose people to more quickly jumping on the bandwagon of war. Clearly we don't need to look back at the crusades; this is current. Second, I saw the risk that strong faith also predisposes people to assume that everything is in their god's hands, that they're too small to make a difference, and that therefore they don't need to take any of our earthly challenges seriously, much less urgently.

I've known some believers who do a generally good job self-monitoring against falling for the above two risks. A third risk, which far fewer are able to avoid, took me longer to put my finger on, and requires a bit more background.

In a list of my self-evident truths, I included: "We owe a decent, stable, and (hopefully) enjoyable planet to future generations." To be up to this challenge, we've got to be at our best as problem-solvers.

Taking New Paths *Stories of Leaving Religion*

That requires being honest with evidence, and not simply selecting evidence we like, dismissing what we don't. To cultivate a tendency in that direction, we have to be honest about things that get in the way of that. We must recognize that it's human nature to believe what we want to believe, and expect that our beliefs should be "respected." We must then ask: Where in human experience do we get the most practice at, the most reinforcement for, believing what we want, and expecting that to be respected, to go unchallenged?

I have now spent two decades searching, and a recent year studying anthropology, to find the best answer to that question. I have yet to find a better-supported answer than that comes from typical training within a community of those with sincerely held religious beliefs. From childhood we learn that we don't directly challenge others' beliefs, even while we might try to share our "better" beliefs, and even if within our communities we might call *their* beliefs nutty or dangerous. In exchange expect the same absence of challenge directed at us.

It is a very short step then, in our minds, to expect nonreligious beliefs to also be respected and go unchallenged. This has been increasing in very recent years. Flat-earthers hold conventions and don't like being challenged. Some deny plate tectonics; some of the same promote a very young earth, and don't like being challenged. Some say vaccines, before but certainly particularly including COVID, are dangerous conspiracies, and feel attacked if challenged. Some dismiss climate change, and don't want a discussion of serious physics, or broad evidence, and again, feel that their opinion is of equal weight to the expressed concerns and evidence/reasons given by experts. Habituation does and habits do matter.

Having seen the fabric of civilization fray significantly twice, and smelled the ugly smell of rampant death, I don't want to endlessly delay and deny until we're on the precipice of chaos. I don't think most realize how slippery that slope is. I hope we can build some broadly accepted new habits of being willing to change our minds when the evidence warrants, and of then making different and more broadly inclusive policies aimed to "promote the general welfare," including in a global sense. But this kind of change is not going to happen by accident; it is going to take deliberate, focused, effort.

My Roots, My Journey, My Present

This does impact our politics, and our relationships, and there are prices to be paid. While I have some closer relationships, I also have newly strained relations. It certainly varies by individual case.

I discuss a fourth risk in an essay listed among other recommended reading at the end of this chapter. It is addressed to dual audiences: concerned citizens and anthropologists, and focuses on how honesty is a prerequisite to solving problems in the face of imminent global challenges, and how to improve communication between academics and concerned citizens.

My mom was still very coherent in her mid-eighties when I published my first book. In it, while not promoting atheism, I did promote a hard and honest look at some of the historic negatives of religion, and a deliberate effort on the individual level to be aware of and limit those negatives. My mom got a copy, read it, and jotted thoughts in the margins of various pages and we discussed some of these for a couple hours on a road trip the two of us shared. The bottom line that was worrying her was that she felt, and believed, that my questioning was putting "my soul" in danger of eternal damnation.

I was a parent of three, and understood a parent's love, and the desire to minimize pain and maximize joy and constructive satisfaction. I tried to reassure her by saying: "Mom, you believe that your god is loving, just, fair, knows all, is insightful, can read minds, and hearts?"

She nodded.

"And you believe that he is not insecure or easily threatened?" Again she nodded.

"And you recognize that there have been a lot of historic misunderstandings of him, things like slavery once being okay?" She nodded still.

"So I don't think your god would be threatened by my questions. I don't think he'd be against pursuing improved understanding. And I think he would see how I'm living my life...not destructively, not self-centeredly. It seems that many Christians live a "good" life, and don't ask serious questions, because they want to both avoid punishment and get a reward. If your god can read motives, I think he would see that my motives for trying to make a constructive difference amidst society are less self-centered than most Christians.

"I'm not afraid of going to hell because if there's a god who is

Taking New Paths *Stories of Leaving Religion*

insightful and fair and not insecure, I suspect I'm in better shape to be judged a "safe citizen" for eternity than the vast majority of believers who behave for extrinsic motives, not intrinsic. So I would encourage you to not worry about me. If god is how you like to think he is, I'll be okay."

She smiled, looked at me, looked back down the road, looked back at me, and with a little nod of her head, folded my book shut. I wasn't sure if one conversation was sufficient to overcome a lifetime of believing that this god liked hearing angels endlessly chant "holy, holy, holy" and would indeed condemn some to eternal suffering in hell, but she genuinely seemed much more at peace.

I didn't add that I felt that if this god, in combination with reputed all-knowing insight, was not fair/just, and was easily threatened, that I would want no part in his eternity. I didn't add that clarification because I felt it could undo some of her new sense of peace. I didn't think she was yet ready to think that it's okay to determine in our own minds what we think is worthy of respect, never mind "worship." Likewise with any discussion of "likelihoods."

With my wife, once I stated that I had reached the inevitable conclusion that strong religion was not only not the solution, it was core to our human problems, my then wife and I were on our way to divorce over irreconcilable differences.

I am beyond deeply grateful that our three children, grownups now, in their twenties and early thirties, have come to understand and respect my journey. With my siblings, it's a very mixed bag; it's hard to maintain closeness when most serious topics, far beyond religion directly, are not only unwelcome, but some are explicitly off limits. My point here is simply to be honest with any reader midstream in re-evaluation that—even if one won't experience the direct and complete shunning imposed on ex-Muslims or ex-Jehovah's Witnesses—there can be social/familial prices to be paid.

Fortunately I have formed many strong relationships with fellow-progressives who also share what we owe to future generations, and a simple core of two basic things:

My Roots, My Journey, My Present

1. A progressive has deep respect for as well as a commitment to verifiable evidence. This has implications. We are therefore open to modifying previous conclusions, prior beliefs. We're simply willing to change our minds, to admit when we were wrong. And, we're not preoccupied with maintaining or defending, any tradition. We're open to, and at times demand, change.

2. A progressive thoroughly embraces the idea of "promote the general welfare." We recognize that it's not "all about me and my rights, my ability to get ahead." We recognize the limitations of our pale blue dot of a planet, and we recognize the myriad ways in which the distribution of its resources, and of basic opportunity itself, has not been done with any semblance of equity, or sustainability, in mind. And we recognize that "the general welfare" applies to All people groups, and to future generations. And we're committed to taking concrete steps to do something about it.

I mentioned that in our last year in Rwanda, I didn't even like what I'd realized. But after a decade in a sometimes lonely sort of no man's land, as I now look back on the most recent fifteen years, I'm grateful for the sense of personal honesty, purpose, and responsibility, with which I've been able to live.

Five years ago I spent a year in the country of Oman. Many of my new Muslim friends not surprisingly tried to convert me. Mostly it made for some interesting discussions. In more than one setting I asked my discussion partners to imagine a big hotel to which we bring two people of every faith on earth, including the many offshoots of all the somewhat larger faiths. From each faith, one of the two people must be a top priest, rabbi, mullah, scholar—highly educated in his faith's literature and dogma; the second person need not be a scholar, but should have a reasonable general education and be a very sincere believer.

These hundreds of people of faith, arranged in their pairs, are told that they will be provided with a comprehensive library, internet access, and food and water, and asked to create an initial document listing fifty central, important, beliefs of their faith, while

Taking New Paths *Stories of Leaving Religion*

including distinguishing beliefs which make their faith different than all the others.

"You will all be locked in the hotel until you have met and discussed enough to persuade each other on what TRUTH is, so that you can write out an agreement on ONE list of fifty truths which at least ninety-five percent of you agree on."

"When will they come out of the hotel?" I asked my conversation partners.

They always smiled and said, "Never."

I then asked them to imagine a second hotel, to which we bring scientists who have various disagreements on broad or specific ideas held within science today.

These scientists make their lists of fifty things they hold to be true, again including some things on which they disagree. Again, they are provided with food and water, and library and internet, and laboratory equipment and space as needed, and then locked into this continuous science conference of a hotel where they can meet, argue, go back to their labs for weeks, months, or years, and meet some more. They are told that they can come out when their current lists have changed to where at least ninety-five percent of them agree on ONE list, while readily recognizing that new nuanced differences on new topics will rise as time marches on.

Again, I asked when they'll come out. My discussion buddies have each time been insightful enough to note that while they might be stuck there for years, even for many decades, that they wouldn't be stuck there forever. They've seemed to know that while science isn't perfect, and there are strong egos and disagreements, that science produces a forward movement as it develops consensus around ideas which are very well supported by verifiable evidence.

I'd heard various Americans dismiss Muslims as close-minded and dangerous as a whole group while considering themselves to be enlightened and open-minded, and had used this same illustration back in the U.S. In both America and in Oman, the group response to these two questions and illustrations is neither completely uniform nor always good humored. I've seen people sit in stone-faced silence as others participated in lively discussion. I've seen individuals doing open and honest exploration, with puzzled re-evaluation-in-process written clearly on their faces in both America and Oman. And I've seen that stone-faced silent resentment of any challenge to one's beliefs, and a clear unwillingness to even contemplate change in both our culture and theirs.

This is not meant to defend Islam; it is simply to help Western people of strong faith see that we, too, very often fall flat when it comes to intellectual/personal honesty. Further, some would point out that I didn't choose to try asking these questions surrounded by ISIS, and indeed I didn't. But I'm not comparing this to the Westboro Baptist Church either. Further, and more importantly, fundamentalist evangelical Christianity makes up a much, much greater fraction of America's society than ISIS does within Islam.

Can we learn—to quote Senator Daniel Patrick Moynihan—that "We're all entitled to our own opinions, but we're not entitled to our own facts?" Can we accept that some claims about reality (some beliefs) are indeed actually connected to reality, and some are not? This fact is central to what makes some opinions neither equal nor valid.

Among those in cultures whose first reaction is resentful silence, some have hung around and ended up expressing themselves, and after I've listened to them, some of them have done a little more listening. I've shared that while I realize that I'm stepping on toes and it's often not welcome, that if the Titanic (yes, they know that story and movie in Oman, too) is headed for an iceberg and many passengers are preoccupied with sipping their tea and enjoying the beautiful sounds of a string quartet, that efforts toward alerting more of the passengers (on this "ship" representing a nation, or civilization writ large), who then hire (what the votes in democracy do) a crew who pay deliberate attention to verifiable facts, might turn out a lot better than not disturbing the peace until it is too late to make a difference.

In our recently more polarized American culture (mirrored in many ways by more polarized cultures in many counties, including Britain where I recently studied), some Facebook friends have posted fact-checkably wrong info, and when I challenged the point of their post, they've asked me to quietly move on if I don't like something they post. I've responded by encouraging them to challenge me if and when they feel I'm factually wrong, or on the wrong side of history. It has made little difference. It's as if many now actually prefer their

Taking New Paths *Stories of Leaving Religion*

self-and technology-created echo-chamber. In order to be left alone in theirs, they offer the bargaining chip of leaving you alone in yours.

Politics is ostensibly forbidden territory around the Thanksgiving table, but it has also become off limits if what you're about to do is break into a person's or a group's echo-chamber with other information or perspective. If we're going to avoid the troubled waters and dangerous shoals our ship—or the whole ship of civilization—could face, we need informed, concerned, involved, and aware fellow-passengers who can and will engage in constructive conversations based in real, verifiable, facts. These conversations can't be expected to be easy or comfortable, but they can be civilized, and connected to checkable evidence in science and real lessons from history.

Here we are. I know people who genuinely think that other people of faith X or Y are thoroughly evil and must be fought, or are simply badly deluded and must not be accepted or allowed freedom, while they think that their unique beliefs are right and make them part of their god's special people. They won't engage in an attempt at public dialogue on how we establish truth, won't thoughtfully challenge (very different than dismissing) other belief systems because they don't want their own challenged. But they'll support a general cultural war and a military one aimed primarily at those 'other' people. Is this a solution that is honest with the evidence?

Among the many forks in the road of life, at which intersection is it that our choice can make the most vital difference?

I submit that it is this: every time we— as individuals or as societies—realize that there is a contradiction between what we believe, what we claim as our truth, and what the best evidence and consensus around it says, we have a choice: we can try to impose our beliefs on the evidence by dismissing, manipulating, selectively quoting it, OR, we can impose the evidence on our beliefs, being willing to recognize that we have been wrong, and then updating, changing our minds, and moving constructively forward.

This isn't necessarily easy, it doesn't come naturally. So, considering the intensity of some of the arguments this may generate, we have to ask if it matters. What difference does it make? Well, any scientist who won't impose the evidence on his or her prior beliefs, and change their mind, won't be able to honestly and effectively solve

My Roots, My Journey, My Present

problems, and will become irrelevant in their field. And, with the scale of our challenges today, if enough concerned citizens won't step up to this level of honesty, we, too, won't effectively solve problems, and civilization itself will become irrelevant.

So why do I share my story? Not to try to make atheists out of everyone. With the increasing numbers (especially of those significantly younger than I) in recent decades joining the ranks of "no faith," part of why I share is hoping to decrease the sense of loneliness experienced by those walking a similar path, and hoping that we might be understood better, and feared less. But much more so, my plea is that believers might honestly recognize the real risks, the sorts of baggage, that have come with strong faith, and personally commit to self-monitoring so that those risks don't become realities in their individual cases. This can spread. We can imagine that the passengers on the ship of civilization vote for crew members who will thoughtfully and open-mindedly consider the most verified facts, and consult painstakingly developed expertise, and take seriously their duty to chart a course which avoids the worst of hazards, and that they do this before momentum is too great and the distance or time too short.

I understand that for many, the fear of death, and the hope of living forever, make re-evaluating one's faith initially too painful to pursue past step one. But I was still surprised, twenty-five years after personally leaving my faith, in doing the wide-ranging reading necessary for my anthropology dissertation, to find this honest admission by the great theologian Karl Barth written in 1957 in "An Introductory Essay," to a reprinting of Ludwig Feuerbach's *The Essence of Christianity* from 1843:

> "The existence of God? The interest I have in knowing that God is, is one with the interest I have in knowing that I am immortal. (that is, that I am certain of my eternal blessedness)"

Taking New Paths *Stories of Leaving Religion*

I don't allow myself to place my psychological comfort above the price paid by others if I let these risks become realities.

To my readers here, as stated earlier, I don't ask you to abandon your faith if you find it essential to you; I ask you to self-monitor against the risks that can be a part of fundamentalist faith.

We're in a half-century that I'm gravely concerned is either sink or swim for civilization broadly. Most have seen the bumper-sticker asking "Got Purpose" meant as a promotion for religion. Well, I've got purpose with overdrive. I think we can leave future generations with a decent, stable, and enjoyable planet, in both ecologic and social terms. The question is, will we take the necessary steps of problem solving, and therefore of risk identification and reduction, to make this a reality?

Selected recommended reading:
Religion Explained, by Pascal Boyer
(patience; the most academic book here)

Handbook on Leaving Religion, by Enstedt, Larsson, and Mantsinen

Feet of Clay: A Study of Gurus, by Anthony Storr

For a rich history of a key turning point in the early development science and secular thinking:
The Swerve: How the World became Modern, by Stephen Greenblatt

Particularly for a deeply thought-provoking chapter in which expert witnesses for the prosecution and the defense give their testimony as to how society might make distinctions in the endless gray area between sincerely held beliefs and insanity. This is about a double murder in Utah in 1984. For context, Mormon history is troublingly laid out.
Under the Banner of Heaven: A Story of Violent Faith
by John Krakauer

For many in the west who are very unacquainted with the struggles of

My Roots, My Journey, My Present

those trying to leave Islam, and for Muslims struggling with just that:
The Apostates: When Muslims Leave Islam, by Simon Cottee

Particularly for any who find themselves employed by the organization whose claims they are actively re-evaluating:
Caught in the Pulpit: Leaving Belief Behind, by Daniel Dennett, and Linda LaScola

For Americans who want to learn more of the intersection of our history, politics, and religion:
Fantasyland: How America Went Haywire, by Kurt Andersen

Nature's God: The Heretical Origins of the American Republic, by Matthew Stewart

For both concerned citizens and anthropologists, an essay appealing for greater intellectual honesty and improved academic-public communication:
Fiddling, or Being Willing to Advocate for Unpopular Positions: A Look at a Key Root of the Fact/Alternative Fact Phenomenon. On medium.com search "Doug Matheson" and this essay title.

For those who find sticking with faith to be personally essential:
The Creation: An Appeal to Save Life on Earth, by E.O. Wilson

Taking New Paths *Stories of Leaving Religion*

8
From Mind Control to Freely Thinking
Laura Garcia Lopez

I NEVER THOUGHT I would identify as an atheist at the age of sixty when I was raised my whole life believing, with all my heart, mind, and soul that there is a God. I always can remember I had hope and purpose when I connected with God. My faith was strong even at five years old when I would pray to the Virgin Mary to help me find my lost turtle or I would hold my rosary and promise to share some of my winnings in the contribution box on Sunday if I won the poker pot at my family's card night on Saturday.

Of course, I would find my turtle under my bed that afternoon and I'd happily put a dollar in the contribution basket Sunday at mass. God always blessed me and he always provided. My mom was raised a Catholic and had been taught by nuns all twelve years of schooling, so when I was born and baptized at one month, I, too, was Catholic.

From Mind Control to Freely Thinking

Little did I know that I would be converted to another religion at thirteen years old and the trajectory of my life would change forever.

I was born in northern California in a very poor, crime-ridden neighborhood. I was the youngest of four girls and raised by a single mom; my father died when I was seven. My mom worked hard and gave us the best life she could. She used to call me her shadow because I was always around her. Naturally, her love of the Bible was easily transferred to me.

I remember how she would read the Bible almost daily on her bed at night. I would find myself cuddling up to her and listening to the life of Jesus. I was reminded of the huge children's bible encyclopedia book located at our doctor's office.

She would also read from the book of Revelation, and it all sounded so strange. On many occasions, I would find myself, at eight years old, holding my breath listening to how God was going to destroy wicked people on judgment day. He would use birds that would eat their flesh and pluck out their eyes. I saw God as a very powerful being and I told myself I needed to be a good girl so I wouldn't have such a horrible fate.

Over the next few years, I followed my mom to church every Sunday, prayed the Our Father and made the sign of the cross for just about everything. This was all I knew; my mom, her family, our friends were all Catholic.

Seventh grade was a turning point for me, both religiously and socially.

My mom had recently broken up with her longtime boyfriend who felt like a dad to me. Our hopes of moving out of the projects and having a better life faded away. Her dream—our dreams—were gone in an instant, stuck in a neighborhood that was no place for a young inquisitive rambunctious girl. My days of riding my bike and skating until sunset were over. Most of the childhood friends were transforming, too.

You basically had two choices as you approached puberty in my neighborhood; stay inside the house like a prisoner or start hanging out with the gangs. Men gathered in stairwells to sell and use drugs. So many of my childhood friends were now becoming single mothers. Going to church was sporadic and became less and less important in our family routine, but we still believed in God.

Taking New Paths *Stories of Leaving Religion*

I think this was when my mom started to question God and asked the priests to explain what she was reading in the Bible. She became more and more disillusioned as they used the catchphrase "God is a mystery" for most of their answers. I remember looking out my window toward the stars and asking God that if he remembered me and my family, to please show me a sign.

My earliest recollection of Jehovah's Witnesses was when our neighbor was asked if she wanted a free home Bible study by two women canvassing the neighborhood; later I learned this was called "field service." My mom apparently had listened to them at bus stops and had thus been given a book, *Babylon the Great, The Finished Mystery,* which she placed by her bed next to her Bible. The print was small and the illustrations were frightening.

Our neighbor asked my mom if she could study, too, and use her house for a Bible study. My mom agreed and the following week the two pretty women bought everyone their own personal study material, "The Truth That Leads to Eternal Life" and a green Bible. They also brought me one more book, especially for me and made just for young ones like myself: *Paradise Lost to Paradise Regained*.

Over the next few weeks, they took such an interest in us and I looked forward to their visits as a break in my isolated routine in the house. It was easy to find the answers and underline them, read my answers straight out of the book, and memorize one or two scriptures each week. I was praised over and over again for how fast I was learning and was such an excellent Bible student. I was desperate to learn anything, and they had an unlimited supply of books to read.

Slowly but surely, they prepared us to start going to the meetings and meeting all the other members at the Kingdom Hall. We started to learn many of the special words and terminology that were used among themselves, but somehow nobody else really knew.

For me, I had the attention I craved—a place to go on the weekend, and a bunch of people who showed tons of love every time we walked into the Kingdom Hall or when they came to our house to study the Bible. It was my opportunity to escape from our neighborhood and feel at peace with friendly people who loved me. I could now pray to God by name, *Jehovah*. He had sent these two women to save me. My prayers were answered.

From Mind Control to Freely Thinking

I distinctly and vividly remember my first visit to the Kingdom Hall one Sunday morning after only one month of studying. The talk was entitled, "Will You Survive Armageddon?" They were talking about the book of Revelation, the book that continued to fascinate me throughout my life. The speaker talked about Satan, dragons, and wild beasts who were enemies of Jehovah. I was seeing in my mind the birds eating wicked people who had died at Armageddon.

I did not want to die like that, so when the brother turned our attention to the end of Revelation where it described heaven with beautiful gems, pearl gates, and golden streets, I knew I wanted to be in paradise. For the first time, I found a way out of the projects.

The preacher on the platform even said that all us young ones would probably never die and we could survive Armageddon if we obeyed God. I would not have to grow up in the projects and I could live forever and never die. Wow, God's "promise" was music to my ears. It was everything I didn't have now.

My mom and I both bought this message hook, line, and sinker. There was just one small catch, we had to keep studying if we wanted to be in that paradise. Only baptized Jehovah's Witnesses would survive Armageddon. We had to stick with God's only true organization. All other religions got it wrong. They had "the truth."

As my mom studied, she had to leave behind all her Catholic teachings and her smoking habit. We were learning so many teachings far different from my mother's Catholic upbringing, but it all made sense. She was reading the scriptures from her Catholic Bible and then eventually switched to the JW's green Bible, because it explained things better.

I was young, naïve, and desperate to find hope outside our projects. I was a twelve year old girl who was promised a crime-free world. All I heard was I would live in paradise. Life would never be boring. I could pursue any interest I wanted, travel anywhere on the earth, and never grow old.

I could live in my own house in a beautiful park-like environment, pet wild animals, and have an abundance of food and resources—all free. I studied every week and heard so many in the

Taking New Paths *Stories of Leaving Religion*

congregation talk about paradise in such real ways. I had a scripture for all these promises. I was convinced I had "the truth."

My mom and I quickly made progress and were baptized together in May of 1975, when I was just thirteen years old—just in time. We were absolutely clear, the organization had apparently been buzzing the term, "Stay alive 'til seventy-five." This was the year the world would end.

We made it! Soon paradise would be here. We were completely settled in our spiritual routine, studying for and attending five meetings a week. We preached regularly on weekends, holidays, and during any vacation time we had—for me all summer. My mom cut off all her "worldly" friends and now we only associated with Jehovah's Witnesses.

We stopped celebrating birthdays, Christmas, and Easter, and any holiday you could think of, because they were all pagan or not acceptable to God, for one reason or another. I stopped playing in my school band and no longer participated in winter programs and musical competitions and was encouraged to make spiritual goals my priority.

The attention I received from my congregation kept us focused and faithful. We were so busy that 1975 came and went, with the loud buzz of Armageddon coming dwindling down to a quiet whisper. We just stopped talking about it, and no one questioned the silence.

I don't remember what changed the narrative so quickly, but I do recall a guest speaker from Bethel (New York Headquarters of JW) giving a special talk to adjust our thinking. We, the congregantes, had it all wrong. It was Brother Franz, one of the anointed and a member of the elite Governing Body, who came to our area to give a talk. I was so excited to actually be in the presence of one of the 144,000 who had the only hope to go to heaven and be kings and priests.

I sat in the audience of eleven thousand other brothers and sisters and listened to how he explained 1975 was just the mark of man's six thousand years of existence. We had a new adjustment as to when Armageddon would come. You see, we did not know when Eve was created. Maybe it was a few years later or a bit more.

The mystery time gap was the reason why the end had not yet arrived. But "apparently" God must have made Eve shortly after Adam was created, so though the end did not come in 1975, it was

From Mind Control to Freely Thinking

still imminent. Brother Franz, our direct channel to God continued to reassure us, it would be soon. He pointed out he was old now, and he looked forward to never dying and walking right into the New Order with us. We all stood up and applauded for such a long time, my hands started to burn.

I remember returning to my local congregation and many were still confused about what he meant and when they asked questions, were quickly silenced for talking negatively about God's anointed. I sat there thinking I'd better not bring up the thing I had learned in school, that humans existed for millions of years. It didn't make sense to me either. I walked away scratching my head but telling myself I was promised I would like it in paradise.

This was the start of my cognitive dissonance. What did I know? I was only fourteen years old. I just reminded myself that I needed to study more or just wait on Jehovah to help me understand. It wasn't the teachings that were flawed, it was me.

I continued to be active as a Jehovah's Witness all through high school. Enjoying the summer before my last year of school, I was asked over and over, "What are your plans after graduating?" Was I going to college or be a full-time preacher devoting ninety hours a month going from door to door? The promise of life on earth and being obedient in everything was well etched in my psyche.

That summer we had an international convention in our area, and they were going to feature missionaries from around the world. As I listened to their experiences, it sounded exciting and adventurous. Even when they suffered a hard trial, Jehovah always came through and provided for them. It was at that moment, I knew I wanted to be a missionary, too.

The brother made an announcement after the talk that anyone who was interested to join him during lunch, and he would share how we could do more for Jehovah as a missionary in an underdeveloped country. This was my big chance to serve Jehovah completely.

I barely sat down to hear the speaker say thanks for all the sisters who came, but they were really only looking for eligible brothers who could take the lead in forming congregations. This was

Taking New Paths *Stories of Leaving Religion*

not a role for a sister unless she was accompanying her husband in this assignment.

It was the first time I felt how misogynistic the organization was toward women. I was good enough to do the menial grunt work of vacuuming, cleaning toilets, and wiping down chairs after the meeting. I was good enough to cook meals and prepare lunches at assemblies. I was good enough to help out with secretarial work since many of the brothers did not know how to use a typewriter.

Now, I learned I wasn't good enough because women weren't allowed to preach from the platform, conduct or pray at meetings. It was a no-no for a woman to direct a baptized brother. They were our leaders.

I had three choices as I approached graduating from high school: getting a job right away, pioneering (full-time ministry in my congregation), and going to college.

The latter was frowned on, as we were reminded, we did not need a career in paradise. We had all our life to study and pursue our interests in God's *NEW* Order. I needed to use my vigor and energy to serve Jehovah and fulfill my dedication and baptism.

The pressure was on. I had lived on government assistance all my life and had a chance to get financial aid and scholarships if I decided to go to college. I could even get a student job and help my mom with our finances. I saw members of my congregation work minimum wage jobs and parents supporting them after high school. I did not have that option.

If I stopped my higher education, I would be cut off from all government financial resources and would have to support myself a hundred percent. My mom was already in the full-time service and barely making any money. We could not live on just her income. I had to contribute financially.

So, I rationalized to the Elders that I wasn't moving out to a dorm, and I would pioneer, too, so I would counteract any negative worldly influences that higher education would bring. As long I went to a community college and didn't talk about school to everyone, the Elders left me alone.

From Mind Control to Freely Thinking

Well, two years of community college turned into a transfer to a university. I earned a bachelor's and a master's degree while staying at home and pioneering full time. Now, I could start working and supporting myself. That's when the pressure to stay a pioneer started. The elders reminded me that Jehovah only permitted me to go to college so I could make enough money to work part time and continue with my "real career," pioneering.

Thinking quickly as I sat in the back room of the Hall with three elders, I announced confidently, "I have never intended on stopping pioneering." I needed to work full time to support my mom's pioneering AND I was still going to be a full-time minister. No worries, I was still the obedient faithful servant.

I continued for a few years more. My social life did not exist. I had no time for weekend recreation, I was going from door to door every Saturday and Sunday for at least eight hours each day. My evenings were taken up holding Bible studies from the time I got off at work until 9:00 p.m. in the evening.

I refused to give up a job I loved and wasn't allowed to stop pioneering. Even after fifteen years as a Jehovah's Witness, I was still hoping for Armageddon to come, and keeping a strong spiritual routine while working full time. I was exhausted and longed for paradise when I could take a break and enjoy the "real life."

The self-talk inside my head was incessant: *Personal goals are out of the question. They are selfish. Jehovah chose me to do His will and I have important work to do.* I slowly learned that every choice in my life, no matter how small or big, was smashed or controlled by this organization. My thoughts could not be my own. The pressure to do more for Jehovah only increased as I got older.

I told myself my heart condition is measured by how many hours I spend preaching. Busy must be good; I can't think about a social life anymore. It is 1990 now and the New System will absolutely come before our next century. I have less than ten years and I will gain the prize.

I had daily contact with my congregation, either in field service or meeting attendance. Even at home, alone in my room,

Taking New Paths *Stories of Leaving Religion*

I read only Watchtower literature, and was reminded of what I'd been trained to believe: *One way or the other, this wicked system of things is no place to raise a child. Besides, a perfect husband will be waiting for me in paradise, and I can have beautiful perfect children to raise and love.*

In the organization, dating was only for those considering marriage. I lived at home, exhausted, lonely, and still a virgin. I hadn't even held a young man's hand at twenty-four years old. I reminded myself that the only thing I was supposed to hold on to at this point in my life is God's guaranteed promise. *I need to focus on my blessings. I should be happy serving my Creator in my youth. I am serving a happy God.*

Yet, I was becoming more and more depressed. *Who am I to question any of the organization's lifesaving counsel and directions from God? It isn't all the restrictions this organization places on its members that is making me feel sad. God is not slow with his promises—I am impatient. I'm letting Satan win if I continue to have personal hopes and dreams. I need to pray more, do more, sacrifice more. Then I will be happy."*

I could never acknowledge publicly that I was miserable. I was burnt out and I really didn't want to pioneer anymore. The door-to-door ministry was boring; usually no one even answered the door. People were rude. Dogs attacked. I hadn't had a Bible study in years. It was exponentially exhausting, maintaining the façade that I was content and refreshed.

I had to stand up on the platform and relate to the audience all the blessings I had as a pioneer. They needed to join the ranks of full-time service so they can be happy, too. At times I would mumble to myself, "Jesus preached for only three and a half years, but I'm expected to never stop. Once a pioneer, always a pioneer."

This religion was becoming more and more controlling and all consuming. It was easy and exciting as a child with no responsibilities. But now, more was never enough. I had tapes running in my head all the time telling me to get rid of any thoughts that longed for a relationship, thoughts that said, "stay home tonight, take up a class, or a hobby."

I couldn't give time to worldly pursuits. My life belonged to God now. My joy turned into fear. My behavior became calculating

From Mind Control to Freely Thinking

to avoid yet any shepherding visit from the elders to encourage me to pick up the pace. I had to make sure I kept up the outer image of being a good Jehovah's Witness, regardless of how I felt inside.

I was even convinced that my prayers could be highjacked by Satan if I said them out loud. He would hear my words and I would be his target for persecution. Sadly, I still believed Armageddon would come soon and I would be devoured by Satan or eventually be food for the birds if I did not continue.

Looking back, I was maturing into a woman, and I was extremely lonely. I never really made lifelong college friends. I wasn't even allowed to build friendships from work. I wasn't allowed to understand my own personal desires and consider my own thoughts. I was good, no longer questioning anything that didn't make sense, and I prided myself on understanding all the convoluted reasons for a new belief, an adjusted take on the "truth."

I was self-disciplined to immediately catch a doubting thought and quickly readjust my thinking by immersing myself in our Bible-based literature. I was trying to find new ways to reinvent myself within the confines of the JW expectations.

I decided to join my local JW foreign language congregation. Surely, they could use a pioneer and I would become bilingual. My loneliness was appeased for a while as I kept busy learning a new language, making new friends, and helping form a new congregation.

I pretended I was a pseudo missionary in my own backyard. After a few years, though, and with no Bible studies, driving across town to speak to just one person and then finding out no one was home, I realized I was just going through the motions, counting time, and coming up with no results.

I loved the friends, so service and meetings became my social outlet and it seemed good enough for the time being. A few years went by, and all the single sisters were getting married; I was still single.

I was twenty-six years old and felt like a child, emotionally, when it came to having a relationship with someone of the opposite sex. I worked hard to gain Jehovah's approval and I was tired of waiting. I was still a virgin, living at home, and never been kissed, never dated, or even held hands with a guy. I needed to grow up and figure out who I was.

Taking New Paths *Stories of Leaving Religion*

That year I moved out of the house to my own apartment. I loved living on my own. I felt like a grownup for the first time. I still believed in the Bible and the promise of everlasting life on earth in perfect health. I was still waiting on Jehovah, but in the meantime, I could come and go as I pleased. I told myself, I'd show the elders I could stay faithful living on my own.

After about a year, I went less and less to the Kingdom Hall. I made a few close friends who were not Jehovah's Witness, and I even tried to date a few times. It felt awkward trying to make chit-chat when all I could talk about was work or the Bible.

Then I met a very nice man and started to have feelings for him. I had no intention of having a long-term relationship because he wasn't a Jehovah's Witness, but I convinced myself I wanted to lose my virginity with him, and thought he would be loving and gentle. He was.

My years of indoctrination were daunting, and the guilt was tremendous. I had sinned against my God, and I had to run to the Elders, like a child runs to a parent, and confess my error. I would submit to any punishment they gave me because I did not want to die at Armageddon.

Much to my surprise, I was shown mercy. I took this as a message from God. He was giving me another chance at paradise. I still had time.

I returned to my congregation determined to establish a spiritual routine of meeting attendance, prayer, personal study, and evangelizing every opportunity I could find. I had forgotten most of the second language I had learned, so it was hard to follow what the speaker was saying.

I found myself drifting in thought and not getting much from my attendance, except hanging out with my friends. I wondered if anyone knew what I had done. Did they still think I was a virgin at thirty years old? I felt like damaged goods with no opportunity to find a marriage mate or even have children. My maternal clock was ticking.

I prayed and recalled Habakkuk's plea, "How long?" I had been waiting since 1975. I'd lived through high school, college,

From Mind Control to Freely Thinking

developing a career. Still, how long before I could enjoy paradise? No way would I grow old in this old dying system of things.

Eventually, I met another man who would become my husband. He wasn't a Jehovah's Witness, but his grandparents and extended family were.

He understood where I was coming from and I didn't have to explain not celebrating birthdays, Christmas, or anything. He wasn't scared off by my religion, age, or career. His only observation was why someone hadn't snatched me up by now. We enjoyed each other's company. I felt beautiful and unconditionally loved when I was with him.

We dated for about a year and then got married. Soon we were expecting our first child and I started to think about the importance of raising our child in a religious environment. I still believed, and went back to what was familiar. I had not been in a Kingdom Hall for a few years, so I knew what I had to do.

I crawled back to the elders, confessed my sin, and resigned to accept whatever punishment they dished out. I confessed everything. I told them I had fornicated, but I tried to make it right and so we got married.

I also shared how sorry I was and knew I needed to come back to Jehovah in order to raise my child and give him an opportunity to live in paradise. I still believed this was the truth and I was so sorry for my behavior. I wanted to raise my child as a Jehovah's Witness.

They in turn, asked me about my unbelieving husband. Did I love him? Was I going to leave him? I said I did love him, and I had no intention of leaving him. We got along great, and he had no intention of interfering with my getting back into the religion.

After about a thirty-minute discussion with the Elders and a ten-minute wait, I was asked to come into the room again to hear their judgment. I was dis-fellowshipped, excommunicated. *When in doubt, kick them out.* Dis-fellowshipping is a horrible form of ostracism. I felt even more isolated than before, like an infectious leper. But even Jesus touched a leper and showed mercy. The elders had the final word because they had God's Holy Spirit.

My heart must have been wicked. I was unworthy and had to prove my loyalty now. I obediently returned to the meetings with my son in my arms. I sat in the back of the Kingdom Hall alone for over

Taking New Paths *Stories of Leaving Religion*

a year, not allowed to associate with anyone. These were my spiritual brothers and sisters who were trained to ignore me, mark me like a leper.

I thought to myself, "What happened to mercy?" I had come to them to confess and was hoping that they had empathy and compassion. I was struggling in my loneliness. Instead, I was on display every week as a reminder to the congregation not to marry an unbeliever. I told myself they would not break me.

When I was finally reinstated, everyone who walked past me in disdain now embraced me, as if nothing had happened. I was approved by God again and could now rebuild my standing with all the members. First on my list of congregational expectations was to go out in service every weekend and not miss any meeting in fear I would fall prey to Satan again.

Twenty years later and three beautiful loving children, we were the example Witness family, even with an unbelieving husband. My children were well behaved, they commented at meetings, and accompanied me out in service every week.

Those were the hardest years of my life. I had an unrealistic schedule that squeezed full time work, house cleaning, and keeping both myself and children on a spiritual routine. I was consumed with fear that maybe God didn't really forgive me. There were consequences to staying married to an unbeliever. Even when God forgave David for his sin with Bathsheba, didn't he let his son die as a consequence. I lived for a long time in fear that something horrible would happen to my children.

Forty years had passed since my baptism, and I was married with children and still waiting for Armageddon to arrive. I was now teaching my own children that soon paradise would be here and they could play with wild animals and live forever.

I ignored any doctrinal changes over the years. I had learned to dismiss any question that would rise from time to time. I prided myself on how I could follow the organization's endlessly twisting logic and reasoning. I looked past their made-up definitions, the deletion of scriptures, new coined terms that appeared out of nowhere. I had to believe this was the "truth." My children's lives now depended on believing.

From Mind Control to Freely Thinking

As much as I tried to understand changes in doctrine, it did not feel like the religion I had known at thirteen years old. My children were in high school and they had questions about what they heard from the Kingdom Hall.

They had questions about what they read in the Bible. They saw the inconsistencies, the hypocrisy, the lies. I couldn't explain why God didn't have a beginning when everything else had a beginning. I could not explain why we taught man has been around for just six thousand years when their teachers said the first human lived millions of years ago. How could a God of love have that she-bear kill forty children who teased Elisha?

They had so many questions that for the first time, I really had to think about the answers. The hardest questions came from my youngest child. He asked me if his dad was going to die at Armageddon because he was not a Jehovah's Witness.

My heart sank, but I still believed, and I knew I needed to step up my game. I needed to systematically study the Bible with them like I had in my youth. I was convinced more than ever that my children needed to get baptized. We were in the twenty-first century and Armageddon was imminent. We had no time to lose.

I asked an Elder in our congregation to study with my son, and I studied with my daughter. As we approached the summer assembly where they would get baptized, my oldest son said he needed more time. My daughter got baptized along with three of her friends. She enjoyed all the accolades and praise she got for giving her life to God. The novelty of her baptism faded and soon wore off when she realized that she was now strictly subject to the rules, regulations, and discipline of the elders. She had worked hard to get straight A's throughout high school to get scholarships. Slowly, the elders were persuading her that worldly pursuits were a waste of time. She was expected to make spiritual goals that precluded college or getting a well-paying job.

She wrote a letter of disassociation just before she graduated from high school. I was devastated when her name was announced to all the congregation that she "was no longer one of Jehovah's Witnesses." Loud sighs and gasps filled the Kingdom Hall. Everyone crowded around me to show their sympathy after the meeting. She was now considered dead, and our relationship would be changed forever.

Taking New Paths *Stories of Leaving Religion*

My husband, who was not a Witness, would never understand that I had to show loyalty to my religion at the cost of abandoning my child. My husband had no clue. He never saw the video that was shown at our summer convention a few years back showing a young adult daughter being kicked out of home because she left the organization.

He never saw how parents ignored any type of communication, even disregarding a text from her. It didn't matter if she needed them or not. She had left Jehovah and now had to face the consequences of her actions.

I kept quiet while he allowed her to live at home. I would never tell him now that as a JW father, he would have been expected to kick her out. Whereas our son who never got baptized was never subject to any disciplinary consequences.

In other words, my daughter was doomed to die, but my son still could make a dedication and live. For the first time, I was thankful he was an unbeliever and not a Jehovah's Witness. My daughter could still live at home.

I was in agony every day as I wrestled with my love for my daughter and the requirement to love God more. My heart grieved as if my daughter had died. She was a walking corpse, and I could do nothing about it. I couldn't even tell my husband how I felt now, because it would reveal how cruel shunning is.

If I voiced any disregard for this teaching among my fellow worshipers, I would be marked as weak and no longer good association. God was punishing me, and my children would not be allowed to enter the new system, like Moses wasn't allowed. God could arbitrarily let Satan take my child away.

I remembered the pain of my own shunning two decades before. Now my daughter was ostracized as an evil unrepentant friend of Satan. She would be considered refuse because she chose "the world" over God. Yet, all she was doing was working and going to college.

I was depressed and felt so alone. My family was seen by the congregation as damaged. I don't know how many nights I cried myself to sleep thinking, "What good is the promised paradise if I don't have my family with me?"

From Mind Control to Freely Thinking

It took me several months to shock myself out of this fog of cognitive dissonance and let my natural motherly instincts return. I could not abandon my daughter over this. I was starting to wake up and see this religion as cruel and dogmatic. How could truth be so unloving?

I continued to go to the meetings. This was my whole community. I knew nothing else.

Around this same time, the Organization was restructuring and downsizing, selling property and moving members to different congregations to fill up empty Kingdom Halls.

I complied obediently and now had to drive thirty minutes, when there was a Kingdom Hall ten minutes away from where I lived. I had to show loyalty and I did. I told myself this would be a good start over. I went with only my son now; occasionally my husband would attend for moral support. I was struggling, two of my children had rejected the "truth."

The new congregation welcomed us, and I was a hundred percent involved in all the activities from the get-go. A few others from my old congregation joined in this merge. However, within just a couple of months, one of our faithful older sisters died suddenly.

The move was just too much for her and she couldn't keep up. I had been very close to her and the news that she was found on her floor alone in her home felt like a punch in my gut. I couldn't help but think that the organization killed her.

She was supposed to be an example of an older sister serving Jehovah faithfully and not complaining about her new circumstances. She was in her late seventies and had to start all over finding Bible studies, walking for hours in hot summer weather going from door to door. Then I started to remember all those who had died serving in this religion, many who had refused blood transfusions. They chose death over life, dogma over family, control over unconditional love.

It was getting harder and harder for me to attend meetings. I had too many questions now. The teachings I held dear at one time didn't make sense anymore. I found holes in the JW reasoning, false quotes and straight-out deception.

Taking New Paths *Stories of Leaving Religion*

I learned about the hidden pedophilia trials and how they didn't report child abuse to the local police. I started to recall incidents of incest and child molesting that were overlooked. For example, there was a stepfather who got his fourteen-year-old stepdaughter pregnant.

Both were dis-fellowshipped as unrepentant sinners. I didn't understand much back then because I was so young. I do remember the gossip in our worship groups, and as an adult it started to make sense. Something was not right with this religion. I wondered if this was really "the truth" I was taught to believe all my life.

I had to find out if all the doctrines I was taught were really Bible-based. I started to look at our literature for answers, but soon realized I needed a more objective point of view. I went to my local library and read books on history, archaeology, religion. I went down the proverbial rabbit hole hard and fast. I gave myself permission to investigate the history of the Jehovah's Witness without any filters.

One evening in late November 2018, I typed a search into my computer: "Jehovah's Witnesses." I found a whole community of ExJW with websites. I held my breath and I read. I read for days which turned into weeks. I was a sponge at night taking everything in and trying to process all this information.

My heart dropped as each layer of deception was exposed. The Jehovah's Witness Organization was a CULT. I was brainwashed into a high-control group as a child and remained heavily indoctrinated throughout my life.

It didn't matter if I attended meetings regularly or stopped going for a while; I was programmed to believe this was the true religion, God's hope for mankind. They used mind control, information control, and fear control to keep me mentally trapped in this religion. I was waking up and could not undo what I now learned.

I stopped going to meetings at the Kingdom Hall in January 2019. I thoroughly and completely no longer believed. I was on a path of deconstructing my religious beliefs and deprogramming myself from a cult, layer by layer. I was ashamed that I had been brainwashed most of my life and now trying to raise my children in this Cult.

I was scared because I did not know how to tell my family. I did not know how to make amends for dragging them into this life of control. I connected with other Ex JWs who had walked a similar path of awakening and I reached out to them. I felt like

From Mind Control to Freely Thinking

Dorothy in the *Wizard of OZ*, opening the door after the house landed. I was transforming from a worldview of black and white to one that was in color. I told my family one by one, first my husband and then my children.

To my surprise, they had already come to this conclusion and were just waiting for me to figure it out. I did, and we were on our way to redefining ourselves a family who could love each other unconditionally. It's been over two years since I exited the JW organization. I am thankful we broke free of a high-control cult and my family is whole and thriving. I can finally say, "I have time." I don't feel the pressure to be everything all the time. My future isn't about not dying at Armageddon. It's about being balanced and content. I no longer plan for a future that will never come. I plan with purpose.

The best part about waking up is I can really enjoy a genuine conversation with someone. I especially like the candor I can share with my now-adult children. We sit and laugh now. We can talk about any subject with no hidden agenda. I don't have to agree with everything and everyone, but I can listen.

I don't have to convert, nor do I have to convince. I took them through more than I would ask any child to endure. Yet, their resilience and my love for them has won over indoctrination.

I've finally come to realize it was never me. I was just a little girl living in the projects who wanted love and attention. I have no regrets at this stage in my life because I am the accumulation of all that I experienced. It has made me more understanding and loving. I am good enough exactly the way I am. I had more agency than I realized.

Though I now consider myself an atheist, I do feel connected with humanity on a global level. Our life on this earth is too short to sit idle or dwell on past events. I am a forever student with a love for learning and exploring. My heart is open. My spirituality is not attached to a religion or to any organization. It is living an authentic life. That is all I ask of myself, and it has served me well.

Everything that follows as a result of this choice is icing on the cake.

Taking New Paths: Stories of Leaving Religion

9
My Tapestry of Change
Hekmat

WHAT YOU ARE about to read is simply a short autobiography of my mind. In this story, I share with you how that tapestry has been created, though I still see it as a work in progress. In the course of its eventful history and as a result of several different factors, my mind went through significant stages of development.

I thought it would be a great idea to reflect on how different factors such as people, books, and events influenced my thinking. The reason I was encouraged to write the story of my mind was the fact that my thinking has gone through significant transformations through its eventful journey.

My mind, this private cradle of thinking and learning, began its mysterious journey when I was born into a very religious family

My Tapestry of Change

in Iran in the late 1960s. Like it happens to everybody else, my mind started being shaped by the people I lived with, and the events that happened around me. First of all, let me tell you how the people I lived with influenced my way of thinking.

My late dad was a pious man, fully dedicated to Islamic principles. He was so kind, considerate, and trustworthy that he was known for his honesty and integrity. I could barely find him to ever tell a lie or think evil of others. He always said his prayers at the mosque and was the head of the board of trustees. He proudly took us to the local mosque most of the time.

Reciting Quran at home, on a regular basis, was one of his chief daily activities. He enthusiastically taught his children how to read Quran and say prayers as well. Though my father was a very religious man, he never forced us in any way to say prayers or go fasting.

If I was asleep, for instance, for the Morning Prayer (a ritual Muslims do before sunrise), he would never wake me up. As he strongly believed one should love worshiping Allah, there was no coercion in performing these rituals. His attitude and manners invited us to love Islam as he was a symbol of all the virtues we could desire to have.

When I observed how much people respected him, I felt great pride in being his son. This was the main reason I started loving Islamic principles in the first place. As soon as people realized I was his son, they started demonstrating respect and trust, and these attitudes encouraged me to try to follow in his path. I can conclude this paragraph by telling you that I began loving Islamic principles from an Ethical Perspective. However, this is not the whole story, since I have always had my reservations about this faith from an Intellectual Perspective, on which I will elaborate later.

The second most influential person in my thinking life is my mother. In my family, familiarity with and interest in Persian poetry was a cherished tradition. It was a great hobby for her to recite mystical verses from Hafiz, Saadi, Rumi, and others. My mom knew many poems by heart, and it was her interest in poetry that brought poems to our family time.

We could hardly beat her in the poetical contest of Mushaira. This is a contest in which you recite a verse by heart and the competitor

Taking New Paths *Stories of Leaving Religion*

should respond by remembering and reciting a verse beginning with the last letter of the verse you recited. Then, it is your turn to recite a verse beginning with the last letter. This interaction continues until one of the competitors cannot recite a verse.

I remember my uncle always encouraged us to think more deeply about the poems we memorized and recited. Reflection on the concepts and meanings of the verses was a great mental exercise for us. We always tried to grasp the intended meanings that were being shrouded in symbolism.

I can say this familiarity with Persian poetry created in us a spirit of tolerance and indulgence toward those who believed in faiths different from ours. From a spiritual perspective, this engagement with Persian poetry gave us a sense of spirituality, which took us to a kind of sublime life much higher than what we could experience in normal life. Through Persian literature, I learned to think more deeply about the meaning of life and chose to seek a life of purpose and meaning.

Besides people with whom I lived, there were some important events that played a significant role in shaping my mind. I was about ten years old when the Islamic revolution, led by Ayatollah Khomeini, happened in Iran. This event had a deep impact on the value system of the Iranian people. My family, with its religious affiliation, was among millions of families who supported this Islamic revolution.

Unfortunately, I witnessed as, little by little, people's religious tolerance got replaced by hatred and hostility toward Americans and Israelis. Khomeini started to redefine being a pure Muslim for the people, and millions of Iranians started to follow this bizarre interpretation of Islam.

Khomeini encouraged people that being a true Muslim meant developing hatred and indignation toward America as the Great Satan. He criticized those who did not curse the U.S.A. and called them "Muslims who believed in a kind of fake Islam;" what he started to call "American Islam." He strongly believed a true Muslim should have these revolutionary sentiments.

Undoubtedly, this revolution had a profound impact on my mind as well. It occurred the year I was about to start the second

My Tapestry of Change

decade of my life. This was the beginning of a new wave of Islamic fundamentalism, which started to infect the region for many decades to come. For me, it was an eye-opening experience as I got the chance to see the inside of a mysterious castle that, for a long time, I had seen only its facade. When the mullahs grabbed power in Iran, they started to impose Islamic principles.

It was the time I started to see a new image of Islam, which was cruel and abhorrent. Music and dance were forbidden; hatred and hostility were incited; basic freedoms were suppressed; public executions became prevalent; and inflation and poverty became the facts of life. I noticed how devastating it could be when religions and ideologies take hold of politics.

Another significant event that had a great impact on my mentality was the war between Iran and Iraq. I was a teenager during that eight-year war. State propaganda told people that Saddam Hussein was a puppet, controlled by superpowers and Israel, to defeat the revolution.

The media in my country told people that it wasn't an ordinary war between two countries, but an Islamic *Jihad*, and those killed would be the martyrs as they died in the way of Islam. Many of the revolutionary families sent their youths to this battle to defend Islam rather than Iran.

I still remember the days our classes were canceled, so that students could attend the funeral ceremony of those who were killed on the battlefields. During those years, I started to think more deeply about basic concepts such as nationalism, patriotism, bravery, deception, etc. I noticed how the two sides of the battle used religious sentiments to send the youth to the battlefield.

Without a doubt, my mind got its shape partly by the books I read and the programs I watched. Unfortunately, during the years I was at the height of my curiosity and was truly hungry to learn, our freedom had been desperately limited.

In the 1980s, censorship and control reached their climax in Iran. The government easily deprived people of access to whatever they desired to read. With no internet, no freedom of the press, and only a couple of state-run TV channels, they were busy indoctrinating people to think in a certain way.

I can summarize the whole situation as living in the dark

Taking New Paths *Stories of Leaving Religion*

because we were doomed to watch only state-controlled TV channels that reflected official ideology. Books and newspapers were published under the strict supervision of the Ministry of Islamic Guidance.

When I write these lines, I am reminded of what I read in George Orwell's book, 1984. Those years, I realized what was wrong, but I had no clue as to what was right. I could see how the situation was getting worse day by day, economically, culturally, socially, and politically. I could see how devastating religion could be when it grabs the power to rule a country. I could see the brutality of the faith I once cherished for its beauties. This was the milieu I grew up in and where I spent the first two decades of my intellectual life.

What I am so proud of is my success in outgrowing the norms of society. This paragraph will open the window to the Intellectual Perspective I mentioned earlier that consists of two main parts. Two key elements cooperated to bring my mind to the level it is now. One was my thinking ability, and the other was the knowledge I could gain from books. These two elements acted like two wings, which allowed my mind to fly beyond superficiality, superstition, and dogmatism.

Although in my first decade of life, under the influence of my father, I was impressed by Islamic principles, I remember even those years I couldn't accommodate some beliefs the clerics threw at people. Even as a kid, when I went to the mosque to learn Islamic principles and perform its rituals, I was barely convinced by what the clerics told people.

So many of the ideas seemed nonsense to my mind. I couldn't believe so many of the anecdotes and miracles they narrated from the history of Islam. For example, I could hardly believe the story of Imam Mahdi, who had disappeared many centuries ago and suddenly will come back to bring justice to the world.

Honestly, those years, I sometimes thought myself captivated by some satanic forces, which were meant to deceive me. I didn't dare tell others how I saw things. My mind was full of doubts, but I didn't find any companion with whom to share my ideas. I was dubious and full of mixed feelings. One side of the coin told me I

My Tapestry of Change

was on the right track, and the other side warned and scared me into thinking I had been captivated by some evil forces.

For example, when I was a child, I started thinking about the reasons behind some rituals such as Prayer of Signs (*Namaz-e-Ayaat*). This prayer becomes obligatory when some natural phenomena such as lunar and solar eclipses (partial or total), cyclones, hurricanes, earthquakes etc. occur. I always thought, "Why are lunar and solar eclipses grouped with earthquakes and hurricanes?

Muslims perform Prayer of Signs for natural phenomena that are scary and dangerous. But eclipses were nothing to be scared of, as they are predictable. I expected the prophet of Islam to explain these phenomena to the people.

Let me share with you another matter that really bothered my critical mind. Some Muslims consult Quran when they want to make an important decision. They close their eyes and open the book randomly and based on the verses they see at the top of the page interpret if God likes this decision or not. In many books of Quran one sees the words "Good" and "Bad" at the top of the page. So, you don't need to interpret the verses any longer. Just open the book randomly, if it says good, that is a good decision. It seemed so irrational to me.

I do believe that two main factors should interact properly so that one's thinking can evolve: one is a rational mind, and the other is sound knowledge. These two interact in a very intricate fashion. Each one is built on and completed by the other.

I started using the logic of my mind to determine the validity of ideas I encountered. In order to do that, I needed some reliable standards. These standards would enable me to distinguish sound knowledge from fake data.

The sound knowledge I obtained this way provided tools for the elevation of my rational mind. Nothing is worse than false knowledge. Nothing is worse than misinformation and superstitions for a healthy mind. Some people mistakenly believe it would be better to accept some religious ideas. If they are true, we go to heaven. If they are false, we don't lose anything. The fact is that believing in irrational ideas has real impact on the mind and causes it to lose its balance.

Taking New Paths *Stories of Leaving Religion*

Since early childhood, I had noticed my mind could not accommodate some ideas related to God and the history of Islam. I didn't have any special knowledge about these subjects, but the point was my rational mind couldn't accept and believe such ideas and anecdotes. In fact, those standards immunized me from being afflicted with misconceptions.

Now, when I look back, I feel so excited to see how, without relevant knowledge, my curious mind could dismiss these irrational ideas. Sometimes, I tried to suppress this rationality as I thought maybe it was some evil force giving me a mistaken impression of truth. This feeling of doubt and uncertainty was with me for a long time. I knew what I needed was more authentic knowledge to decide if it was rationality or deviancy.

I knew I needed to free myself from the chains of ignorance. I started reading different books and embarked on learning English. I found out that in order to free myself from the limitations imposed by the government, I needed to learn English.

It was the best decision I ever made, and I am so proud of it. In the era following the Islamic revolution, finding Persian books with a critical approach toward Islamic principles was obviously impossible. They didn't allow books with a critical attitude toward the established religion to be published or distributed.

Actually, the greatest development in my way of thinking started when I gained the ability to read in English. The decision to choose English literature as my major at the university was a big move. It made a great contribution to the criticality of my mind. It is practically impossible to provide an exhaustive list of the books I have read, but I name a few to shed light on this aspect of mind growth.

One book that had a lasting impact was *Jonathan Livingston Seagull* written by Richard Bach. I read this book when I was a junior at Kerman University. This book was full of insight and inspiration.

I felt I shared lots of sentiments with that bird. I was different from the rest of the flock. I didn't want daily routines to dumb my soul. I didn't want to pursue an unexamined and unreflective life. I wanted my soul to fly beyond the clouds of a boring life. Life was more than eating and sleeping and praying and studying. These daily routines could not satisfy my rebellious soul.

Another book I found illuminating was *The Story of Philosophy*

My Tapestry of Change

by Will Durant. Reading that book familiarized me with prominent thinkers of the world. Among them, Socrates captured my soul with his intellectual virtues and his dignified method of questioning. I was fascinated by his attempt to establish an ethical system based on human reason rather than theological doctrine. In fact, it was Socrates who brought me to the realm of Critical Thinking.

Later I read many books from critical thinkers such as Richard Paul, Lipman, and Bertrand Russel. Another prominent thinker who inspired me very much and to the extent that I can say I owe him my awakening is Spinoza.

Whenever I was talking to religious guys and they told me that the human mind is incapable of grasping the idea of God and therefore we need to rely on what we received from God's messengers, I reminded them of Spinoza and his great approach in analyzing the scriptures to decide if they are man-made or God-made. In addition to his method of analysis, I was so absorbed by his character. He refused professorship and even financial bribes to keep quiet his views, though he was living in abject poverty.

When I look back, I am so grateful I got to free my mind from the chains of superstitions and fallacies. I hope sharing my story inspires others to break the chains of superstitions and enter the realm of wisdom.

Taking New Paths: Stories of Leaving Religion

10
Who Am I?
Maroun Al Hourani

I WAS BORN IN and live in, Lebanon, a small country in the Middle East. I was raised as a Christian Maronite (not to be confused with Mormons), and like all the other Christians my age, I was taught how to practice my religion. Religion was so crucial for me; I saw it as the essential truth, a place where hearts feel no pain and minds navigated in the space of freedom and tenderness. Living in Christian surroundings influenced me very much; it kept me caged in my comfort zone. Religion had all the answers to questions people ask:

>The origin of the universe.
>The purpose of the meaning of life.
>The sense of love.
>And much more.

Who Am I?

I saw religion as something amazing and unique, a sacred place for the seeker; this is why it was so hard leaving it.

Growing in a Christian community made me blind about every other religion globally. I was taught that was I was living in the truth, and there is no different truth. All of this was hitting hard my critical thinking, and long ago kept me in the same place.

As Richard Dawkins said in his book *The God Delusion*: "Do not indoctrinate your children. Teach them how to think for themselves, how to evaluate evidence, and how to disagree with you."

Unfortunately, I didn't have the chance to explore the religions and ideas of the world in my childhood. I was a prisoner for a long time, of a vision and philosophy that I never chose. I was blinded and didn't have the opportunity to see the world as it is.

When did I start to doubt?

As a teenager, the world began revealing a little of itself more every day. Around the age of fourteen, I had my smartphone and a more open social life. As soon as I entered high school, I saw diversity in race, ethnicity, age, and most importantly, diversity in religious beliefs. That situation made me realize that the world was a much bigger than I thought. Indeed, there I learned about and saw many different views, firm believers, and many theories. It was a weird experience, and I started to have friends from other backgrounds and religions.

One day I was walking in the streets of Beirut, and I heard the sound of Mosques and the prayers; they disturbed me! I never saw something like that before—people praying and having faith in their own religion as much as I did in mine. I wondered how, thousands of years after Judaism, it was possible that people still have different beliefs? Is there something wrong about that?"

As soon as I came home, I opened my smartphone and searched a bit about Islam on the Internet. I realized that it is as severe as Christianity. Millions of believers, mosques, and apologists worldwide are trying to understand the world, believing only they have the absolute truth.

Taking New Paths *Stories of Leaving Religion*

Starting to think this way made me fear a little bit. I didn't want to simply believe, or doubt, my religion, but I wasn't able to ignore that. I had a strong feeling of disappointment, and I knew inside my heart that there was something wrong about that.

I realized that all religions can be false, but they cannot all be true and I asked myself one crucial question: "How can I justify my beliefs rationally to other people? And what makes me a Christian but not a Muslim or an atheist?" I had no rational explanation and I lived a long time with that feeling of confusion inside myself.

When I started having atheist friends I was taking a Christian theology class in high school. There were two boys who always sat in the back of the classroom, and they always grabbed my attention. They never seemed to care about what was going on in the class.

After a class I went and asked them why. My classmates told me that they were atheists. I didn't know yet what atheism meant, and they explained to me that atheists are people who do not believe in any God.

I was shocked, for I hadn't ever expected to meet anyone who didn't believe in God. I didn't even know they existed! I started to wonder if they were good people, as they seemed to be. I was curious to know more about what they thought, believed, and disbelieved. So, my curiosity led me to more discussion with them.

They helped me discover a new way of thinking. Even if I didn't like some of their reasons and their conclusions, I liked the process of discussing new ideas. We talked about many subjects, and I was shocked by some of their answers; they were knowledgeable people! But humans do not have answers to every question.

They didn't always provide me with answers when I asked a question, and that is why I didn't take them too seriously. At that time, I didn't know yet that to have a reason to believe, we should have some answers, and not just answers we should believe.

I came to see that it is beautiful when you accept your weakness and ignorance of this world and say, "I do not know," instead of imagining irrational theories. Science is here to make us understand the world much better every day.

Who Am I ?

Be skeptical; always look at all the points of view and their arguments to make your conclusion.

The problem of death is something for which we all seek answers. As a child I never thought about death because it was terrifying to me, so I always avoided it. I had no experience of losing someone you love until it happened to me. My grandmother started to have severe health problems. She was taking many medications and constantly going from one hospital to another. It was heartbreaking seeing her like that.

I couldn't accept reality or think about it until one day it hit me in the face, and I could not avoid it anymore. My father called us and told us that my grandmother had passed away. Starting then I experienced depression and stress, I didn't understand what was going on, and I expressed myself with tears.

I wanted so much to make sure that my grandmother was in a better place, in heaven. I started reading the Bible more deeply, praying more, and asking questions of pastors every time I got the chance. I did all of this to create this feeling of security inside myself. But I never got the answers I was searching for, even though I tried to be satisfied with the responses I got.

I want to say that sometimes sudden changes in our lives will make us look and search for something. For me, I called it searching for the truth and making sure my grandma was in a safe place, a better one, and that I would see her again. All that was an additional point that made me search more for answers about religion.

I admired scientists. Once I watched a fantastic documentary that was about the theory of relativity. Einstein made me realize something vital: the things around us may look so simple, but reality is much bigger than that. I was surprised by the fascinating theory that changed all physics and upgraded it to the next level, letting us better discover the world and understand a little more the complexity of time and space.

Taking New Paths *Stories of Leaving Religion*

I saw beauty in the natural world. It was so amazing to read about the theory of relativity. It is beautiful, but moreover, it is real! We didn't need a supernatural power to be satisfied. And I cannot describe what I felt more without quoting Richard Dawkins: "There is real poetry in the real world. Science is the poetry of reality."

At the age of sixteen, I was already doubting, but there was that fear that didn't leave my heart—the fear of calling myself an atheist. This was something terrible to society, to my family, and my friends, who always encouraged me to read the Bible more if and when I have any questions, even though they never finished reading half of it, themselves.

Nonetheless, I took their advice seriously and started reading the Bible more and more. Surprise; nothing changed! On the contrary, I started doubting more and more, and realized, seeing from an objective point of view, the real things that are in the Bible—the stories and morals that no priest ever had the courage to tell us about. I am especially referring to the Old Testament in general, and some of the New Testament as well.

If religion is true, why never discuss the Old Testament in Sunday church? Is it too dangerous to tell the people the reality? Should we avoid that for better explanations, or just try to imagine our own interpretation? Or tell people to have faith and God will give you the answer? Or maybe claim that this was God's way of doing things back in time? Perhaps say that God revealed himself to humanity through the ages until he was incarnated, or just throwing out all the Old Testament, saying that it is almost all wrong, and that is why we have the new one, with Jesus.

What I have just shared are some of the different interpretations people choose to believe.

Let's look at Matthew 5: 17-20 The Fulfillment of the Law (NIV) New International Version:

17. Do not think that I have come to abolish the Law or the Prophets; I have not come to abolish them but to fulfill them.

Who Am I?

> *18. For truly I tell you, until heaven and earth disappear, not the smallest letter, not the least stroke of a pen, will by any means disappear from the Law until everything is accomplished.*
>
> *19. Therefore anyone who sets aside one of the least of these commands and teaches others accordingly will be called least in the kingdom of heaven, but whoever practices and teaches these commands will be called great in the kingdom of heaven.*
>
> *20. For I tell you that unless your righteousness surpasses that of the Pharisees and the teachers of the law, you will certainly not enter the kingdom of heaven.*

So clearly said, I can't understand why people still interpret this passage as they wish. Even though Jesus wants to fulfill the law, he himself contradicts the law many times.

In addition to that, I had to ask if the Bible has really been kept in its true meaning. No one knows how much the scripture has been affected by translations, and copies after copies after copies of copies. Some claim that we can clearly analyze the work of the holy spirit by keeping the holy book in its original form nowadays.

Let's take a look at two different well-known translations. (New International Version (NIV), King James Version (KJV))

Isaiah 45:7 (NIV) *New International Version*

7. I form the light and create darkness, I bring prosperity and create disaster; I, the Lord, do all these things.

Isaiah 45:7 *King James Version (KJV)*

7. I form the light, and create darkness: I make peace, and create evil: I, the Lord, do all these things.

Did God really create evil? Some Christians try to solve this problem by reflecting on another translation of the Bible, hoping they find another word easier to interpret.

Taking New Paths *Stories of Leaving Religion*

But this doesn't solve the problem at all.

First, this creates a new problem: Why are translations different? Which one should Christians read and trust? Isn't the Bible a holy book? So why do they differ? Has the holy spirit failed?

I will not be surprised if some pastors say that it is the fault of humans, or human sin, because they see everything bad as coming from sin, and everything good from God, with humans in a very low position. They are described as creatures that can't and will never do anything by their own will, needing help and salvation coming from above.

Second, by rejecting the King James' translation for Isaiah 45:7, and trying to explain the other version (the NIV version) they, too, didn't solve anything. First, darkness is not a matter, darkness is just the absence of light, so how could God create darkness? Did he miss a physics course? Second, if disaster originates from evil, but is created by a perfect, omnipotent, omniscient being, you must ask how that is possible.

For a normal human, sometimes causing disaster may be because of choosing to avoid a different disaster, or of having a bad intention in the first place. I have never met a perfect person. Imagine a boy wanting to help his mother at washing the dishes, but instead he breaks a glass. He is not to blame because it came from good intentions; instead, the mother should teach her child to take more care for the next time.

Now imagine with me that by chance you learned of a mafia plan. You know where the mafia is located, and they are going to commit the biggest crime ever in the city—they are bombing all the city. You don't have time to call the police, the mafia is located just ten minutes from you, and the bomb will be detonated in fifteen minutes.

You have two options: put your gun on and go kill each one in the mafia, or try to escape. In case you choose to go and stop this crime from happening (what everyone else should do), you are going to make a different disaster by killing all the mafia, men that have families. too. But you did this in order to a avoid a bigger disaster, so in that case you are understood; moreover, you are a hero to all the city.

Who Am I?

If you were an omniscient being, you would have assured the safety of every innocent person.

So, let's talk now about the origin of sin.

Everyone knows the story of Adam and Eve, the story that explains why humans are suffering and why evil exists from the perspective the three Abrahamic religions: Judaism, Christianity, and Islam.

They pretend that God created everything perfectly. He created Adam and Eve perfectly, without the ability to compare good and evil, but because of a talking snake, which represents evil, that led Eve and Adam to eat from the fruit of knowledge of good and evil.

God punished all humans that succeeded Adam and Eve for something Adam and Eve didn't know was wrong. They didn't know disobeying God is wrong because they didn't have the ability to compare between good and evil, and because of that, over seven billion humans are suffering just now in 2021, because of the evil in their free will and in nature (earthquakes, tsunamis, natural disasters). I don't call that a perfect creation, but the rather biggest failure I have ever seen.

We are taught since we were young that we are weak and need to be saved because of our sins. We are seen as pathetic creatures, creatures that cannot do anything without the holy spirit: find cure for cancer, master the piano, cook, get amazing grades at college, program a computer windows app, etc. without the holy spirit to give us the abilities that we didn't have to do all that.

Another problem that we face is, where did the snake come from, where did the first evil come from? No answer. If you want to interpret the snake by calling it evil, then you have to explain its origin, if you think that God created everything perfectly. And if you want to say that God was testing Adam and Eve (which is not the case in the Bible), then you have to explain the omniscience of God for knowing what they will do *or* putting limits to his omniscience whenever it fits your belief.

But there will always be the same problem and we will always go back to it: If God really created everything perfectly, evil will

Taking New Paths *Stories of Leaving Religion*

not have entered the world. Why, do you have to think, to accept, to believe, and to have faith that when you go to heaven there will be no evil at all, because everything will be perfect with God? At the same time, you believe the irrational story of Adam and Eve, which doesn't solve anything, and instead makes us pose many more questions to which we can't find answers in the Bible at all.

The story of Adam and Eve is a big failure of creation; I would expect it to come from a demon instead of a perfect, omnipotent, omniscient being.

I have always realized that religion has an impact on many social issues, and one of them is animal rights and the questions of a vegan/vegetarian diet.

Religion and especially Christianity have unconsciously put the idea in people's mind that eliminating meat and dairy products from our diet is depriving ourselves from essential and delicious food; this leads people to think that eating animal products is very normal and acceptable. This idea put some blocks for thinking more about the vegan diet.

As a vegan, I have many times discussed with people about veganism and why I think eating meat and animal products is unethical. I have realized that almost everyone I've talked to has religious reasons for eating animals. So, I have asked them a question: "Why would God choose to create animals in billions to be eaten by animals or humans? Why, if they are food, make them feel suffering just as humans do?"

I couldn't understand their definition about an all loving and caring God. It seems that they don't even want to think more, to ask themselves questions. They seem blocked, locked down, in their minds, and one must ask, why? While Jesus ate fish and didn't mention anytime that eating animal products is not a necessity, many scientific researchers have proven that eating meat and animal products is unnecessary. In fact, The American dietetic association and the British dietetic association stated the following:

Appropriately planned vegetarian diets, including total vegetarian or vegan diets, are healthful, nutritionally adequate, and

Who Am I?

may provide health benefits in the prevention and treatment of certain diseases. Well-planned vegetarian diets are appropriate for individuals during all stages of the life cycle, including pregnancy, lactation, infancy, childhood, and adolescence, and for athletes.

Indeed, Jesus wasn't the best example to follow.

Quitting religion required me to clear my mind of all that I learned in Christianity, and start to think on my own. It was more difficult that it seems. It takes courage to admit that all of what I thought to be the absolute truth might be totally false.

It is hard to leave all that, and at the same time live in a system that reminds you of that wherever you go—on the radio, in family reunions, in college, with your friends, and even on the street—you hear the sounds from the churches or the mosques.

I felt rejected by most people, many still frustrated hearing the word "atheist." One of my best friends refused to talk to me because I was skeptical about his religion, Christianity, and he assumed that I was attacking his religion and he can't tolerate that from anyone.

I never chose to be a Christian, and people were judging me for leaving that choice that I never made. It is really weird. I just want to think on my own, I want to think from scratch and arrive at my own conclusions and own decisions.

It may seem weird and strange for some people to know that an atheist still goes to church, but I still do for several reasons.

First, I am curious to see what is happening in churches and what is being told to people every week. As an atheist, I want to continue to gain some knowledge in religion. I want to read the Bible and study it with professionals; this should increase the critical thinking of a person when it comes to religion and give him the ability to debate effectively with a religious person when needed.

Secondly, I love the community in the church. To be honest, there are some people in the church that I like having discussions with; they are respectful, calm, and open minded, and the feeling of being around them can be good sometimes.

The problem of evil remains and religious interpretations regarding it remain. Looking around us, we see a huge amount of

Taking New Paths *Stories of Leaving Religion*

suffering wherever we go: explosions, death, car accidents, poverty, disease, animal suffering—the list is long.

The "evil" we can see around us can be divided into two parts:
1) Suffering caused by humans;
2) Suffering caused by nature.

Would an all loving, all-powerful god really create all that suffering? Could God have created humans with free will but without the ability of doing wrong? Does God really intervene in miracles like the holy fire, but not intervene with other major problems to solve them? Those all are questions we should ask ourselves, reconsider our beliefs, and search for answers. The amount of suffering in our world is huge, and we cannot turn a blind eye and ignore it.

In conclusion, we are all sentient beings. We don't know everything about all the mysteries of the universe, but we are trying our best to understand the things that happen around us. It is our nature. It is a privilege to be alive, to be human, the most developed species that can think, discover, and create new ideas. We should be amazed by the universe we live in, and by its complexity. We should use all the power that we have as humans, all that makes us different from other species, to think on our own, to think from scratch, and to even create our own new understandings, fresh ideas.

Long ago, slavery was acceptable, but now it is a literal crime. An example like this should make us reconsider every aspect of our lives, every idea, and everything we do and consider as normal. We should ask ourselves questions, be skeptical about everything, and always search for the truth, using strong evidence and critical thinking.

I am a normal guy who quit religion gradually for several reasons. I am not so special, but I like to think in my own proper way, not simply what society tries to teach us.

My purpose for writing this short essay is to encourage everyone to think about religion again, on his or her own. Make your proper research independently; look for different and opposite points of view, and in this way hopefully achieve personally honest conclusions...whatever they may be.

Precarious Faith; Rethinking Spirituality

11

Precarious Faith:
Rethinking Spirituality Through Inhabiting Multiple Religious Identities
Lih Yui Khoo

THE CONCEPT of religion in the Southeast Asian nation of Singapore is largely associated with culture and ethnicity, and is at times driven by ideals of capitalism, meritocracy, and even superstition. In a society that maintains collectivist attitudes in the midst of progress, it is not uncommon to see that familial ties and interests are being prized above other forms of kinships.

This applies to the field of religiosity as well. Like the majority of Singaporean millennials, the very first religion I adopted was that of my family's, and it shaped a significant part of my upbringing, where moral education drew from religious beliefs and superstitions.

Taking New Paths: Stories of Leaving Religion

In Singapore, the term "free-thinker" is loosely used to refer to atheists or individuals who choose not to belong to any specific religion or faith. In my childhood years, I was taught that having a religion or faith system is necessary for one to achieve a sense of purpose and stability in the everyday. As my mother would say, "free-thinkers are non-thinkers." Religion was not only a gateway to learning about my own Chinese and Southeast Asian heritage and their traditions through myths and storytelling, it provided my family with a source of comfort in times of adversity or misfortune.

The act of worshiping a divine being in return for wealth and good luck seemed reassuring to them; and educational and economic success are highly sought-after attributes in many Asian societies.

While the notion of faith had established itself as a monolithic presence in my formative years, it eventually became one of the most fluid and ambivalent aspects of my life. At twenty-six years of age, as of the writing of this chapter, I have inhabited five different faiths and religious identities. As such, I am receptive to the possibility of impermanence in religious belief systems, and that faith and spirituality can transcend institutional constructs.

Living in Singapore's multi-cultural and multi-racial society, I was fortunate to have gained exposure to a heterogeneity of cultures and religions. Many of my elementary and middle school field trips consisted of visits to temples, mosques, and churches to learn about the histories, traditions, and architecture behind each of those sacred spaces.

Up until I was six years old, I was put in the care of my maternal grandmother during the day when both my parents went to work. My grandmother had been a devout Buddhist her entire life. She instilled in me teachings of Buddhist practices and rituals from a young age, though not its philosophies.

The most repetitive and ritualistic element of Buddhism that I was taught as a kid was to offer three prayer joss-sticks to a porcelain figure of a Buddhist deity known as the Goddess of Mercy, Guan-Yin, which was displayed on an altar. This was done every morning, and each time before I left the house.

My grandmother told me that Guan-Yin was like a direct aide to Buddha and offering her joss-sticks would ensure protection from external dangers, as well as earn us divine favor from Buddha.

Precarious Faith: Rethinking Spirituality

Along with Guan-Yin, we would sometimes offer joss-sticks to photographs of our deceased family members during special occasions and anniversaries to seek their protection and blessings. This was a way to remember and respect our elders by allowing them to be involved in our lives, even after they had passed on.

The ritual appealed to her as it allegedly came with a promise that no harm or bad luck would befall on her as long as she offered daily joss-sticks. I committed to this practice and even knelt down before the figure to ask for forgiveness on the days in which I had forgotten to offer my share of joss-sticks.

Over the years, I grew accustomed to this ritual, and became physically and psychologically conditioned to feel a sense of insecurity if I did not perform it. I later asked my mum to purchase a Guan-Yin figure to place in our own home so that I could do the same when I was not with my grandmother\.

My grandmother turned to the subject of the afterlife as a guiding principle for her own mode of being, as well as to educate and discipline my cousins and me as children.

Most Buddhists in Singapore and Southeast Asia believe in the concepts of karma and rebirth after death, whereby our present lives are a result of how we lived and behaved in our past lives. An individual who had committed grave sins would, for instance, be reborn into a hideous animal or insect in their next life. A kind philanthropist may stand a chance to reincarnate as a wealthy person in the distant future. Above all, the main goal is to attain nirvana after death—a transcendent state free of suffering and desire, which releases one from the effects of karma and rebirth. Such principles helped steer us away from misbehaviour and misconduct, and reminded us to always treat others with compassion and respect and pursue more charitable acts—all in the pursuit of nirvana.

When I asked my grandmother why she had chosen to become a Buddhist, she explained that her own mother was a Buddhist and it is natural for us to follow in our parents' footsteps, as an act of obedience and filial piety.

While the rituals came as an integral part of Buddhist worship to honour the gods and deities, my grandmother believed that they would also ensure that our Buddhist ancestors or deceased family

Taking New Paths *Stories of Leaving Religion*

members will be rewarded abundantly in the afterlife in exchange for our devotion to the faith.

A large part of Asian culture places emphasis on values of respect towards our elders. This extends beyond the private sphere of the home, encompassing all areas of day-to-day exchanges including our professional and social relationships.

I have heard stories of friends having to practice Buddhist rituals in their workplace, as their Buddhist bosses would organize yearly mass prayer rituals in the office in hopes of the company being blessed with better luck or greater financial revenue.

Through time, being Buddhist became an obligation to my grandmother rather than a genuine undertaking of the faith. I continued to practice Buddhist prayer rituals and lived by my grandmother's teachings until I entered middle school.

I sometimes wonder if my grandmother had unknowingly indoctrinated me as a child. Buddhism has its share of rich and inspiring philosophies that can potentially provide useful life advice. It was unfortunate that I was never given insight into this, despite being brought up by a devout Buddhist.

Messy Worship: while performing inter-religious rituals during the Buddhist phase of my life, I participated heavily in several Taoist rituals alongside my grandmother and mother, even though none of us are of the Taoist faith. We did so because we have deceased relatives from my maternal grandfather's side of the family who were Taoists, and we had to pay our respects to them through Taoist ancestor and deity worship, as part of being filial to our elders.

As we had no knowledge of Taoist philosophies and religious teachings, we performed these rituals based on information passed down to us from previous generations of family members. I was always under the impression that these Taoist rituals were a part of Buddhism, and only learned at a later age that Buddhism and Taoism and two entirely different religions.

One of the more prevalent Taoist customs in Singapore is the Hungry Ghost Festival, which my family and I took part in every year. In addition to being a religious event, the Hungry Ghost Festival is one

Precarious Faith: Rethinking Spirituality

of Singapore's well-known local cultural festivals. It is celebrated as a yearly national affair throughout the entire country, often in outdoor public spaces.

Taoists believe that in the month of August, one's deceased ancestors would be allowed to return to the earth to pay their living family members a visit, and more importantly to eat their fill of a years' worth of food, earning the festival its name.

For the whole month of August each year, Taoists burn offerings made of paper for their dead ancestors as part of the festival's offering ritual. These papers, known as "hell money" or *Kim Chua* in a Singaporean dialect, resemble ancient Chinese dollar notes. It functions as currency for the afterlife. The burning of *Kim Chua* takes place in Taoist temples, as well as large communal metal bins which national Town Councils have installed in neighborhoods to prevent fire hazards.

The more *Kim Chua* one burns as offerings, the wealthier and more well-fed their ancestors would be in the afterlife. *Kim Chua* in Singapore is specially designed and printed by shops selling Taoist religious products. In recent years, to capitalize on this phenomenon, shops selling *Kim Chua* also manufacture and sell mobile phones, gadgets, cars, and even food made of paper for people to burn as offerings.

The Hungry Ghost Festival was something that my cousins and I looked forward to each year as children, although we should have known better—that it could have significant negative impacts on the environment and our own health in the long run. For us it was interesting and fascinating to see the latest designs of hell currency and paper items that shops would produce for this occasion.

If we were lucky, we could even enjoy a free and exciting *Ge-tai* performance: a traditional Chinese opera show performed in makeshift tents built around various neighborhoods in Singapore during the Hungry Ghost Festival to entertain the ghosts who have dropped by for a visit. The loud instrumental music accompanied by colorful costumes in *Ge-tai* performances brought a festive and carnivalesque atmosphere to this religious event. Presented as part of local culture in Singaporean society, the Hungry Ghost Festival has become familiar and accessible to Singaporeans of all ages and backgrounds.

Taking New Paths *Stories of Leaving Religion*

Although none of my present family members are Taoist, the Taoist version of afterlife seemed much more effective in enforcing discipline amongst children. Unlike the sublime and metaphysical Buddhist afterlife; Taoists in Singapore believe that they would all be sent to hell after death, where they would be judged for their sins and wrongdoings. Taoist hell consists of eighteen levels, like an eighteen-story building built underground.

The more severe your sins, the deeper you would go down into the depths of hell. "Minor" misbehaviour, like telling a lie meant being sent to level 1, where punishment was extremely subtle. "Moderate" sins like stealing would place you in the middle floors, and extreme crimes such as murder would immediately send you to the lowest level with the worst forms of medieval torture.

Elder members of my family would reinforce these ideas of Taoist hell to the younger generation, including myself, as a reminder that we should always remain righteous and meritorious in our ways.

Another less commonly known ritual that I participated in annually as a child was the *Bai Tian-Gong* ritual, loosely translated from Mandarin as the ritual of praying to the God of the skies.

My family conducted this ritual once a year, on the eighth and ninth days of the Chinese Lunar New Year. On the eighth day my parents and grandmother would wake up early to prepare a huge feast usually consisting of an entire roast pig and at least ten other dishes, as an offering to the *Tian-Gong*, or God of the skies. The food was displayed on a table for twenty-four hours until the next morning.

While this ritual is commonly performed by Taoists in Singapore, it has its roots in historical contexts originating from the Song Dynasty in China, which I only discovered in recent years. It was performed in ancient Chinese by the Hokkiens to pray to the heavens for protection against external threats and disasters.

The Hokkien people are a Chinese sub-ethnic group that originated from China's Fujian province and spoke their own dialect language distinct from Mandarin. Today, significant populations of people with Hokkien ancestry can be found across Southeast Asia,

Precarious Faith: Rethinking Spirituality

including Singapore, due to emigrations of Hokkiens of China in the past. Historically, the Hokkiens in China prayed for the heavens' protection against invasion from the neighboring Mongol Empire.

Adapting this to the modern-day context, my family performed the ritual to pray against possible misfortune, illnesses, and accidents that could occur in our daily lives. We eventually abandoned this ritual as it took up too much time and was generating colossal amounts of food waste.

When I turned seven, my mother had enrolled me into a Methodist Christian missionary school for my elementary and middle school education. Students attended compulsory daily morning prayer sessions and weekly chapel sermons. Christian teachings at school sounded refreshing compared to the Buddhist and Taoist rituals that I grew up with. Christianity preached about love, forgiveness, and salvation, which could perhaps provide an escape from karma, rebirth, or hell.

There was also a much-desired sense of freedom in the way Christians conducted their prayers, as opposed to Buddhist and Taoist worship rituals. Unlike the tangible presence of the porcelain Guan-Yin figure that I was accustomed to, the Christian God is without physical form and iconographic depictions, precisely because of his omnipotence.

I very much enjoyed the exciting new idea of being able to pray at any time and place, especially when I was facing a dilemma which required immediate attention, such as during a school examination.

The hallmark of many Christian texts is the monotheistic almighty God. If I were to adopt the Christian faith, I could no longer commit to my Buddhist practices passed down by my grandmother. At the same time, my grandmother would certainly not be pleased if I were to abandon my Buddhist faith that she had shared with me.

I led a double life for the next two years where I learned about Christianity at school but would still carry out my daily routine of offering joss-sticks to Guan-Yin at home. I would hide myself in the toilet when I wanted to pray to the Christian God, believing that it was

Taking New Paths *Stories of Leaving Religion*

the only private space where the Buddhist deities could not catch me in the act of "betrayal."

My grandmother eventually noticed my diminishing commitment to Buddhist rituals and grew suspicious about the likely change in my religious allegiances. My mother, on the other hand, was supportive in my exploration of other religions, despite our familial obligations that had influenced our Buddhist faith. With her blessing, I began reading the Bible in secret.

Aunty P. (pseudonym), a close friend of my mother's, is a Catholic who often did evangelism work. When I was ten years old, Aunty P. came to visit us one day to share about Catholicism. Although Protestant faiths and Catholicism are two different branches of Christianity, it was a good opportunity to learn more about the Bible and its teachings, as the Protestant and Catholic Bibles share many similarities.

Through Aunty P., I understood in greater depth the Christian ideologies of God and the spiritual divine and modes of prayer, keeping in mind the differences in Protestant and Catholic interpretations of the Bible. As a Catholic, Aunty P. prayed to God through Mother Mary, who played the role of an intercessor between man and God.

This was unlike the teachings from missionary school, where one was permitted to speak directly with God. An ordinary daily Catholic prayer can be accomplished using a Rosary, usually consisting of fifty-nine beads and a Cross pendant. Every day, I recited the Lord's Prayer fifty-nine times, each time holding on a single bead on the Rosary.

It was indeed an exhausting process, but Aunty P. reminded me that persistence and dedication are crucial to prayer, and it was also a way to instill God's word in oneself.

The meditative qualities of this mode of prayer were at times reassuring, as it provided a physical method of communicating with God. The corporeal nature to the act helped bridge the gap between the abstraction of the divine in Christianity and the materiality of Buddhist rites.

At a young age, it was difficult to visualize and comprehend a

Precarious Faith: Rethinking Spirituality

deity that was invisible and immaterial, especially since I was brought up surrounded by tangible religious objects that I could see, touch, and use. The tactility of the Catholic prayer ritual with the Rosary reinforced the existence of an invisible God.

While I did not pursue the Catholic faith any farther than its method of prayer and the few conversations I had with Aunty P., I still have the rosary as a power object and reminder of a physical manifestation of God's presence. I have never attended Catholic church proper, aside from the one or two church weddings that I was invited to. This was perhaps one of my more momentary fleeting explorations of a single religion thus far.

I first formally joined a Christian church when I was twelve years old. Prior to that, I was undergoing a series of extremely traumatic experiences and events that lasted for more than a year. I fell ill and often had to take time off from school.

Taking the advice of a teacher who knew of my struggles, I began seeing the school counselor for counseling and therapy. She also happened to be a pastoral staff member at a nearby local Methodist church. During our counseling sessions, she shared more about Biblical parables and verses in hopes that these literary promises of God's strength, guidance, and healing would be empowering for me.

Prayer and reading the Bible became sources of comfort and motivation, which drew me to the Methodist church that my counselor attended. Naturally, I had a series of long discussions with my parents before my conversion to the Christian faith.

Seeing how it had helped me through a difficult period of my life, my parents were receptive to my change in faith. Over time, my parents developed an interest in the faith and made the decision to adopt it as well. They grew deeply involved and attached to church activities and the community. Their physical and emotional commitment to Christianity and the church easily surpassed mine in due course.

We broke the news to my grandmother a couple of years later when we wanted to get baptized as a family at the same Methodist church. She was furious about our decision and was even more horrified to learn that I had discarded the Guan-Yin figure that I'd

Taking New Paths *Stories of Leaving Religion*

purchased years before. A cold war between us and my grandmother ensued in the following months. I figured there were a couple of main reasons for her resentment towards our choice and her antagonism about the Christian religion.

First, she was apprehensive about the contrast between Christian and Buddhist worship practices and concepts of afterlife. Secondly, she perceived Christianity as a "White man's religion" and felt that we were dishonoring our culture and traditions. The very first Christians that she'd met during her childhood were probably Caucasian missionaries. Third, and possibly the most significant reason behind her discontent, was the absence of rituals in Christianity.

Buddhism encompasses a significant number of rituals that revolve around the basis of familial kinships. As Buddhists, we were also permitted to perform other Taoist and Chinese rituals to pay respects to our ancestors or elders. Such rituals do not exist in Christianity and would perhaps be frowned upon by other Christians who stand by a monotheistic God. As such, my grandmother was afraid of an impending emotional disconnection between us, and that we would sever ties with her after she has passed on.

In the last few years, my grandmother moved in to live with my parents and me, as she needed our care and assistance in her old age. Living together once again, I was able to reassure her that my values remain unchanged even as I had adopted a different religion. It took a long time for her to understand religious faith, kinship, and culture, and to overcome our religious differences. In time, my grandmother and I grew much closer, and the subject of religion became something we could discuss casually and unreservedly. More so than what religious faith and rituals reinforce, the relationship I had with my grandmother has created for us a valuable form of kinship.

As a joke, I would tell her about a Christian "ritual," the Holy Communion, which I termed "the God-eating ritual." Holy Communion took place once a month at the church I attended. It is a symbolic re-enactment of The Last Supper that takes place in the Bible, as an act of remembrance of Jesus' sacrifice for our sins.

Following a series of prayers led by a pastor, each member of the church congregation consumes a small piece of crackers and cup of juice. These items represent the body and blood of Jesus Christ and

Precarious Faith: Rethinking Spirituality

are believed to be able to cleanse our sins and infirmities through their ritualistic consumption.

In her witty response, my grandmother would jest that I would have no need for any hell currency in the future, since I have my fill of crackers and juice awaiting me in the Christian afterlife.

The Christian phase of my life proceeded in a rather pleasant yet uneventful manner throughout my middle and high school years, but eventually started showing cracks. In my experience, Methodist teachings are highly structured and organized, with strict rules and hierarchical systems to adhere to.

Just as with any other institution, the institutionalization of faith could inevitably result in the rise of internal structures that discriminate against individuals outside of it, and even those within who do not conform to social norms.

Many of the folks at the church I attended displayed intolerance towards the non-Christian Other—the LGBTQ community, believers of other religions and faiths, people outside of their social circles, and even other churchgoers who might interpret Biblical texts in a different way. I found myself rejecting the hegemonic grand narratives of the Methodist church for a more postmodernist outlook.

On countless occasions, my life choices and opinions were deemed as radical by the church community. Power struggles were common within the church circle. At the youth group, pastors and leaders showed favoritism toward selected individuals, who would then exercise this empowerment over others.

Decision-making revolved around their personal preferences and lacked empathy and consideration toward other members with very different circumstances. Derogation and slander were common amongst those seeking power.

The sacred space of worship and healing became a site of negativity and toxic politics. Such attitudes of exclusivity shaped the evangelism practices of the youth group. We were often encouraged to invite our non-Christian friends to church, albeit in an over-zealous way where people would strategize on how to entice others, almost

Taking New Paths *Stories of Leaving Religion*

as if it was a competition. In Sunday School service for younger children, they would be rewarded with gifts every time they brought along a non-Christian friend to church. This further enforced a boundary between self and Other—Christians and non-Christians, or non-members of the church.

This division between the inside and outside spaces of church was more pronounced when it came to the day-to-day behavior of the members and attendees of my church. As the church was a partner organization of the Methodist missionary school I went to, a large proportion of my churchmates were also my schoolmates.

Their persona of the ideal saint-like Christian on Sundays would somehow vanish during the rest of the school week, where they took part in bullying, acts of racism, and petty crimes such as theft and vandalism. This was perpetuated by the fact that these students, who came from a privileged upper-middle class community, were oblivious to the people around them.

I had witnessed Christian classmates speak to students of a different race or economic background in a derogatory manner. Standing up against them would in turn make me into their new target of bullying.

Despite the fact that Christianity helped me overcome a difficult period of my childhood, the church no longer felt like a safe space. I was first drawn to Christianity because it spoke of love and acceptance but failed to address the antagonism within it. I recall questioning a pastor at church about the extent to which church can be a safe space when it enables attitudes of prejudice and biasness towards people who embrace alternative lifestyles or life choices.

Unsurprisingly, his response was unenthusiastic. I had brought up a controversial issue that he had been trying to avoid addressing. His curt reply went along the lines of "We'll just have to pray harder for these people and hope they'll come to the right path." Other similar encounters have led me to become disillusioned toward the Christian faith.

Although I continued to rely on prayer as a coping mechanism, I had entirely stopped attending church by the time I entered university, after an extended period of church-hopping.

Precarious Faith: Rethinking Spirituality

Just as my religious explorations were beginning to look bleak, I was introduced to the New Age Movement and the metaphysical trinity of Body, Mind and Energy by a classmate during my time in university. While origins of New Ageism can be traced back to ancient astrology and animism, this classmate of mine claimed that it can be viewed as a set of guiding principles for a metaphysical way of life in our modern era.

He had noticed that I was suffering from frequent anxiety attacks and paranoid behavior, which were remnant effects of my childhood trauma, and he felt that New Age practices could perhaps help mitigate some of these unhealthy tendencies.

According to him, the New Age beliefs are built on the understanding that one's body contains different spiritual energies that correlate with one's lifestyle, habits, and interactions. One needs to maintain a good balance of these different energies by practicing reciprocity, and not just in physical gift-giving or material exchanges.

For example, overworking or associating with unpleasant people may cause one to manifest their negative energies. In exchange, one can spend some time in solitude or find means of relaxation to release negativity whilst inviting positivity back into our spiritual minds. As with the laws of nature, our internal energies should be in a constant flux.

In simpler terms, these abstract practices can be seen as a way of managing our emotions, life choices, and relationships. As our external lives and surroundings are influenced by these internal energies that we manifest and project, it is important to regulate our energies in a way that best suits our needs. Parts of these concepts resonate with the Law of Attraction Theory, where positivity brings more positivity and negativity breeds misfortune.

When I first engaged with New Age ideologies, I was holding on to a lot of repressed anger and unhappy memories that stemmed from childhood and were carried forward into adolescence and even adulthood. This may have caused a significant build-up of negative energy in me, which was detrimental to my work, health, relationships, and my general wellbeing.

It was important for me to embody thoughts and emotions that are self-empowering, in order to bring about changes in my personal life. One must note, though, that toxic positivity, or an obsession

Taking New Paths *Stories of Leaving Religion*

with positivity, is also dangerous as it may result in downplaying or neglecting pain and misfortune, among other risks.

New Age has provided me with a neutral platform for self-care and reconciliation with my turbulent past. It has allowed me to feel at peace with myself and come to terms with my inner demons without the use of institutional religious doctrines.

Many proponents of New Age believe in the healing power of crystals. Crystals are regarded as transformative tools through which we can channel energies into and out of ourselves.

Beneath their beautiful glistening exterior, crystals are essentially naturally formed rocks that have been excavated from the Earth, before being processed, polished, and sold. As objects of the Earth's natural ecosystem, crystals derive their energies from their molecular compositions that give off certain vibrations and frequencies resonating with each individual in a unique manner.

Thus, different crystals have different mineral properties and healing abilities. For instance, Fluorite is used as a stress-reliever, while a Dumortierite crystal is excellent for patience and communication. A Chalcopyrite is believed to aid stimulating new ideas and beginnings, and a Tourmaline enhances self-confidence.

Following the advice of my classmate, I keep a range of crystals in my collection to help in various aspects of my life. They can be worn as an accessory, meditated with, or displayed in an indoor space. Through them, one can draw strength and harness the energies of the Anthropocene—the sun, moon, land, and oceans.

During a trip to Japan several years back, I met with a family friend who is a Christian missionary based in Kyoto. She worked with local organizations to provide counseling and assistance to youths and young adults at local universities. Her personal philosophy in religion is drawn from notions of believing and being.

Among the Japanese youth that she works with, many are keen to learn about Christianity in hoping it can provide them with a new source of direction amidst their personal struggles. However, they often choose to not attend a church or participate in church activities, as a lot of them grew up in Buddhist or Shinto household, the most

Precarious Faith: Rethinking Spirituality

common religions that Japanese families adopt with deep-rooted ties to local culture.

They are thus not comfortable with being too physically involved with church institutions. As a result, they often worry about the validity of their Christian faith. Her response is the reassurance that physical acts alone do not affirm one's faith; and faith exists by simply knowing, believing in, and living by that God's teachings.

Hearing about their experiences, I began to reflect on the necessity of the physical church and its institution. In my experience, the physical site of church tends to create divisions.

Churchgoers in Singapore often make the effort to evangelize by inviting their friends to attend a church, forgetting that some may not have access to the church itself due to personal circumstances, such as limitations in time, means of transportation, and family commitments, among other countless possible factors. Taking into account these considerations, faith that is spatially-bound may in turn cause more harm than good.

Faith has been very personal to me throughout all my religious explorations, and I believe that it is subjective to each individual's circumstances and way of life. It is almost irrational to have to confine faith to a specific religious site or limit its definition to a set of rules written by religious leaders.

Rooted in personal thought and spirit and exhibited through one's principles and values in the everyday, believing and being for me are far more powerful than institutional definitions of faith. In my own Christian faith, I wanted to pursue a spirituality that transcends manmade boundaries.

Following this line of thought, New Age appealed to me precisely because it allows spirituality to transcend the boundaries of religion and religious institutions, into an entity that is metaphysical and reflective of one's inner mode of being. It can be incorporated into any other religion or be simply practiced as a way of life.

As I wanted a more informed and reflexive approach to my religious explorations, New Age practices encouraged me to reconnect

Taking New Paths *Stories of Leaving Religion*

with my Christian faith from a spiritual perspective that focuses on prayer, meditation, and raw emotions. Drawing reference from New Age, I now regard Christianity as a source of positive energy from which I draw my strength and inspiration.

At present, I do not attend church or any church-related events. Rather, I choose to read the Bible and pray independently in my own private space, in order for the religious experience to become a more personal and meditative one.

Through prayer, I release any negative emotions to God, sometimes with the aid of healing crystals; and I attempt to seek positivity from Bible verses or even Christian worship music that provide a contemplative space and serve as a guide for difficult situations in my life.

My grandmother passed away in March of 2021. The funeral was a week-long affair and held in a rather elaborate traditional Buddhist style of funeral proceedings. As part of Buddhist funerary customs, there are a series of rituals that immediate family members of the deceased must perform on a daily basis, several times a day.

The funeral arrangement was rather detailed, consisting of many elements and objects that had to be utilized in the rituals. In front of my grandmother's coffin were several large altar tables with her photograph, displayed alongside porcelain figures of Guan-Yin and other Buddhist deities. These were accompanied by items used for offerings and ancestor worship: censor bowls for burning incense and joss-sticks, floating candles placed in bowls of oil, and fresh food and fruit. Buddhist-themed decorations and flowers were displayed around these tables as an additional touch to the overall space.

In the morning of the first day of the funeral, my family and I were briefed by a group of Buddhist monks about the rituals we had to complete, in an almost spontaneous crash-course fashion.

Buddhists in Singapore and parts of Southeast Asia believe that the soul of a person would still be present on earth for the next forty-nine days after his or her death, hence the need to perform these rituals as meticulously as possible to pay our respects, and more importantly to put the soul properly to rest.

Precarious Faith: Rethinking Spirituality

Each morning for the duration of the entire week, we offered joss-sticks in two different censer bowls for the Guan-Yin figure and my grandmother respectively. For Guan-Yin, we used a spiral shaped joss-stick that had to be burnt in a clockwise direction, and for my grandmother, we used a thick large joss-stick specially crafted for funerary ceremonies.

Throughout the duration of the funeral, we had to ensure that the joss-sticks did not burn out before we lit a brand new one. An empty censer bowl with burnt-out joss-sticks is believed to be harmful to the soul of the deceased. The oil in the candle bowls had to be refilled frequently to keep the candles lit. These candles are symbolic of enlightenment as well as reflective of the impermanence of human life.

Following the offering of joss-sticks, we had to prepare a small bath set-up for my grandmother using a small pail filled with water, bar of soap, and toothbrush. This would wake her spirit up, in a metaphorical sense, to prepare her to receive her offerings each day. Lastly, we replaced the food and fruit offerings with new ones twice a day, at breakfast and dinner times. The food had to be meatless—vegetarian or vegan—as a sign of respect for all life forms.

Every evening, monks from a temple would drop by the funeral site to chant a series of Buddhist prayers for about thirty minutes. These prayers not only put the deceased's soul to rest, but also help guide other neighboring wandering or lost spirits to the afterlife. These spirits would then in turn express their gratitude to my grandmother by returning her a favor in the afterlife.

My parents were apprehensive about taking part in these rituals at the beginning, perhaps fearing judgment or criticism from their Christian friends and relatives who attended the funeral. While Christian teachings do not normally condone ancestral and idol worship, I regarded these rituals as a way of respecting and honoring my grandmother.

At the same time, it became a method of coping with death and loss through routine. In performing these funerary rites for my grandmother, I felt that I was establishing a sense of physical and spiritual connection to her departed soul. Exodus 20:12 in the Bible tells us to "Honor your father and your mother, so that you may live long in the land the Lord your God is giving you."

Taking New Paths *Stories of Leaving Religion*

In the past, my grandmother often expressed her hopes that we would be willing to undergo Buddhist rituals during her funeral, regardless of our religious differences. Knowing that her religion meant a lot to her, I am glad that I was able to fulfill her wishes and, in the process, propose a reconciliation between religious differences.

In all my religious explorations thus far, faith has repeatedly presented itself as a complex and open ended plurality of possibilities, like "a house with many rooms," as described in the novel *Life of Pi* by Yann Martel.

As my experiences, identities, and relationships changed through time and space, my beliefs were altered and shaped according to my everyday realities. Throughout my recollection of the religious identities that I had inhabited, the subject of "kinship" came up quite frequently. These networks of relations revolving around family, friends, and religious organizations often led to moments of self-evaluation, decision-making, and gaining the courage to let go in my encounters with faith.

This precarity of faith has made it more meaningful than ever. Many times, I had hoped to establish an attachment to permanence and routine by leaving one religion and settling on the next, only to realize how little control I had over the nature of believing and being. It was in times of doubt and uncertainty that I could unravel and further make sense of my own faith—a phenomenon that remains undefined and a perpetual work-in-progress.

Suggested Readings:
God: A Human History, Reza Aslan
Jesus in Disneyland: Religion in Postmodern Times, David Lyon
Religion, Modernity, and Postmodernity, Paul Heelas
Religious Pluralism and the City: Inquiries into Postsecular Urbanism, edited by Helmuth Berking, Silke Steets, Jochen Schwenk
The Life of Pi, Yann Martel
The Unconscious God, Victor E. Frankl
Waiting for Godot, Samuel Beckett

Two Changes Before a Final Exit

12

Two Changes Before a Final Exit
Casey S. Corbridge

I HAVE SPENT NEARLY all of my life holding strong religious beliefs of one kind or another. I was born into the Mormon church and was a very active participant in that faith until age twenty-one. Four years later, at twenty-five I converted to Evangelical Christianity. I was very passionate and involved with that faith until that unraveled for me as well, twelve years later, at age thirty-seven.

As stated, I was raised in a Latter-day saint (LDS/Mormon) household in Layton, Utah. My family on both parents' sides have been LDS for generations. Mormonism is truly a culture just as much as it is a religion, particularly so in Utah where an overwhelming sixty percent of residents are Mormon, (if you can imagine) with most everyone living in tight-knit Mormon religious communities.

It seemed I scarcely knew anyone growing up who was not of the Mormon faith, and there wasn't any part of my young life that wasn't completely shaped by Mormon teachings and culture.

Taking New Paths *Stories of Leaving Religion*

Most people are familiar with Mormonism's missionary effort; it's an unmistakable image of two nineteen-year-olds on pedal-bikes donning black slacks, short-sleeve white dress shirts and a tie, with a backpack full of copies of the *Book of Mormon* they are more than happy to disperse to anyone who'll take them. The image is even more recognizable following the success of the satirical musical *The Book of Mormon* by South Park creators, Matt Stone and Trey Parker.

Mormon culture expects that following high school, every "worthy" male is to serve one of these full-time missionary efforts for two years to win converts (females can serve as well, should they choose, but there's no expectation or pressure, and their service is a reduced eighteen months). The church headquarters in Salt Lake City, chooses by "divine revelation" where each young man will go; the applicant has no say.

My father was ordered to serve his mission in New Zealand and looking up to him as a youngster it never once occurred to me growing up that I would not go on one of these missions when the time came. It was just seen as the expected next step between high school and college.

It didn't even seem like a decision to be made. It was just… what you did. Additionally, all my friends served missions and, interestingly enough, I was the only one who happened to be assigned within the United States. I was sent to Rochester, New York, while my friends found themselves in the Dominican Republic, Germany, Romania, Chile, and a variety of other countries.

These missions were no joke. We were compelled to be with a "companion" missionary at all times; we were to never to be alone or leave our companion's side for literally any reason (other than the two obvious exceptions of toileting and bathing).

The list of rules we were under strict orders to adhere to, seemed endless. For some examples, our haircuts had to be approved, non-LDS music was outlawed, there was to be absolutely no watching television or movies, no talking to females, no swimming…on and on. It was regimented for us what time we woke up in the morning, to what time the lights were to go out at night.

We were to report nightly to our superiors concerning the daily

Two Changes Before a Final Exit

activities accomplished, to make sure our daily quotas were achieved. We were given one half-day per week for preparation (called "P" day), which was the only time allotted for shopping, cleaning, laundry, etc.

We were not even allowed to call home to speak to our families (the only two exceptions being Mother's Day and Christmas). We could only write letters to loved ones. Bestowed upon each missionary was a miniaturized rule manual, that was to be always kept with us, dubbed "the little white book."

This was a very emotionally difficult and depressing time for me. Although I deeply believed in the cause, and the importance of what I was doing…obviously, this is not what any nineteen-year-old would prefer to be doing with their life at that age.

I actually packed up my suitcase and arrived at the mission leadership's home in Rochester, ready to go home. He shoved me some Prozac, and basically told me "It's now time to get back to the Lord's work, soldier." The pills went promptly in the garbage.

Shortly after beginning the second year of my two-year requirement, I began to be confronted with information that gave me pause about the veracity of church doctrine, and seeds of doubt began to sprout and flourish.

The nature of these winding, mounting concerns is not worth going into depth here; however, there was one pivotal moment I think worth relaying. To understand my frame of mind, I do have to sidestep into a brief explanation about Mormon theology concerning the nature of God.

It will certainly go unnoticed that Mormons use exclusively male pronouns when referring to their god, because all the Monotheistic Abrahamic religions do this very thing, so we're used to this. However, Mormonism is unique among these religions in that, for them, the male pronoun is not a figure of speech or artifact of language construction. Mormons believe their god is actually literally physically anatomically male.

The founding prophet of the religion, Joseph Smith, supposedly, through divine revelation, announced that god was once born as a mortal human on some unknown distant planet, and through

Taking New Paths *Stories of Leaving Religion*

his obedience (a process they call "progression"), he evolved into a "glorified man," i.e. a god. He is now one of these "glorified" humans, living on a distant planet revolving around a star named Kolob.

He apparently also has a goddess wife Mormons don't particularly like to discuss, but if pressed they call her the "Heavenly Mother." In fact, the church leadership used to declare via divine revelation that the Mormon god is actually a polygamist with many goddess wives.

Mormonism is henotheistic, that is, they posit the existence of countless humanoid-gods throughout the universe, but they are only to worship one of these god-man deities—the one whom they call "Elohim," or most commonly "Heavenly Father."

Here I'll state a crucial pivotal fact: the end goal of becoming a god (or goddess) is the beating heart of Mormon doctrine, and is considered by them the very purpose of life (though surprisingly this is never overtly stated at Mormon church meetings; thus a visitor to any typical Sunday morning Mormon service would never be aware of this underlying foundational doctrine of deification).

This unique and bizarre doctrine about the nature of God affected me a great deal towards the end of my mission. Throughout each missionary's two-year tenure, we are moved around to different "areas" and change companions every few months.

My final assignment was in a little perfect cottage out in the countryside, complete with a nice outside porch situated with a couch, facing directly towards "Silver Lake" in Wyoming County, New York.

I remember sitting out there during the nights of early autumn (well past when it was "lawful" for me to be awake), looking out over the lake, and up at the starlit sky. I'd stargaze and contemplate the grandeur of the unimaginably distant stars and invisible galaxies I knew were out there.

I was totally taken in by the peaceful and incomprehensible beauty of it, and felt overwhelmed contemplating the unimaginable numbers, sizes, and distances of these celestial objects. As I did this, I found myself becoming completely disenchanted with the Mormon doctrine that there could be a glorified, but bodily human, man living on some distant planet near a star ridiculously called Kolob…and that this man is "god." The wizard behind the curtain.

From his planet he sits there—governing, sustaining, moving,

Two Changes Before a Final Exit

and manipulating time and space with his "divine power," and magically possessing total omniscience of the past, present, and future of the entire universe in his "exalted" brain, enclosed in his "exalted" skull. Equally absurd was the notion that at that moment, he was reading my thoughts—also simultaneously the thoughts of seven billion other people on this tiny planet, light years away from wherever he actually was.

My mind ventured to even further absurdities nested in these notions, such as the idea that this man, "Heavenly Father" has a "plan" for my life, and also a unique plan for each one of the other seven billion other earthlings, and from his distant planet he is manipulating events on earth like a puppet-master to bring his plans to fruition.

As I dwelled on this, it all began to seem a totally irrational and preposterous scenario. I knew there was no other-worldly man in my head, nor in the heads of anyone else that was not in need of medication. My disillusionment had almost become complete.

So, during the final six months that remained of my two-year stint I was quite jaded. But returning home early from one's mission was enormously shameful within LDS culture. I would become a pariah—a disappointment and embarrassment altogether in the eyes of my parents, family, friends, and home congregation.

Around this time, I started experiencing some strange, severe, unmanageable headaches. On Halloween 2001, just two months shy of when I was supposed to have completed my missionary service, I went to the hospital for evaluation. I was CAT-scanned, and subsequently diagnosed with a brain tumor.

I was immediately flown home to Utah for emergency brain surgery. After my craniotomy, the biopsies of the tumor revealed it was benign. Though I was prepared for the worst—literally to face my own death—I was relieved, as was my family, that it wasn't cancer. I needed no further treatment, radiation, or chemotherapy.

A short time after returning home from the hospital and I was mobile again—to my astonishment and horror—I was informed the church leadership were contemplating sending me back to New York to complete my last month of service (even though I looked a mangled mess reminiscent of Frankenstein, complete with a half-shaven head and huge staples along the swollen and bruised seven-inch incision in my scalp).

Taking New Paths *Stories of Leaving Religion*

I was so happy to be home even under the worst of circumstances, though I was mortified at the notion of being sent back. But, to my enormous relief, in the end, they chose to offer me an honorable release,

Once home, I continued spending a lot of time grappling with my spirituality internally. I found the standard three-hour Mormon church services painfully repetitive and tedious, and spent most of those hours doodling cartoons about how ridiculous everything being said was.

In a relatively short period of time, I concluded the church just couldn't be true. Within six months of returning home from my mission, I had stopped attending Sunday services altogether. Noticing this, my parents approached me in a very mutually uncomfortable conversation.

Somehow, I found the courage to inform them I had lost all faith in Mormonism and was for all intents and purposes an atheist. I then put religion out of my mind completely.

I joined a very short-lived screamo-metal band and began enjoying after work drinks with my co-workers—truly engaging in what would be seen by "the Church" as all kinds of egregious transgressions; but I felt emancipated to just...not...care.

This went on for a few years, as I started my college career. Eventually I began taking many diverse biology courses prepping for graduate school to earn my Doctor of Pharmacy post-graduate degree.

I took several General Biology courses, Cell Biology, Genetics, Biochemistry, Physiology, Immunology, etc. Although these classes were all taught from an evolutionary point of view, it nonetheless reignited spiritual questions within me, such as: Why is there something instead of nothing? How did life arise from non-life? How did consciousness arise? How could natural selection (with its only fuel being random mutation) explain the astounding complexity and diversity of life on earth?

Even though I was being presented with evolution being the assumed, when not overtly stated, paradigm in my coursework, I

Two Changes Before a Final Exit

nonetheless started suspecting that perhaps there was possibly something "more," that perhaps I had been too hasty to identify as an atheist.

For a short time, I had some shallow interest in Eastern Religion, but I didn't really put in any real effort towards learning or understanding it. Eventually I found myself gravitating back towards the idea of monotheism, as a more familiar and comfortable worldview from my upbringing.

Though I regarded Mormonism to have no truth value, I began considering the tenants of my former rival: main-stream Christianity. Christians seemed to do "good things" prompted by their beliefs, so I thought, I might as well tentatively align with that. But I didn't truly know much about Christianity other than the clashing theological points of conflict I argued with them while on my LDS mission.

Now for this story to all come together, I must rewind back to my New York mission experience to an event that would turn out to be the most important and pivotal moment of my entire life—my introduction to my future wife.

Eighteen months had gone by since I had started out, and a certain evangelical Christian girl, seeking to get to the bottom of Mormonism, started talking with the missionaries. She was disturbed by Mormon doctrine, as it departed so sharply from Evangelical ideals, and thus she believed we were all absolutely doomed to eternal hellfire for our mistaken and heretical beliefs.

I was introduced to her, and despite our faith differences, we made fast friends, and a mutual attraction was palpable. Breaching the highest order of missionary codes of conduct and anathemas, we met often, and continued telephone contact even after I had been transferred to my next area. If any of this were to be discovered by leadership, I would undoubtedly be sent home in total disgrace.

After returning home, she and I continued to talk frequently, and a few months later I flew back to New York for us to spend some private time together, unhitched from my missionary state of mind and behavior restraints. I had fallen deeply for her.

However, eventually she severed our relationship out of a conviction she needed to be with a like-minded Christian and saw our

Taking New Paths *Stories of Leaving Religion*

faith incompatibility as a deal-breaker. I was heartbroken. A few years went by with no contact.

Then out of the blue in 2004 she contacted me, and the flame was reignited. This time around, as I previously related, my worldview had evolved to where I was no longer Mormon, had a new spiritual gravitation that I happened to choose to label as Christian. I thought I knew much more about Christianity than I did, but the truth was, I had never ever even once attended a single Christian church service, nor any other non-LDS service, for that matter, in my whole life. I certainly did not grasp Christianity as she saw it.

But I used the magic word "Christian" and that was enough for her. With no further investigation into my flimsy faith-claim, we resumed daily phone calls and cross-country visits, culminating in a marriage proposal and a move back to Rochester in January of 2005. We were married later that year.

So, when my young bride and I had settled in an apartment back in Rochester, I suddenly found myself under compulsion by my spouse to attend weekly church services with her at Victory Baptist Church. Regular church attendance wasn't in my plan when I moved across the country. Obviously, I had not thought this through carefully enough. But there I was.

It was a very different experience from the strictly traditional LDS services I was accustomed to. I'd never heard any other instrument played in church other than an organ or piano. But to my astonishment this Baptist church was fit with a deafeningly loud drum kit, electric guitars, basses, and a whole band. After jamming their hearts out to the Lord, the audience would clap their approval as if they were at any other rock concert. In an LDS meeting, if a person were to clap their hands they'd probably be escorted out.

Following the performance of the "praise band" (a new phrase to me) the pastor would take the stage. He was a skilled dynamic preacher, furiously shouting out with conviction the "word of god." He'd have his audience laughing at one point and he'd turn deadly serious the next. It was great showmanship, I suppose. The LDS have their own brand of showmanship, too, but at the other extreme. In a Mormon church you will find congregants taking the pulpit to burst into contrived tears in order to display their undying affection towards founder Joseph Smith (and sometimes Jesus, too). It was seen that the

Two Changes Before a Final Exit

depth of a Mormon's spirituality was proportionate to the quantity of tears that could be mustered up.

Quite contrary to this experience, having the gospel yelled at me on a Sunday morning was a jolting new experience. Initially I felt very out of place. People would be swaying, clapping, singing, holding their arms outstretched...all the while I looked on standing still, silent, and hands clasped firmly behind my back. Even though I had supposed I was some sort of Christian, prior to this, I didn't really buy much into what I was hearing. But I listened, nonetheless.

For a year and a half, my wife and I attended Sunday services, Sunday School, and mid-week services as well. All those times I'd take in this "Pastor Joe" character. He was a master orator, very well educated, and had a magnetic personality and infectious smile.

Ironically, he was also a sixty-year-old mixed martial artist, the church property housed an MMA training facility, and they boasted of training the Rochester police department in fighting techniques. He and his son Paul led a ministry called "Karate for Christ" and the church was even documented in an HBO special called "Fight Church" (on which I can be spotted sitting in one of the pews!).

I thought all of that was so cool, having an aged-ninja for a pastor whilst HBO knelt filming in the aisles during Sunday service. Though I felt like a fish out of water there at first, eighteen months of listening to this man's preaching started getting some hooks into me, and I started to become drawn in by it, but remained unsure of what to really believe. (Interesting side note, both "Pastor Joe" Burress and his son Paul Burress pastored that church...and they are, likewise, both now registered sex offenders, both having separately plead guilty to multiple child sex charges. Go figure.)

During that same time, things were wildly unraveling in my marriage. I had left my whole life in Utah behind, moving across the country to pursue a relationship that began with such absolutely fairy-tale romanticism. As it would turn out, the whole thing would turn out to be a nightmare I couldn't have ever dreamed possible. The details here I will omit...but it was traumatically hellish. The whole situation sent me into a spiraling depression, complete with thoughts of suicidal ideations. I felt like a prisoner. I was a poor student with barely enough money for the basics, living in a distant state from my family and with zero support system, nowhere to go and no one to turn to.

Taking New Paths *Stories of Leaving Religion*

And for whatever reason I still felt like I deeply loved this person with whom things had gone so completely south. I thought, naively, that things could and would magically get better. It's not worth going into more detail than this…but suffice it to say that life got very, very unimaginably bad.

In the midst of my emotional turmoil, my thoughts turned to Pastor Joe's weekly preaching, emotionally imploring me that if I would only pray and ask Jesus to forgive my sins, I'd step into a personal relationship with God and become "born again." I thought maybe that is what was missing in my life. Maybe that was what was missing in my marriage. Maybe *that* was what was going to fix everything.

So, late one night in July of 2006, sitting in a separate room from my wife after a typical cataclysmic fight, I prayed to Jesus for salvation, and asked him "into my heart to be the Lord of my life" as I was instructed each Sunday to do. At this time I began to actually believe I had been "saved," chosen by God, and that I had secured irrevocable eternal life.

I believed God would bless my life and my situation would improve along with it. This began my journey into evangelical Christianity…a journey that (spoiler alert) would end twelve years later at enormous personal cost, emotional turmoil, and the loss of friends, community, family, all support—and ultimately—a devastatingly ugly divorce.

At the time of my conversion, in addition to thinking my new Lord was going to right all the wrongs in my life, I also believed that as a "new creation in Christ" I would eventually enjoy the bliss of heaven, while the majority of the rest of the world would be doomed to an eternity of torture—burning in a lake of fire in hell forever.

Of particular concern for me at the time, when looking through the lens of Evangelical elitism and snobbery, Mormonism appears so thoroughly heretical, Satanic even, that certainly all Mormons are strapped aboard a spiritual rocket-ship aimed right into the heart of hell.

Two Changes Before a Final Exit

I struggled with the thought that all of my friends and family were blindly marching into eternal torture...but bafflingly I accepted this, nonetheless. I strained a lot of relationships nearly to the breaking point, trying to preach Jesus to them, in an attempt to save them, in the way I thought I had been saved.

After all, now I knew the truth (in the same fashion as I thought I did when I was a Mormon) and was under a compulsion to share that truth (again, in the same fashion as I did when I was a Mormon). The psychology of religion is really quite astounding.

Some people less familiar with Mormon doctrine may not fully understand why most Christians would be so eager to exclude them from their camp, and even insist LDS beliefs would certainly send them to hell. When examined, Mormonism and Christianity share many terms but with polar opposite definitions.

For instance, consider just the word "Jesus."

To Christians, Jesus is the divine incarnation of a monotheistic deity who exists (contradictorily) as three persons comprising the "Trinity" as it is called. The Christian Jesus has existed for all eternity, is equal with the father, and is the *ex-nihilo* (out of nothing) creator of the universe.

In stark contrast, the Mormon Jesus was a more or less recent "creation," born as a spirit-baby to the Heavenly-Father and Mother on their home planet in outer space. Jesus was born there in the same way we all were: humans, demons, and even Satan (Mormons call this realm the pre-existence). We're all part of one big family from Kolob.

The "good" spirits, like you and me, get sent to earth to inhabit bodies with the hopes of becoming gods, the bad ones get sent here as invisible demons to tempt us away from that goal. (Digging deeper, you must know it was taught that the valiant spirits go down to earth to get white bodies and the less valiant inhabit black bodies. It is repulsive how little is known about how thoroughly racist Mormon roots are, but that is for another essay.)

In an act of blasphemy in the eyes of a Christian, Mormons affectionately call Jesus their "elder brother," and this Jesus is also the brother of Satan (Evangelicals have a conniption over this), and Jesus is likewise a separate and subordinate being to the father and is not to be worshiped. Mormons heretically deny the Trinitarian doctrine outright.

Taking New Paths *Stories of Leaving Religion*

Additionally, Mormon Jesus didn't *"ex-nihilo"* create anything, but was rather the project foreman of many "helpers" that formed the earth out of pre-existing materials. All of this, of course, constitutes total blasphemy to the Christian; all reasons Mormons are seen to be destined to hell for believing in a false Christ.

"Salvation" is another important term redefined. Christians (at least the lot I came from) tend to hold to the Ephesians model of being saved by grace through faith apart from any personal works of righteousness. If you believe in Jesus, you are awarded heaven—if you don't, you go to hell.

Mormonism refutes the whole paradigm. They have this inordinately complicated progression from living as spirits on a planet in outer space, subsequently being sent to live and die on earth, then they are whisked away to yet another Spirit World to await judgment when the second coming of Christ occurs, at which time they get admitted to one of three different "kingdoms" of heaven, depending on their degree of faith and righteousness.

Hell has been dispensed with altogether as being far too distasteful, and it is replaced by a realm of "Outer Darkness" reserved for Satan, demons, and Mormon apostates (poor me).

Lots of other terms are redefined too, to the Evangelical chagrin. Another example: "baptism." Evangelicals generally see "baptism" as a public pronouncement of faith and an act of obedience. Mormons see "baptism" as the first necessary magical ritual required to gain entrance into the highest of the three heavens (and the first of at least four, possibly five, Mormon rituals needed to attain the status of godhood). Yet more blasphemy!

All of this is more than enough for most Christians to declare Mormons absolutely hell-bound, and the list of irreconcilable differences could continue on ad nauseam and fill volumes, as it already has.

But for my last point, Christians tend to be very uncomfortable with two specific Mormon claims: First, that they have ongoing revelation from God through living prophets and apostles (who are not to be questioned upon threat of excommunication) and second, that the Bible is thoroughly tampered with and is only to be trusted as far as it agrees with modern Mormon revelation and scripture.

Two Changes Before a Final Exit

Therefore, though Mormons see the Bible as useful and canonical, they read it with an eye of distrust; whole books and passages within are dismissed when found at odds with LDS theology (which occurs suspiciously often). Such notions are intolerable to mainstream Christendom.

The amount of general public knowledge about the religion is only the tiniest tip of a great hidden theological iceberg. There is a great deal about Mormonism that is intentionally withheld from outsiders, and even from new converts. Mormons are forced to swear oaths of secrecy about their clandestine god-making rituals once performed, and they are found to strictly adhere to these oaths of silence. Prior to 1990, a Mormon ritual participant, when swearing these oaths of secrecy, had to also agree to accept a death penalty if they were to breach this sworn silence.

There is so, so very much that could be said about Mormon beliefs, practices, and doctrines here; it is an extremely complicated and dizzying subject, and volumes upon volumes of books have been written on the matter. It is an absolute bizarre maze of ever evolving beliefs and teachings. Such is not the aim of my essay. But take the above as the most cursory of overviews.

If you are interested in more: during my time of zealousness to reach Mormons for the "truth" of Christianity, and to expose their bizarre secretive doctrines to the unsuspecting public and potential converts, I personally wrote, animated, voiced, produced, directed, and released two exposé cartoons on the subject. They were successful beyond my wildest expectations, one with well over three million views. They are on YouTube under my pseudonym, Mason the XMormon.. The first is entitled "Mormon Secrets: What the Missionaries Don't Tell," and the second is "Mormon Secrets 2: Race, Racism, and Revelation." So, all that is a brief explanation of how I could have possibly been convinced that those closest to me throughout my life (including my own parents) would burn forever and ever.

But still…though I was a passionate and committed believer, over the course of years doubts began mounting, in a similar way as how I began doubting the LDS church, but at a much slower pace. I was motivated to believe, and I put in a lot of effort to assuage my doubt.

Taking New Paths *Stories of Leaving Religion*

To keep myself in line I would read, listen, and watch media from all the heavy-hitter Christian apologists like William Lane Craig, John Lennox, Frank Turek, James White, Hugh Ross, Ravi Zacharias, Tim Keller, etc. I would pour over articles of pseudo-science released by ICR (the "Institute for Creation Research") and AIG ("Answers in Genesis)" and I basically worshiped Stephen Meyer and regarded his work *Signature in the Cell* as my secondary Bible.

Despite my best efforts to maintain the brainwashing I'd succumbed to and had allowed to overcome my critical thinking, there were still theological "snags" that tripped me up. For example, I always had a problem with Noah's Flood story.

Even during my Mormon years, the story was incredibly difficult to swallow. It was unnerving to have found myself dealing with the same doubt over the same thing, now as an Evangelical, which ultimately makes sense, given that the story is ridiculous. The large majority of Evangelicals and many other Christian sects make authoritative claims that the Bible is perfect in every way, including its historicity.

Then you open the book to read about a five hundred year old man building a "magical zoo boat" (as Aron Ra so eloquently phrased it), that was to hold two of every kind of all the countless animals of the earth for an entire year while the "God Who is Love" (1 John 4:8) massacres every man and woman on earth: the elderly, the young, the children, the newborns, and unborn fetuses as well. In an act that would make Hitler green with envy, in God's version of the "Final Solution" he snuffs out all of humanity, except his chosen band of eight people floating along on the magical zoo boat.

As if that weren't enough, the God-Who-Is-Love was so lovingly furious he drowned along with the evil humans all the innocent kittens, puppies, koalas, and those super-cute Tamarin monkeys, too. He slaughtered every living thing.

As the story goes, the waters eventually recede, and the ark finds land. No explanation is given as to how all these animals, once unloaded off of the ark, were to survive on a barren drowned planet. Every single meal of two hungry bears or tigers would mean the extinction of an entire species. The herbivores were in just as tough a spot—because there wouldn't have been anything to eat.

How is it that people believe this?!? I can ask that incredulously

Two Changes Before a Final Exit

now, but during my years under the Evangelical hypnotic spell I'd have gladly gone and visited Ken Ham's Ark Encounter Theme Park and allowed Mr. Ham to lull my doubts to rest.

I had similar hesitations over the Jonah story, or all the other over-the-top miracle stories to be found. I was troubled, not only trying to convince myself these could have been actual events, but also struggling trying to explain where the miracles all went. I spoke to my pastor about it; he gave me some cursory answers, urged me on in my faith, and sent me on my way.

Fast forward to January 1, 2018. My marriage, which had started out horrendously, was hardly any better thirteen years later, and I was still under this crazy illusion that if I could just get closer to God or behave more righteously it would all get better. But my motivation wasn't merely believing in something to get something. I truly did believe it, regardless of Earthly benefit or lack thereof. I felt distant from God and yearned for a deeper connection with him, so I determined the best way to accomplish this would be to get deeper in his word, the Bible.

So, as a 2018 New Year's resolution, I began a close reading of the Bible cover-to-cover, in a reading plan that was to span one year. I had read most or perhaps all of the Bible before, but in piecemeal fashion, never straight through.

As I began the reading plan, something unexpected started happening: I began to see how transparently outrageous the text actually was. I can't explain why I didn't see it before or why I was seeing it then, but suddenly it leapt off the page to me how obviously (if not comically) purely mythical the stories were.

Getting through the creation story in the first few chapters of Genesis started making me feel insane to think that I believed such things were an actual historical account. But I kept reading, day after day, week after week, into months.

There were many memorable moments that left my jaw agape and eyes wide in disbelief. One in particular that sticks out in my mind, was the story of Onan. If you're not familiar with Onan, the story reads that this man inherits his dead brother's wife but doesn't want to have kids with her. So, he takes full advantage of the pull-out method of contraception, "spilling his semen on the ground" as the

Taking New Paths *Stories of Leaving Religion*

text puts it in Genesis 38. Apparently, this was such an egregious sin, God killed him dead over it.

Stunned, I stared at the page for a while, then re-read the passage several times to make sure I was understanding correctly. Was this the "holy writ" I was supposed to believe in? I put this nonsense in the back of my mind and moved on.

Then I came to the next book, Exodus, and stumbled upon the passage about Zipporah, Moses' wife. Apparently at this junction in Exodus 4, God was so enraged with Moses about some stupid thing or other, that God tries to kill him. But Zipporah, being the fast-thinker that she is, decides the best method to quell the wrath of God was to take a knife, mutilate her son's penis with it—circumcising him—and then touch the dismembered foreskin to Moses' feet.

Apparently, her inexplicably bizarre plan worked, as tickling Moses' toes with the boy's severed naughty bits actually appeased the vengeful deity. Thus, God left Moses alone and allowed him to live. Magical foreskin.

Again, I was dumbfounded. Who is this God I had dedicated my life to? Why do I hold this Bible to be so pivotal in my life when this is the kind of nonsense I'm reading?

Still trying to preserve my faith, I created within my mind a "mental shelf" to store all the things that didn't make sense to me, so I could set them aside, go on maintaining my belief, figuring I'd find the answer in the years to come if I'd just study harder, or perhaps it would be revealed to me in the next life where I'd surely get to sit down with God and play a round of "ask me anything." This was the same futile mental process of "shelving" I performed when trying to maintain my crumbling Mormon faith.

Even surrounded by mounting doubts, I still somehow held to the *Sola Scriptura* view, and believed in the notion of absolute Biblical inerrancy. I had to "shelve" all these things I already mentioned, like Noah and Jonah, but many more to come.

I put on that shelf: talking snakes and donkeys, magical fruit, a man living to be over nine hundred years old, every word of the entire ridiculous narrative in Judges about Samson from start to finish (his trademark magical hair isn't nearly the only preposterously absurdity in that ludicrous tale).

Two Changes Before a Final Exit

I shelved the passage in Joshua 10 where supposedly God stopped the entire earth from rotating for a full day, so that the sun would stay still in the sky and enable Israel to win their battle in the daylight. I ignored tales of fireballs falling from the sky, staffs being turned into snakes, seas parting, falling manna, the falling walls of Jericho, etc., etc.

But one of the crowning moments of mythical comic relief I found actually comes from the New Testament. I was reading about the resurrected Jesus; Apparently having grown weary of his post-mortem partying with the disciples, he decides to make his grand exit by flying up into the clouds and out of view—as if he was a zombie-Clark Kent, flying off like superman to who knows where… outer-space I guess.

I couldn't believe it had never occurred to me before how silly this was. This also led me to think about the "rapture" so embraced by evangelicalism, where all the Christians will one day take flight into the sky at the Lord's (overly long awaited) second coming. It stands as another notion difficult to avoid mockery. But yet, I'd believed it.

In retrospect, I find it strange that I was able to continue in a faith for so long, which now seems so absurd to me. But at the time I was very much bogged down with strong confirmation biases, group-think dynamics, and trying to hold my crumbling marriage together, using Christianity as some sort of foundation.

Also, during the mounting years of doubt, when things just didn't make sense, I would always return to two verses from the Bible (the theological basis for my "shelf"): Isaiah 55: 8-13, and Proverbs 3:5-6: "For my thoughts are not your thoughts, neither are your ways my ways," declares the LORD. "As the heavens are higher than the earth, so are my ways higher than your ways and my thoughts than your thoughts. This will be for the LORD's renown, for an everlasting sign, which will not be destroyed.

"Trust in the Lord with all thine heart; and lean not unto thine own understanding. In all thy ways acknowledge Him, and He shall direct thy paths."

Taking New Paths *Stories of Leaving Religion*

Above I've listed a few examples of the overtly mythical stories that were piling up in my head, and my faith was suffering over them. However, these implausibilities on their own did not completely shatter my faith. It was the revealed character of the Judeo-Christian God that broke me. It was the malevolent, violent, vengeful, unjust, and morally bankrupt character of this wicked deity that finally broke my mental shelf—caving in not only my faith but my entire life along with it.

Every day, multiple times a day, for years I'd pray to this deity, as if he himself were my own father, omnipotently (magically) tending after my best interests. It was constantly being instilled in me from the pulpit that God was this perfectly merciful, benevolent, loving Eternal-Father-figure.

But in reading the text I quickly discovered he was actually an absolute psychopath; a blood-thirsty, vengeful, jealous lunatic of a tribal deity, issuing out orders to his tribe to carry out the most horrific acts imaginable, including mass murder and genocide, infanticide, slavery, sex-slavery, and rape.

He was a dreamed-up excuse for depraved men to justify their acts of depravity, molestation, and violence (if any of these recorded events had even actually occurred). This megalomaniac in the sky was said to have issued forth pestilence, plagues, famines, and floods—and he was worshiped for this.

Indeed, the only way to placate the YHWH (Yahweh, the Hebrew name of God) deity was through death and blood. The whole Bible, beginning to end, is just the story of an evolving cult of sacrificial "blood magic" (to borrow the phrase).

Many cultures for centuries before and after Israel have made sacrificial blood offerings to their deities, in attempts to either placate them, or to win their favor. There was nothing fresh or unique about Israel's invented god, the tribe just copied the already pervasive belief, that killing stuff pleases gods.

In retrospect, it's such a strange notion to me that I ever believed that, in order to obtain forgiveness from sin, the blood of one (be it animal or human) must be sacrificed to procure the forgiveness of another. When I started thinking through this, it became clear that it was not only completely void of any coherent sense of justice, but it was also detestable.

Two Changes Before a Final Exit

I began to think about how I could best communicate my thoughts about this to a fellow Christian, and I came up with an analogous scenario. I conjured up a man, Joe Blow. I had Mr. Joe Blow horrendously rape, torture, and murder a small child. Blow gets arrested with irrefutable damning evidence against him. During his court trial he gets sentenced to death.

Now, let's continue pretending I happened to be in the courtroom during his sentencing. Feeling especially merciful that day, I stood and pleaded with the judge, "Your highest honor, please execute me in Joe's place, that Mr. Blow may go free. I volunteer to shoulder his judgment of death."

I would imagine once the judge stopped laughing, he would certainly explain to me that's not how it works. Justice isn't met by killing any random innocent person. Justice is met when the offender gets his due. How would Joe Blow's victim's family feel if the judge were to allow me to step in allowing ol' child-murderin'-rapin' Joe to walk free? Would you guess they'd feel justice was served on behalf of their brutally murdered child?

As absurd as this concocted scenario is, it is the same scenario billions of Christians think is going to save them from the furnaces of hell, that someone else is taking their punishment for them and that this somehow spells j-u-s-t-i-c-e. Similar to the deluded thinking of primitive Israel for thousands of years, believing that sacrificing scores of animals would vicariously absolve them of sin.

The late but notable Christopher Hitchens once said in his work *Letters to a Young Contrarian*:

> *"I find something repulsive about the idea of vicarious redemption. I would not throw my numberless sins onto a scapegoat and expect them to pass from me; we rightly sneer at the barbaric societies that practice this unpleasantness in its literal form."*

Recently I heard Ph.D. Philosopher and Biblical historian Dr. Richard Carrier discussing the Jewish Yom Kippur and Passover traditions. Paraphrasing him, he said something to the effect that the atoning effect of animal blood only had "weak magical mojo," which is why it had to be repeated every year. But the book of Hebrews tells

Taking New Paths *Stories of Leaving Religion*

us that a human sacrifice (or rather a deity incarnated as human being sacrificed) had much stronger magical mojo, that it would only need to be done once and would then last forever.

In another lecture Carrier stated, "God needs blood to fix the universe, but only his own blood had enough magical power to do it, so he gave himself a body and then killed it." Though phrased jocularly, it is spot on.

Lastly, if you'll allow me to paraphrase Matt Dillahunty as well, he summed up Christian theology as thus: God decided to send himself, to sacrifice himself, to himself, in order to serve as a loophole for the rules he is in charge of anyway. Stripped bare of all else, Christianity is nothing more than a cult of human sacrifice. There is no way around this.

Toward the end, I started seeing this for what it was.

I previously mentioned my 2018 "Through the Bible in a Year" reading plan. I had made it through to July…when I came to a particularly jolting passage in 2 Samuel 21 concerning a rival tribe-nation known as the Gibeonites. In this passage, clearly God accepts human sacrifice as placation for his mysteriously misplaced fury against Israel.

I panicked, and immediately started reading about the context of the passage to make sure I wasn't misunderstanding. But the more I learned about this story the worse it got.

It was that day. I was done. No more of this nonsense.

It occurred to me within a moment's time—I didn't believe it anymore. Any of it. In my mind, in one day, the Bible fell from its status as the inerrant Word of God—to utter rubbish. Genesis to Revelation, all of it. Garbage. I felt a fool for ever having believed in any of it.

Shortly after, I announced this to my (then) wife, that I was no longer a Christian. Without expounding further, I'll just say that didn't go well.

I then had to grapple with the aftermath of a second worldview shattered in my lifetime. What of the afterlife? What of morality? What of origins? I was initially very fearful. Particularly of

Two Changes Before a Final Exit

the notion of hell I'd been brainwashed into believing. I would guess for most deconstructing Christians, ridding themselves of the heavily indoctrinated fear of hell is a common challenge.

There is always the thought, "what if my intuition turns out to be wrong, and I end up being toasted in hellfire by the Devil and his demons forever and ever, tortured endlessly with no hope of reprieve? That's a scary thought. The fear hung around in my mind for around a year or so, and I had to constantly remind myself of how nonsensical the entire belief system was in order to relieve the fear that I might actually be eternally doomed.

But, as it does for most, that fear has totally abated. I now fear stubbing my toe in the twilight infinitely more than the prospect of being pitchforked by demons whilst being burned by fire for eternity.

In addition to fearing hellfire, I was also thoroughly indoctrinated that without God or the Bible, there was no objective basis for morality. Hundreds of hours listening to Ravi Zacharias's sermons and speeches by William Lane Craig pounded this into my brain convincingly and repeatedly. I realized if I were confronted and asked to explain the basis for my moral compass untethered from God, I would not be able to. This bothered me a great deal for a while. But listening and reading from notables like Sam Harris, Matt Dillahunty, and others gave me some great insights. One quote that stands out in my mind was from the atheist magician, Penn Jillette during a SiriusXM studio interview with Ron Bennington in 2012:

> *"The question I get asked by religious people all the time is, without God, what's to stop me from raping all I want? And my answer is: I do rape all I want. And the amount I want is zero. And I do murder all I want, and the amount I want is zero.*
>
> *The fact that these people think that if they didn't have this person watching over them that they would go on killing and raping rampages is the most self-damning thing I can imagine. I don't want to do that. Right now, without any god, I don't want to jump across this table and strangle you. I have no desire to strangle you. I have no desire to flip you over and rape you."*

Taking New Paths *Stories of Leaving Religion*

If I may also bring back Matt Dillahunty to offer another quote, because I found this helpful on the topic:

> *"I get my limits from a rational consideration of the consequences of my actions, that's how I determine what's moral. I get it from a foundation that says my actions have an effect on those people around me, and theirs have an effect on me, and if we're going to live cooperatively and share space, we have to recognize that impact. That's where I get my limits from. I get them from an understanding of reality, not an assertion of authority."*

During my deconstruction from Christianity, I quickly realized that the Bible is actually a very poor compass for morality. It has some valuable sayings, such as the golden rule: "Do unto others as you'd have them to do to you" (a saying actually far pre-dating its quotation in Bible in Matthew 7:12).

But The Bible also instructs that if a bride is found not to be a virgin on her wedding night, she is to be brought to her father's porch so rocks can be thrown at her until she's dead (Deuteronomy 22). Or that disobedient children (Deuteronomy 21), or those found gathering sticks on the sabbath (Numbers 15) are to be fatally stoned. Any person found worshipping any other gods than YHWH were to be murdered. It says it's okay to beat your slaves as long as they don't die within a few days, as they are your property (Exodus 21).

Any book that contains any one of these things, forfeits any claim to being a moral guide of any sort. It is morally bankrupt.

Moving to the next point of difficulty I faced by abandoning my faith was the loss of meaning. That is to say, if when we die there is no afterlife, our actions truly can have no meaning. Stoic Philosopher and Roman Emperor Marcus Aurelius was quoted to have said "what we do now, echoes in eternity."

If this is not so, i.e. there is no eternity, then "what we do now" doesn't matter. There is no meaning to life. In the end, we all suffer two deaths. The first death is when our heart stops beating within our chest, and we grow forever cold. Our second death is when we are forever forgotten.

Two Changes Before a Final Exit

We are each buried a second time alongside the last living person who had any living memory of us when they too join us in death. In this context it would seem true meaning ceases.

The prospect of death as a finality is another adjustment. As a believing Christian, I always assumed that the godless must be wallowing in continual fear of their own death; and perhaps worse than this, is what they must experience when enduring the loss of a loved one. The grief and despair of the occasion would be compounded exponentially, knowing there will be no future embrace with this person waiting them on the other side.

Because it was so drummed into my head that this is how I would inevitably feel without the promise of a blissful eternity reunited with the departed, I ignorantly assumed this is how every non-believer must feel. I thought the godless were hiding their continual depression and hopelessness staring into the face of meaninglessness.

Jumping the fence onto truly greener pastures, this notion all turns out to be false. I suffered far more depression under the yoke of religion than after I've been psychologically free from those shackles. And concerning the fear of the finality of death, surprisingly for me this resolved shockingly quickly.

The realization that I had no eternal spirit residing within me, that death was final in every way—surprisingly—didn't incite the horror within me that I had assumed it would. I actually felt a strange sense of comfort in it.

I do fear the inevitable process of dying, as we all certainly do. I can't imagine this final exit is likely to be very comfortable; but I almost immediately lost the dread of "non-existence."

Shortly after coming to these conclusions, I lost my grandfather whom I dearly loved. Honoring him and giving him a very final farewell carried no more sting for me than if I did believe I'd see him again in heaven. It was an unexpected experience.

Along the lines of maintaining a sense of meaning in the face of the finality of death, I adore a fantastic expression from British comedian and outspoken atheist, Rickey Gervais. He said, "It's a strange myth that atheists have nothing to live for. It's the opposite. We have nothing to die for. We have everything to live for."

I love this.

Taking New Paths *Stories of Leaving Religion*

Realizing this often-difficult life isn't just the dirty doormat at the foot of the door on into eternity, but rather that this is all there is, has me feeling more compelled to live my life to the fullest and be grateful to have the life I do have. As far as personal meaning goes, it is my position that my life has all the meaning I give it, and how I choose to live my life. I don't spend an ounce of effort pining that death has robbed me of that meaning.

If I were to guess, the majority of people in our culture would see religion as just best left alone, something not to be discussed. Religion is seen as a benign offer of comfort for those who would rather not face the inconvenient truth that what we see is all there is, or that God is seen as a convenient genie of sorts, answering prayer-wishes. Or the even more mistaken belief that society cannot be "good" without god (whether "he" be real or not).

Conversely, many others have bravely championed the idea that religion is a thoroughly pernicious institution. It debases the progress of our species, and hampers discovery and intellectualism. Beyond the promise of false hope, it brings little more than division, hatred, and at times war and violence. Religion's entire history has been penned in blood; though Christianity's bloodthirst has been mostly quelled, we see the same pattern as we look Eastward today.

Within my own life, even after shedding religion, it continues to be a malicious force. Though my exit from faith would serve as the catalyst to end my marriage (that was doomed from the beginning) in dreadfully painful ways, its effects are even more damaging than that.

Upon announcing that I had discarded my faith, I agreed with my wife not to interfere with my children being raised Evangelical, an agreement which I have upheld to this day. But already, my seven-year-old is expressing dire consternation that I don't go to church or pray, and demands an explanation. This sweet, sweet boy has been pleading with me endlessly that if "you don't love God then you won't get to be with me and my sister in heaven!"

It both breaks my heart and infuriates me at what he and his sister are being taught. It's rubbish…and it's harmful rubbish.

To conclude, if anyone reading this finds themselves struggling

Two Changes Before a Final Exit

with the fearful feelings of their faith slipping away, I would like to reassure you that it will get better. Questioning your own beliefs will always be daunting, sometimes frightening. It may also feel a lonely road to travel at times. But, may I say it's all worth it, and ultimately unimaginably freeing. Indeed, the truth will set you free, this much of the Bible is true.

During a conversation with my mother once, she actually told me that if her religion wasn't true, she'd rather just not know. I think that is so incredibly tragic! There's so much life to live without devoting your time, energy, emotion, thought power, and funds to an antiquated, unsubstantiated, and often dangerous set of ideas.

Keep learning, researching, reading, questioning, and thinking. Reach out for help. Many have been down this path and are eager to help. And finally, take it easy on yourself. Let go of the guilt. Such are the artifacts of indoctrination.

It's okay to question; it's okay to live your life in the way you want to live it, untethered from what you've been told the eye in the sky wants you to do, or not to do. There's nothing wrong with doubting…or living. Question everything and learn all you can from all points of view. Live your life to its absolute fullest.

Taking New Paths *Stories of Leaving Religion*

13
Comparing and Questioning
Doug Matheson based on interviews with Kunal Arora

KUNAL GREW UP within an hour of Delhi, assuming zero traffic issues. His dad was and is a Sikh, and his mom a Hindu. This mix didn't make for conflict though, in his home. He describes his childhood feeling of the Sikh faith's ten great Gurus easily fitting in as essentially among the many levels of Gods in Hinduism's pantheon; "You almost prayed to these Gurus as if they were Gods."

His father was a strong personality, and the final authority in his home. Seeing him, with his mom, bow the knee and worship "God," whomever that was, gave him the sense that there was only certainty to everything about this being, or these beings. Certainty and strength didn't, however, generate fear in his heart and mind.

Comparing and Questioning

That his parents had some differences in understanding of and approach to their Gods, but didn't have active conflicts about it, created a positive approach to both faith and gods.

This in turn led to him "feeling a fondness" for these various deities, even perceiving Shiva, the Destroyer, as having a good side.

"My parents would take me to temples with them. I enjoyed it, and they always encouraged me in this. They would appreciate my participation in the goings on. So slowly I got conditioned to follow, to explore, my family's combination of faiths."

The traditions wrapped in various festivals stand out in his memories of childhood. Kids will focus on having fun if given a chance, and he certainly did. Understandably, in his look back, Holi and Diwali still provide the most vivid memories of being great fun. Being able to throw colors, in liquid and/or powder form, at friends and strangers works well for a kid, as does lighting up all manner of fireworks.

But it wasn't all just fun and games. Absorbing the ideas of the circles of life, the potential upsides, but also the distinctly undesirable downsides to reincarnation was part of shaping his attitudes and behavior. He states that not wanting to be reborn as some sub-human animal "created a sense of urgency to follow my faith with all my heart."

One of the first areas that generated questions in his mind was the active remains of the caste system. He remembers in roughly the 6th standard (grade) his class was filling out some form asking for various demographic information: parents' occupations; family income; number of siblings; etc., and Caste. There were options listed: General; OBC (other backwards castes); SC/ST (scheduled caste/scheduled tribe).

This, not being a formal exam, he remembers students checking with each other and some quiet talk going on while filling it out. He didn't know what caste was, or what to put down for himself, so he asked a friend. His friend told him that he was "General." He frowned his puzzlement, and asked, "Wait a minute. I don't know my caste; how do you know my caste?"

He remembers being distracted from his friend's answer by some noisy activity mixed with embarrassment in part of the room. Two classmates he considered his friends, who were popular, good

Taking New Paths *Stories of Leaving Religion*

students, good young athletes, and habitually confident, were suddenly cowering on the receiving end of direct and malicious teasing.

There were whispered questions and answers among the rest of the class and he quickly learned that the victims were "SC," including the lowest castes, and that that was somehow socially terrible.

At home, his parents gave an almost non-response to his recounting what had happened. They didn't justify or deeply explain the caste system, but they also didn't condemn it. He had learned that he was among the upper, not the lower and vulnerable, and so didn't have anything to fear. As a kid, he remembers being bothered by the unfairness, but he didn't then make any connections between this caste system and the religion of Hinduism.

He realized that he, personally, didn't need to worry about discrimination, coming from an "upper" caste, and learned that the modern government in India had long-since made caste-based discrimination illegal. That he wasn't personally disadvantaged, however, didn't make him comfortable with others being unfairly treated, and some years later this began to make him wonder about the ethics supposedly worked out between these deities his parents believed in and humanity.

He was in his twenties before he saw caste as more than "a social problem." Ultimately though, he couldn't help but see a religious system that justified and promoted discrimination, raw human unfairness. The promise of reward in one's next (hopefully "higher") reincarnated life, for being a "good" and patient member of a discriminated-against group, now seemed to be more manipulation than reality.

Backing up to his late teens, he had become aware of elements of Islamophobia in the society around him. He had his own two religious traditions, and a general awareness of Christianity's existence, but interestingly, rather than internalize anti-Islamic sentiments, he consciously wondered if maybe they might be hated because they were somehow right about at least some things.

So, for the first time, he seriously explored beyond the blend of traditions he had grown up peacefully surrounded by. This exploration lasted several years, and for a while had what he calls "an almost romantic" touch to it, after which he began to reach a somewhat broad, but at that point tentative, conclusion.

Comparing and Questioning

Internal contradictions and a god obsessed with power were part of what he found in this search. He quite quickly picked up what he calls "an obsession with all kinds of behavior control." He found it very bizarre that Mullahs would teach that raping a woman was a lesser sin than failing to pray five times per day. Whereas he had grown up in an environment in which questioning was not only allowed but (at least by his parents) encouraged, he was struck by how his Muslim friends tended to shush questioning. One specific issue which friends repeatedly quickly avoided was how there was no Quranic direction requiring that women wear the *hijab*, but so many Muslims require it. He began to see the same misogyny he had seen in Hindu society.

He had started out personally expecting various stereotypes to be easily corrected, but he found reinforcement of several: The Muslims he got to know really did have a visceral emotional reaction against Jews, and, interestingly, Sunnis had this reaction against Shiites, and Shiites against Sunnis. He couldn't help but question the objective, intellectual, factual, foundations of a system that cultivated such emotion-based hatreds.

He heard the oft repeated claim that Allah was "merciful," but couldn't reconcile that with the many threats of earthly punishment and the descriptions of horrific and prolonged punishments in their version of hell.

He accumulated many more serious questions than substantive answers about this explored religion to add to those of his starting-point religion. But more so, he seemed to intuitively wonder if it was possible that any of the many religions he was becoming aware of were likely to separate themselves from the crowd, and stand out as much closer to Truth, while the rest of them would clearly fall behind. All of this he intended to measure with evidence which could be confirmed.

Overlapping in this time period he was also reading *The Ocean of Love: The Anurag Sagar of Kabir*. Initially he felt he was refining, and changing, elements of understanding from Hinduism.

But, as his awareness of the multiplicity of gods and faiths in all of human history (and in contemporary societies) continued to rapidly grow, his suspicion that it was exceedingly unlikely that one

Taking New Paths *Stories of Leaving Religion*

among the thousands would turn out to be well supported by evidence and logic, also became almost overwhelming.

At that point he had the opportunity to pursue a graduate degree in Canada. Thinking that the religion about which knew the least—Christianity—just might harbor the objective and experiential truths he hoped to find somewhere, he explored Christianity in a culture that seemed primarily Christian.

Alas, the more he saw and the more he learned, his prior suspicion that no faith, in any god, would end up being able to stand out as a relative island of truth in a sea of conflicting and confusing unsupported claims, seemed to be confirmed. Even if it wasn't welcome in his own head and heart, let alone broadly.

Part of India's internal politics played a role in his evolving awareness and thinking. The 2014 rise of the BJP (Bharatiya Janata Party) party's Hindu Nationalist approach made him stand back in active re-evaluation. He saw there what he could also see elsewhere: A rather defensive reaction to anyone questioning your sincerely held beliefs, and anything connected to your sense of identity. And he noted that it went further: It included falling for the temptation to impose one's beliefs and practices through politics, on the whole of the society.

What now? While focusing primarily on developing his career, in his chosen profession, he at least had to decide how to let his new insight impact the way he lived his life.

He could suppress the understanding he had developed, going back to something he had held or considered along the way; he could acknowledge and accept what seemed to be reality, but just keep it internal, not bothering others with unwelcome ideas; or… he could choose to share the importance of what he was becoming convinced of.

He had noticed along the way that all communities of faith seemed to draw limits to what they considered "appropriate" questions. Either some things simply shouldn't be asked, or standard answers (which aren't really answers) were expected to be accepted. He, on the other hand, was coming to see questioning things as a right, and

Comparing and Questioning

vital to any progress in understanding, or in how societies organize themselves and attempt to change for the better.

Internally, he had to face his own question as to whether or not he could "accept the fact that there appears to be no god at all." He leaned toward being honest with that, with what he assessed as the evidence and the probability.

He didn't like that "frequently atheists make fun of believers," but knew he didn't have to participate in that; he could still play a role in encouraging open questioning, of everything.

Rather than live "in the closet" and pretend that he still finds some god credible and supported by evidence or logic, he has chosen to be an honest advocate for a questioning approach to life. He found that he was able to "help my parents come to better understand religion in a broad sense."

And, more broadly, he recently chose to regularly publish a discussion on YouTube (https://youtube.com/c/KunalkiRaay), and interact with members of many faiths, but especially the Hindu and Muslim faiths, which dominate in India.

This isn't an easy path. Some of the faithful in every faith take offense at having their claims questioned. If humanity is to make progress, to take on the problems of our times, Kunal is convinced that this willingness to question things, and to seek honest and supported answers, is simply essential, and is worth the price of sometimes having to deal with frustrated and angry adherents of any faith.

Taking New Paths *Stories of Leaving Religion*

14
From Shattered Pieces
to
Freedom and Inner Peace
Kathy Marshall

WHEN I WAS TWO my parents and I went to Singapore as Seventh-day Adventist missionaries after Dad's graduation from the College of Medical Evangelists (Loma Linda University). Mission blood runs rich in my family. Dad was a doctor at Youngberg Memorial Hospital, in Singapore. His father had been a doctor in the remote south China city of Nanning, near the Vietnam border. My mom's parents went as missionaries to Japan in 1921, and she was born in Tokyo while her dad was studying Japanese in preparation for his job as Japan Mission President. Mom, her parents, and her older sister and brother, were present for the devastating 1923 earthquake.

From Shattered Pieces to Freedom and Inner Peace

The story of how my mother, at age nine months, was miraculously saved from being crushed by the fireplace during that earthquake was written in *Uncle Arthur's Bedtime Stories*.

My early childhood was healthy and happy in the affirming environs of the mission family and church community. I felt a deep sense of warm security belonging, and even a budding sense of family pride.

At age four, while my father was spending a year as the sole doctor for sixty bed Youngberg Memorial Hospital (YMH/YMAH), I contracted polio which paralyzed my legs. My parents and I were flown back to White Memorial Hospital in Los Angeles for rehabilitation treatments. It was highly unusual for Adventist missionaries to fly in those days, but the brethren felt it was important for us not to spend six weeks on a ship to LA.

After a month Dad flew back to Singapore and Mom and I followed at the end of three months. My life continued in happy nurturing ways, albeit with various iterations of leg braces which didn't seem to slow me down any. My playmates and schoolmates were kind and supportive, first in the church's elementary school, and then, as the years ticked by, at the academy.

The only fly in the ointment was that except for three instances during my four years in academy, I didn't have any dates. It hurt to be 'an old maid' with no dates or steady boyfriends like most of the other girls had.

My only life dream was to be a missionary wife, and since that didn't look like much of a possibility, I resigned myself to the idea of being an 'old maid' with fifteen cats!

Once through high school and back in the U.S., I took nursing at Walla Walla College. Because of my admiration for my dad and my exposure to the medical and other elements of our church's work, I had come to believe that the only 'sanctified' Adventist professions were doctors, dentists, nurses, teachers, preachers and secretaries. With a nursing career I could get back to the mission field as a single person.

During my teen years there was a prominent movement within the church teaching the ABC's of Prayer: Ask, Believe, and Claim the Bible promises. I was born with an independent nature and a 'can do'

Taking New Paths *Stories of Leaving Religion*

happy attitude that was fostered by my parents, especially in the face of my polio handicap. I chose not to dwell on marriage because if it didn't happen, then I would be all the more depressed. So only once during my college years did I let myself claim the ABCs of Prayer for a husband.

My world revolved around mission work, God, and the Church, which I believed to be the truest interpretation of the Bible.

During my final two quarters of college, I met Terry, who was on a Sabbatical from nurses training at Southern Missionary College (SMC) and working in Portland Adventist Hospital. He was tall, handsome, fun and talented. We began dating and were married the summer after I graduated. It was a feather in my cap that I had married, and to a good-looking guy.

My survival as a person with a handicap had depended greatly on leaning on God to get me through. It was deeply tattooed in my brain that God loves people as a father, and He never gives bad gifts. I considered it a direct answer to prayer that God had reached out his scepter and deemed that I could be married. Adult mission field surrogate aunts and uncles even told me how they had been praying that I would find someone and what a miracle it was that God had given me such a wonderful husband.

I had followed church standards carefully and devoutly. Since I didn't have boyfriends, I had very little chance to hold hands or kiss as a teenager and I was a virgin on my wedding night. I had done as God wanted and saved myself for marriage.

I had waited eagerly for someone to love me and to experience the joys of physical love. On our wedding night, my new husband said, "We've had a big day; it's late and we're tired. Let's just go to bed and sleep." Not how I envisioned my wedding night! After waiting all my life for love, I was beyond waiting anymore and 'pawed' at him until we eventually had sex. The next day we spent a lot of time in bed. Every time he would start to get up I'd suggest we play some more. He said, "but we just did that. I want to go for a walk instead."

Nothing in conservative Adventism in the '50s and '60s had given me any exposure to homosexuality. It was frowned on to hold

From Shattered Pieces to Freedom and Inner Peace

hands, pet or kiss—actually given almost the same spin as having sex. I thought my fiancé was being a Christian gentleman. I had no context for suspicions of homosexuality.

Because of my physical handicap I came to think that his lack of interest in sex during our thirty-three years of marriage was because I was not womanly, sensual or sexy enough. It was easier to suppress my own sexuality than to build anticipation and then suffer disappointment. Sex during those years of marriage was anywhere from every two to six weeks. Naturally when we did have sex, I was hesitant because I never knew if it was really going to happen so I held back and was guarded. Then he blamed me for taking too long and his libido running out. By the end of our marriage, I had suppressed my sexuality to the extent that when I stood naked in front of the mirror my mind fogged out my boobs and pubes as they do in news reports.

I felt depressed and trapped. I needed extra affirmation because of my physical handicap and instead was being denied a full marriage experience. I saw the way other happy couples looked at each other with deep cherishing and physical longing in their eyes. I wanted that for myself. His filial love, pride in who I was, and my talents were not enough without the deep physical attraction being returned to me.

I began to think of divorce, but how does one divorce because the sex isn't good enough when a prominent part of my tight conservative religion—where 'half the world' knew who I was—was a community that says sex is God given in marriage, but at the same time speaks of a celibate life as a virtue?

In spite of his reticence to have sex, we had two sons together. At age twenty-one our youngest son, Sidney, revealed he is gay. Then my husband told me he had always suspected it. Surprising to me was my husband's ability to accept our son's gayness. He had been very critical of our son for his worldly music and his earrings. How could he accept him, unconditionally, when he revealed he was gay?

It didn't take me very many months of hearing Sid's story, heart cry, and pain, and then meeting his gay and lesbian friends and hearing them tell of their struggles, to come to the conclusion that homosexuality is NOT chosen, but rather biological and/or genetic. Until I came to that knowledge, I had grieved as if Sid had died—he would never be accepted in our church or welcomed in the community

Taking New Paths *Stories of Leaving Religion*

again. Slowly I came to see that he was the same kid he'd always been. I still grieved deeply that life would be hard for him, and that I would most likely not have a daughter-in-law or grandkids from him.

I've always been close to my kids. When Sid came out, he sat with me into the wee hours of the morning while we worked on a project. He talked of the fear that homosexuality carries. People threw things at him and his boyfriend as they walked down the street. People on bikes tried to run them over. Sid spoke of all the beautiful, fun, talented girls he had dated in high school. He was tall, handsome, musical, funny, interesting, intelligent, the life of the party, and basically could have dated anyone he wished. But, he said, "they were all soul sisters, Mom. I had no sexual feelings for any of them, but when a good-looking guy walks by on the street, the chemistry is there unbidden!" He talked of how he had known since grade school that he was attracted to boys and was able to name his crushes. He said, "There is no way that I would choose to be gay and put myself in this danger and hurt you and Dad the way that this hurts you. I didn't choose this, and can't make it go away."

This all happened while we lived in a small backwoods town and attended a church where many members were suspicious of the broad world-perspective we had gained during mission service. Their religion was very rigid and unbending. I began to feel like I was attending church in Russia where one never knows if there are KGB in the congregation that are waiting to pounce. I was withdrawing more and more.

When our son came out, I realized that was the last straw with that congregation. I went into the 'closet' with them about Sid and made every excuse to absent myself from being an active member of that church community.

Within a few months I became a very strong advocate for LGBTQI individuals. I could identify with them on a deep level in three areas of emotions:

1) I had grown up as a Third Culture Kid, wanting to be accepted into the community of locals in Singapore, but

From Shattered Pieces to Freedom and Inner Peace

continuing to be different from them. When I was in the States I wanted to fit in as an American, but had differing perspectives and life views from my fellow American peers. I was an amalgamation of two cultures and not fully fitting in either one.

2) I had a physical handicap I hadn't chosen and couldn't change that strongly defined me just as a differing sexual orientation defines the LGBTQI community. I can feel their pain and desire to fit in.

3) Because of my lack of dates and attention from the boys in my expatriate community, I developed feelings for a local boy and he was attracted to me. Because our religious community viewed a mixed racial relationship or marriage as 'being unequally yoked" according to their interpretation of the New Testament counsels against it, we had to hide our feelings for each other.

I believed in that era and community a 'mixed' relationship would have ruined the missionary reputations of my four grandparents, my aunt and uncle, and my parents. I had seen it happen to others. I was convinced that it would shame my family. So our attraction had to go underground and consisted of a secret relationship; conjuring up benign situations where we could be together; secret looks; holding hands once and him giving me a goodbye kiss on the cheek when I left for college in the U.S.

But I was left with a feeling of deceit and dirtiness for something innocent and pure. I felt like a slut. Much the same way the LGBTQI community in past generations has had to sneak around, live a double life and carry a feeling of shame and dirtiness, I could personally empathize with them: basic human attractions viewed as wrong and dirty; feeling shame for something that wasn't shameful. I could identify with the LGBTQI challenges and emotions of wanting so much to belong and be loved and accepted. The Seventh Day Adventist Kinship family and Sid's friends became my new community.

Then five years after our son came out and after thirty-three years of marriage, my husband revealed that he is gay and has known since he was a child. He learned in dormitory worship that he should marry a nice straight girl and all those homosexual feelings would go away. He married me in great anticipation but discovered that his homosexual feelings didn't evaporate.

It hadn't been about me! Nothing was wrong with my womanliness, femininity, sexuality and sensuality! I couldn't believe what it had taken for him to be in the closet and pretend to be attracted to me. I knew that I could never pretend to be attracted to a woman and live in a lesbian relationship. I knew from the knowledge I'd gained from Sid's journey that homosexuality wouldn't be prayed or counseled away.

This would be the eventual end of my marriage. But I resolved that I wanted to remain friends, and to one day be a friend of Terry's Mr. Right when he found him.

Through those first months after Terry came out, I was a deer in the headlights. I cried for months. Couldn't sleep. Had to live in the closet myself for nine months, telling only my kids and a couple of cousins. My mother had just experienced an aneurysm a few months before, leaving her in a state of dementia. My father's health was tenuous with all the stress of my mother's situation, so I hid out in my house a lot.

I couldn't trust anyone with the news that Terry was gay. The grapevine in the church would have reached my dad. I was alone, sifting through the rubble of what had been my life like a Hurricane Katrina survivor sifting through the wreckage for any small piece of their former life and identity. I now had to separate my life from my former identity as a wife, church pillar, leader, missionary and mentor. My journey with the church was tenuous after my son came out, and it was completely finished when my husband came out.

The Kinship family and Sid's friends understood my pain and loss and I leaned hard on them. Nine months later when my dad's health allowed, Terry and I came out to him. We were very grateful that even though he was a conservative Christian of German descent and in his eighties, he cried with us, accepted both of us in love, and had a willingness to keep an open mind. He came to believe that homosexuality was genetic and/or biological.

From Shattered Pieces to Freedom and Inner Peace

Over the course of the first year after Terry came out, I began to realize that I also didn't fully fit in the Kinship family or with Sid's gay friends either since I was a heterosexual woman. They remain family to this day, but my involvement in their community has decreased.

I was and still am very angry at Christianity and God. My sense of betrayal by God was overwhelming. I couldn't hear references about God, religion, his fatherly love, his omniscience, omnipresence, omnipotence or any religious music without feeling that I was suffocating. I've never been raped, but I imagine my emotions around God and religion were parallel to those of a rape victim when thrown back into the presence of the rapist again.

I had trusted God and He let me down. He couldn't find any husband for me (a handicapped girl) besides a homosexual 'fake' husband—to me the very definition of kicking someone when they are already down. If Christianity/SDA Biblical interpretation is so wrong about homosexuality, why would I have any trust for the rest of their Biblical interpretations such as women in ministry, the Sabbath, tithing, dress, diet and behavior?

I have been in a church only two or three times since my divorce, for things like my Dad's funeral or my uncle being in town and preaching. Religion of any kind has become to me nothing but other people's mental crutch and delusion, a way for rulers, leaders and powers to hold sway over the populace. The Bible to me now is a book of fables and fiction. Prayer now holds the same meaning to me as the Easter Bunny and the Tooth Fairy. It is an exercise that one does to trick their mind into a sense of control and complacency—pie in the sky!

If God truly existed and was all loving and accepting, why would one need to request thousands of people around the world in prayer chains to beg God to do something. Why would thousands of prayers have more power than my single prayer?

My belief system has evaporated. I'm not even sure there is a higher power. I do think there is energy in the universe. The best way I can describe myself is as an atheist. I'm repulsed by the con tactics

Taking New Paths *Stories of Leaving Religion*

of religions and their proselytizing methods; by the way children are brainwashed into Christian perspectives and thought processes before they can even think for themselves.

I find the crucifixion the most macabre story that could be told. A father who is all-wise killing his only son because he can't think of any other way to save a universe?! Easter and Christmas feel hateful to me. It feels like fawning over a fake to me while other people blindly follow along in awe.

My former faith community conditioned me from my birth to think that those who left the faith carried a heavy mantle of guilt. I've found in leaving the religious community that there is amazing freedom and peace. I've left nothing behind to return for. I will never again be able to stop seeing through the guises and find any truth. It is all mirrors and mirages.

No religion, or community of any kind, will ever 'own me' again. My previous community felt it their right to claim any or all of my time, talents and resources; shame me for not attending every gathering or activity; shame me for not using any and all possible talents for their cause; claimed the right to question my every decision; demand that I must take on every job they dreamed up for converting the world; claimed the right to dictate how I thought and believed.

My closest friends now are those who can also poke fun and see the ridiculousness of religion. Angry that my youth is gone and my only experience at a true marriage is in my 'old age' when my body is waning, I'm sad that I don't share the experience of having and raising children with the true husband I have now.

I determined about eighteen months after Terry came out that I had never experienced a real marriage and didn't want to go to my grave never knowing what it was like to be married to a straight man. So, I did a lot of online dating and began taking ballroom dance lessons. I met some nice and some awful men. Where does a non-drinking and non-religious person meet men? I was coerced by a girlfriend to sign up on eHarmony after months of meeting losers on other sites. I resisted because I thought it was a religious site. Turns out it isn't and I met my straight husband, Jim, on eHarmony.

From Shattered Pieces to Freedom and Inner Peace

I miss my parents and other relatives very much. They were an affirming, loving safe haven. But I feel relief that my grandparents, parents and aunts and uncles are gone now, and I don't have to explain to them or disappoint them with my apostasy. My children and most of my extended close family have also apostatized and we find much camaraderie in that.

At the time I severed my ties with the church my mother was in a state of dementia in a nursing home. My father was in his late eighties and still of sound mind. I was open with him about my experience of marriage to a gay man and my anger at God. He was sad for me and surprisingly understanding about why I'd be angry. For a time he would send me messages of concern for my eternal destiny and quote Bible texts.

I replied that if he had that kind of faith in God, he could leave my soul and its destiny with God—it wasn't my dad's concern. He got it and stopped trying to influence me, saying just, "Don't stay away too long. The longer you stay away the harder it will be to come back." I explained to him that at that time God was still the rapist and religion was very toxic to me.

A wise gay friend helped me to see that taking care of myself could mean distance from toxicity. I have learned better boundary principles (something that Christianity doesn't teach and in fact runs roughshod over), and ways to deflect the religiosity of my well-meaning religious friends.

One insisted in telling me in every communication that she prayed for me every day. Eventually I wrote back that if it helped and comforted her to pray, then go ahead, but to me it meant nothing. Now she keeps her praying to herself! If I'm a friend only for them to proselytize and not for my personal qualities then it is a friendship that is meaningless. The idea that they can have friends who are in different thought boxes and that not all people need to think alike in order to be okay, is a very foreign and impossible concept for many Christians.

My roots as a missionary's kid, my own experience as a missionary myself and my years lived in foreign lands are a deep, rich and treasured heritage. I claim the positive lessons and outlooks I gained, but leave behind the dogma and control over my mind and decisions. I'm free to be me in my retirement years. I still find joy in

Taking New Paths *Stories of Leaving Religion*

helping people in need, but without telling them how they need to think, believe, behave, or dress. I can explore and respect their cultures and beliefs without labeling them as pagan, heathen, or ignorant people. I view the world around me as neutral; beautiful, fascinating, filled with wonder and science. I find it prattle when every experience, sentence and sensual stimuli must include a reference to the amazing, loving god that they feel created it.

I'm still proud of my ancestors and heritage even though it centers so exclusively around missions. I no longer respect or believe in the goal of getting the whole world to think or believe a certain way, I still enjoy and can admire the faith and endurance of my missionary ancestors and mentors; their spunk and ingenuity for their causes; their leadership abilities; their ability to mingle; and treat other nationalities with respect as equals. I'm fortunate and glad to have had those role models. I still enjoy Facebook exchanges with former missionaries, classmates and friends reminiscing about the old days and memories. Those experiences shaped who I am today, and it would be impossible to exist in a state of separation from all that molded me.

My apoplexy around religion has eased enough that I can sit through the blessing of the food at a friend's table or family worship when visiting in the home of long-time friends, even though it is nonsensical to me.

One curious thing is playing the piano. My childhood piano teachers were straight-laced musicians, not teaching me any pop songs or pop style music. I played hymns much of the time and became the most at ease with that type of music. Now when I play the piano (only occasionally) the easiest thing to sight read through is the hymnal. I'm now able to play the hymns without triggering, enjoying the tune, rhythms, and harmony but ignoring the words.

I tell my story and its personal details for several reasons. I feel my family is honorable and lived their lives and careers of faith in sincerity and concern for others. Those who were still alive to see my son's journey and the end of my marriage were open-minded enough to learn about homosexuality and embrace my son and my ex with unconditional love.

From Shattered Pieces to Freedom and Inner Peace

There are many others in my life and former community who were/are not open-minded. My hope is that in telling my story, others will come to love all people of all races, colors and orientation unconditionally and with equality. They will walk in our family's shoes enough to see the person rather than the dogma of religion and tradition; they will feel the cruelty of telling homosexuals to 'just marry a nice straight person and it will go away.' What parent would want their child to be trapped in an experimental marriage to a homosexual and experience the years of heartache that I carried those thirty-three years.

There is a high price that comes with belief in miracles. What parent deep down wishes their child to live a life of lies conforming to doctrine that is man-made, Biblically twisted, and soul destroying? Who wants to be part of a community that proclaims publicly that one's honest, loving, talented, generous loved ones are going to be lost at the Second Coming and locked out of 'heaven' for something they didn't choose and can't change? That is not an organization I want to be part of or associated with.

I wanted to spare my father the pain of hearing others' remarks about me removing my name from church membership, so did not ask for my name to be removed from the church books until after my dad and my aunt and uncle had passed away. One consistent thing in this world is the Adventist grapevine! I removed my name because I don't think, act, believe or talk like an Adventist anymore so have no wish to be identified as an Adventist. I've had enough of that community hinting that my faith wasn't real—there must have been rottenness somewhere in my core or I wouldn't reject the truth and God.

But I can reject their guilt trips, text spewing, pointing fingers and dogma without rejecting them as people. I am able to be friends with them for the sake of past memories, adventures and connections outside of their doctrinal beliefs. I actually feel pity for the brainwashing they've had and the delusions they believe, the narrowness of their world, and the constant fear of judgment they live with.

A recent email letter from my continuing life experience:

On Nov. 9, 2020, at 12:19 p.m. xxxx wrote:

Taking New Paths *Stories of Leaving Religion*

> *Dear Kathy,*
>
> *I know this lady: compassionate, smart, and from what I hear, a very good counselor. She pretty much sums up how I feel about things. I understand a little of how you have been feeling...the fear. Neither of these candidates makes me feel safe. The only relief I have from the ad nauseam of the managed media and the natural fear of the future of our country is to refocus on the Rock cut out without human hands that will strike the image on the feet of iron and clay and fill the whole earth (Daniel 2).*
>
> *You and I have a very bright future to look forward to! I often think of how you will love heaven more than the average because you are such a lover of beauty here.*
>
> *So...I pray you will let the Shepherd pick you up and carry you back home (assuming you aren't back already). I absolutely know He is after your heart because I pray for that every day...if I may be so bold as to say so. :) And if you are a praying person, please pray for me as well. The Lord knows I'm weak and need a lot of His lifting and carrying, too.*
>
> *With a lot of love, xxxx*

Attached was a lengthy political/religious blog from this counselor she mentioned. I don't recall opening the door to a political discussion really, except that I mentioned some serious concerns about our country and our polarized politics.

I was upset by her email and was leaning toward ignoring it. On Nov. 11 I got this voice mail from her in a teary voice:

> *"Hi Kathy. This is xxxx. I was hoping to connect with you on a lonely rainy afternoon, and also to tell you that if I was in any way offensive with my note about praying for you and wishing you back home to your family roots, I am so sorry. I love you enough to ignore all such things in the future if is uncomfortable, 'cause our friendship means an awful lot to me. So that's why I called just hoping for a chat and we can avoid any uncomfortable subjects if you prefer it that way. I've always wondered exactly why you left and*

From Shattered Pieces to Freedom and Inner Peace

we can talk about that at another time. I have ideas but I do sometimes wrong (sic). Anyway, love you lots. Talk to you later. Bye"

My email reply 11/13/20

Dear xxxx,

I heard the angst in your voice message, but I truly doubt that your angst holds a candle to the anxiety, hurt and pain that your email caused for me. I've been derailed from my landscaping since it came. I couldn't sleep the night your message came in until 3:00 a.m. My blood pressure skyrockets. I had just returned home from choosing, among others, your birthday card when I read your email. It was all of the intense pain of my handicap plus the pain of the whole Terry thing ripping my heart out again. It was bright flashbacks to the abuse. I cried reading your email and have repeatedly since.

You asked how I got to where I am. I know I have explained it to you until I'm blue in the face already. I've poured out my soul without reserve trying to help people understand, but to no avail. I will try one last time, but not on the phone—in writing, so that you can read and reread *ad infinitum*. It is too derailing to repeat and repeat and it doesn't feel respectful that I have to. So even if after reading this you don't understand, that doesn't change my reality. My journey is not based, regulated, steered or governed by whether people understand or not, or by whether they approve of it or are uncomfortable with it.

I'm sure this will not be an easy or comfortable read, but since you asked, I hope that you are prepared to hear the answers, and cope with the anxiety it may cause you. Not only was I highly offended by your email, but even worse, was deeply hurt. I am a person outside of my religion or lack thereof. Many other people can and do love me, accept me, affirm me, and find me personable even if I don't fit their personal belief boxes. They can be my friends without trying to fix me.

Taking New Paths *Stories of Leaving Religion*

I'm telling you as I did my dad when he sent a parallel letter about heaven and me returning "home." My soul and my salvation is not your responsibility. That is a mistaken belief in the church. Your only responsibility is your own soul. If your God and your faith in him is as you profess, then you can turn my soul over to God and leave it to him.

You appear over the years to have fixated on perfection to the point that you can only be at peace when you can order your world and those in it to fit neatly into the box of your belief system. In a world with unbounded examples of diversity of peoples, plants, animals, and organisms, I can not accept that there is only one path or belief system for all souls—that all brains are wired alike and will only be right if they think the same and fit in identical boxes.

So, fasten your seatbelt.

My life experience and my brain wiring has taken me to a place where my faith in a deity or his writings are meaningless and irrelevant. The Bible is merely a book of fables, myths, and a smattering of history. It is only stories written down mostly years and centuries after being handed down orally. Certainly, there are some nuggets of wisdom hidden there, but it is not sacred or inspired to me anymore. If it was a message from a God of love and caring then he wouldn't leave the script uncorrected for all these thousands of years causing so much discrimination, pain, and suffering to those he is purported to love—homosexuals, women, slaves, etc.

Whenever the deep pain of being handicapped or being married to someone who didn't fully love me washed over me through the decades, I leaned on the writings of that book; the supposed promises from that all knowing, all present and all wise God.

He was my lifeline until I learned it was all a devastating trick. The miracle of a husband for me (as so many called Terry) evaporated, crumbled and was just a pile of ashes and tears. It had all been a bad gift and a sham. Any scrap of trust in or credibility in that God has been destroyed forever. Before you point it out as others have done—yes I'm

From Shattered Pieces to Freedom and Inner Peace

thankful for my boys, but wonderful children would have been on option with a straight, real husband as well.

The church that touts itself as having the most pure doctrine; the voice of God; the highest standard of honesty and representation of love continues to trod on unknowing, helpless straight people by telling homosexuals to marry a straight spouse thus live a lie. It continues telling homosexuals they can't have a soulmate, a lover and a companion because of biology and/or genetics they have no control over. It still denies that women are equal and believes they aren't fit to be pastors even though they had a woman prophet (higher in rank than a pastor). In so doing they have zero respect for the souls of the spouses trapped unknowingly in those marriages to closeted, deceiving homosexuals.

The church's "precious" doctrines are more sacred than our souls. They condemn the homosexual spouse and in doing so don't even stand by their own heterosexual members married to homosexuals. Their pride in their beliefs and interpretations are more important than love for people who are hurting through no choice of their own. My personal standards for integrity and honesty are higher than that of the church.

There is a high cost to believing and preaching miracles. When the miracle crumbles so does the soul who was led to believe in them and depend on them. (This whole subject was discussed in a sermon I heard from a revered SDA minister before Terry ever came out, by the way. I am Exhibit A for his sermon.)

Rather than live my life tempering the present joy and world I live in for a far-off promise of heaven or paradise, I will live my life in the here and now honestly, lovingly, respectfully and with care for others to the best of my ability. When I die I'll be like a bouquet of fragrant flowers fading away to dust. Having blessed people while I was alive, I will be gone as the puff of a dandelion is gone. Eventually there will be no one alive to even remember me and I'm okay with that. Do I miss my parents and others who have died? Yes I do. Do I salve my grief by telling myself that I'll see them

Taking New Paths *Stories of Leaving Religion*

again? No. I can accept that they are gone and I can replay my memories in my mind's eye until I'm gone.

I will forever be hugely scarred to my deepest core and have post-traumatic stress syndrome from the deceit, distrust, and disillusionment caused me by religion, the church and its God. This will be painful to you and probably unfathomable to you, but you asked. If you have ever had a close friend or patient who was raped, you will know that the rape victim suffers extreme trauma when they re-enter the presence of their rapist and abuser.

My journey with the God of my roots and "home" as you say, is as extreme a pain and trauma as that of a rape victim. God has been my abuser and a rapist to me. The Shepherd became the betrayer. Hearing others recite his wonders, love and perfect attributes causes me extreme angst, anxiety, and pain. I get physically ill—apoplectic, I break out in a sweat, can't think, and concentrate, and my blood pressure shoots up.

When people insist on quoting the very texts I leaned on and then found out to be empty words during my journey, I go back into the same PTSD I experienced when Sid and Terry came out. My world was built on that God/Shepherd and those "promises" until it collapsed as surely as the World Trade Center collapsed.

I'm sure it is unthinkable to you that I blame God, and to you it is probably an indicator that my faith never really was real in the first place. I haven't forgotten the common illustration of the beautiful apple that had a rotten core. Think whatever you need to if it comforts you and preserves your belief in the God system.

If you find comfort in praying, please do. But please don't spew texts, Ellen Gould White, your religious beliefs, or boasting of your prayers to me. They represent all that defines the abuser. Those things are all very toxic to me. I choose to take care of myself by removing toxic things from my life. Religion is like a penis. It's a perfectly fine thing for one to have and take pride in, but when one takes it out

From Shattered Pieces to Freedom and Inner Peace

and waves it in my face or shoves it down my throat, we have a problem.

If someone wants to be in my life they can, but on the condition that they will not be toxic to me. I will remove myself from the toxicity.

Personally, for years, I have had a problem with the dissonance created by the idea that getting a prayer chain going or asking dozens of people to pray for a certain thing will be a greater influence on God than one person praying and will increase the chances for results. What kind of God is that who needs hundreds of people to beg and nag at them before he answers a prayer or not? When I see those requests on FB it makes me nauseous.

Whether you realize it or not, trying to fit me into your belief box and announcing your prayers is a way to feed your ego; placate your perfection insecurities, show others what a wonderful Christian you are, a way to get the results that make you comfortable and at peace, and a manipulation by heaping guilt on another person. Prayer is meaningless to me personally. It is mind games to soothe the person who does the praying.

We were always led to believe that backsliders are eaten up with guilt. You should know that I have no guilt. I feel more free and clear than I ever have in my life. My reaction to your email did not come from guilt. It is anger and grief that I'm not acceptable to you unless I meet your standards—that I'm not good enough and need fixing.

For many years I have been unable to wrap my mind around the belief that a supreme being who is all wise, all knowing, all present, and all powerful would have no other solution than to sacrifice his own son and call it love, that he'd be unable to find a better solution to prove to the universe that he is love—putting our world through six thousand years of sorrow and pain, death, and suffering. Him sacrificing his son on the cross is the most macabre thing I can think of.

Because of the prudish sexual hang-ups of Christianity for centuries, and the Adventist church in particular, I was

Taking New Paths *Stories of Leaving Religion*

robbed of my vital innate (God-given) sexuality. I was fed the line (by the church culture, not my parents) that sex is abhorrent but somehow positive and wonderful at the same time.

The church treats sexuality like it is something we all have to put up with, shoved away in a closet instead of a beautiful, vital, necessary part of our deepest being. I saved myself, as the church said I must, for my husband, only to have it trodden and tromped on and left to spend decades of my life thinking I was second class. I was trapped by doctrines which downplayed the biological importance of sex. I was denied the option of divorcing because sex wasn't working with Terry.

Social church stigmas and taboos meant that doing so would have ruined my family's reputation. Can you imagine the church's reaction if I had divorced because "the sex wasn't good enough?" I never had the joy of an unsullied wedding night.

After years of counseling and a very understanding second husband, I still struggle with the scars of the sexual rejection I experienced and the negative flashbacks it causes. The church had as much to do with that as Terry did. I will carry that loss and the scars to my grave.

I sense that sex isn't something very high on your list. You are more comfortable with cuddling. Because of church teachings and doctrines surrounding sex and sexuality, it wasn't until Sid came out when I was fifty years old that I dared to even let myself examine my sexuality.

At that time, I allowed myself to do what one should do in their youth—examine their own attractions. Could I think of any girl or women that I had been attracted to physically? Were my feelings for boys and men just because of society's expectations or were they deep in my soul? Was I at all attracted physically to women?

After several weeks of contemplation and letting myself journey back in my mind to my early sexual awakenings, I came to the firm conclusion that I am heterosexual. Men and their bodies are attractive to me. I suspect that like me, you

From Shattered Pieces to Freedom and Inner Peace

never allowed yourself to do that. It was unthinkable that we would not be heterosexual and too dangerous or foreign for us to even entertain. I do not respect the way religion, specifically Christianity and Adventism, handled this and continue to mishandle it. The way they counsel gay men to just "marry a nice straight girl and it will go away'" as Terry was told.

Now late in my life journey I am learning to protect myself from toxicity. To not be driven by what people think of me or think I should or should not do. I have learned what boundaries are and that it is alright to set them. If you truly love me, these are my boundaries of friendship:

1. Don't evangelize me.
2. Don't poke your nose into my soul and my salvation.
3. Don't treat me as if I'm eaten up with guilt.
4. Don't try to guilt me back to your thinking box of the church "fold" and beliefs.
5. Don't quote the Bible and EGW to me.
6. Don't lace religion/doctrines into all the conversation. It makes no difference to me whether you took a walk on Sabbath or any other day. Let me enjoy your pictures without toxicity and agenda. The only reason to mention that it was a Sabbath walk is to try and jerk my heart strings. I'm savvy enough to see through those tactics.
7. I'm still nauseated by all the church politics and in-fighting. I don't need to hear about it. It is none of my business and only your choice to put up with it. I think it is poppycock that leaders are elected by God—especially Ted Wilson and Trump.
8. Other people's religious inspirational musings are irrelevant to me and feel like a manipulation.

Taking New Paths *Stories of Leaving Religion*

9. Stop projecting the idea that I will ever return to Adventism, Christianity, or any organized religion. The blinders have fallen off my eyes. That train has left the station and gone over the cliff.

Here are some relevant quips I have saved that are meaningful to me and my friendships:

• Sorry is not enough. You actually have to change.

• You must love in such a way that the person you love feels FREE.

• I may not be someone's first choice, but I'm a great choice. I may not be rich, but I'm valuable. I don't pretend to be someone I'm not, because I'm good at being me. I might not be proud of some of the things I've done in the past, but I am proud of who I am today. I may not be perfect, but I don't need to be. Take me as I am or watch me as I walk away.

• What you believe is not the problem. What you think I should believe is the problem.

• Just because I do not believe in your god does not mean that I do not believe in anything! I believe in compassion, kindness, love, logic, equality, empathy, myself, integrity, honesty and more.

• Anything you can't control in your life is teaching you how to let go.

• *"The beginning of love is to let those we love be perfectly themselves, and not to twist them to fit our own image. Otherwise we love only the reflection of ourselves we find in them."* Thomas Merton

I would feel very sad to lose your friendship. We have precious memories going back almost as far as we can remember. Your family has been my family. But my blood pressure skyrockets with toxicity. So here are answers to your questions that have taken me two days to write out. I leave it in your court. Is the cost too high or can you "bend" your religion and doctrines enough for you to still be my friend?

15
My Journey as a Muslim Apostate
Hakim Naved

I WAS BORN AND BROUGHT UP in a conservative Muslim home in South Africa. At age thirteen, I was sent to study at seminaries in Pakistan and India. I spent nine years there. At the time, I believed the Islamic creed to be "gospel-truth." I had some doubts, but not very radical questions lingering in my mind. I thought these to be musings from "Satan," so I worked hard to dispel them.

I then got into the business of teaching theology and Islamic jurisprudence (mostly concerning rituals), and I delivered sermons and officiated as an Imam for plus-or-minus eleven years. However, just two or three years prior to enrolling at a University for a religious studies program, I began reading up about Muslim philosophers such as Farabi, Ibn Sina, and Ibn Rushd.

I did not have access to any of their original works.

In addition, I began reading books by current Middle Eastern

Taking New Paths *Stories of Leaving Religion*

`ulama (Wahba al-Zuḥayli and Abu Zahra), who advocated the contextualization and adaptability of the *shari`a* for the modern era.

Consequently, I began raising questions about "*Shari`a* Law reform." This is when I began encountering resistance and hostility from the Muslim clergy, as well as from the general public, more so from the merchant class sector, who donated the bulk of the monies for the construction and upkeep of the mosques and *madrasah*s (religious schools).

I was flabbergasted. The reform I sought to promote, after all, was for the "good of my society at large, that they may be free from the manipulations of the clergy." But alas, they were as complicit in persecuting me for my views, as were the clergy. I was initially persecuted by being often dismissed from teaching jobs. This naturally, was always orchestrated by the `ulama (clergy), who used to pressurize the donors and managers of these institutions.

These `ulama, with the very generous help of the merchant classes, eventually went on to set up powerful `ulama bodies called *jami`ats*, "Islamic" secular schools, and *halal* (lawful) trusts that regulated food production and consumption for the Muslim community.

After my initial altercations/challenges to the `ulama, I began reading more critical literature, such as Nietzsche's *Human All Too Human*, Bertrand Russell's *Why I am not a Christian*, and other similar works of Western philosophy.

I read Joseph Schacht's critique of *hadith* and the *isnad* (chain of narrators) system. By the time I got to University some two/three years later, I had already lost my faith in the Muslim God (Allah), as well as in all the peculiar and irrational precepts, and teachings of Islam. I stopped praying and fasting.

I only went to mosque on Fridays, (and I still do, albeit not so punctually), just to be safe from harm from the community, as I lived in a predominantly Muslim area. I only retained my faith in those values that cut across religious and ethnic boundaries, call them "secular values" if you like.

After much encouragement from a few liberal-minded friends, I gave up a lucrative teaching post at an Islamic school, and I enrolled at one of the most prestigious universities in my country for a MA degree in religious studies.

This entailed studying the social sciences: anthropology,

sociology, philosophy, etc. *vis-à-vis* religion. My intentions for embarking on the academic study of religion were firstly, to equip myself with the necessary "rational knowledge tools" that would enable me to critique orthodox Islam.

Furthermore, undertaking study for the MA degree served to confirm my apostasy. It entrenched my conviction that abandoning Islam was the right thing to do.

For me, giving up Islam was not really an intellectual challenge, in the sense that I was never very "devout and pious" as a Muslim. I just performed the basic rituals of the five daily prayers, and the fasting in Ramadan. I had already performed one Hajj. I was never one who was very much inclined towards rituals.

I gained more stimulation from reading and discussing intellectual matters. The rational sciences fulfilled my intellectual curiosity far more substantially than Islamic theology, or jurisprudential disputations ever could.

In fact, I found Islamic theology to be an insult to human intelligence, given its contradictory claims and dogmatic nature. To illustrate the point by way of example, in my Friday sermons in the mosque, I always spoke about moral and ethical issues.

I unflinchingly emphasized the humanistic features of Islamic teachings, such as upholding justice, honesty in one's dealings with others, fair treatment of one's employees, as well as loyalty and honesty toward one's employer, kindness, equality, humaneness, etc.

It appealed to some people, who, I might add, were also not the type that were observant of the rituals (they are commonly disparagingly referred to as "nominal Muslims"), but rather, who were interested in social issues affecting the community.

They were particularly opposed to the apartheid policies of the then white minority government. Incidentally, the members of the mosque committees became very uncomfortable with my speeches. These committees are increasingly made up of wealthy businessmen who possessed no knowledge of Islam, or any other field beyond their business, for that matter.

I later discovered how many of these committee members were involved in all sorts of underhanded and illicit activities in their businesses. Many among them were not people of high moral integrity, in that they had no qualms about resorting to these underhanded

Taking New Paths *Stories of Leaving Religion*

financial dealings, tax evasion (it is this "hot money" that they usually donate to the religious institutions), dealing in truckloads of stolen goods, having extra-marital affairs, etc.

They were, of course, the wealthy merchant elites, who came across as very egotistical. They were supportive of the apartheid form of government, since, in their minds, as well according to the thinking of the *`ulama*, apartheid was considered to be a "blessing for the Muslims," since it preserved Islamic morals and practice. Muslims could live in their own "Indian or Malay ghettos," (under the apartheid racist policies of racially segregated residential areas), etc.

Seemingly, they treated their financial contributions towards the mosques and *madrasahs*, more as a form of "expiation for their sins," as well as a means to boost their egos, and flaunt their power in the community, not to forget that they were "securing their palaces in *Jannah* (paradise)."

This class used to frequently appeal to me to deliver lectures that focused more on performing the five daily prayers and fasting—the rituals. They implored me to stay away from discussing politics. They called on me to rather discuss issues such as drug addiction, the free intermingling of the sexes, especially with regard to the young, university-going sector of the community, and the prohibition of music, etc.

As stated earlier, I just never got a kick out of rituals.

I never "felt the presence of god," and the like. I never had any "religious experiences." I also realized later on that I was morally and ethically a good human being who never acted dishonestly or wickedly towards other people, or animals, or the environment. Therefore, what was the need for me to "cry during the night in front of Allah begging for repentance for my sins?" I was no sinner!

Yes, I may have some human frailties, for which I was/ and still am always ready to apologize to the person I may have inconvenienced, or been nasty to, but I never committed any "crimes against Allah." I owed him/her/it no apologies. I felt that if anyone needed to apologize, then it was "Allah," who needs to apologize to me, since she/he/it "directed me to the service of Islam."

I felt that religion was, and still is responsible for "wrecking my life," since it deprived me of enjoying a normal upbringing, free

My Journey as a Muslim Apostate

of religious bigotry, which I believed was the cause for my being deprived of learning the necessary secular skills that are required for one to earn a living through a decent career other than religion.

The major challenge for me has been on the social side rather than on the personal level. Despite the fact that I did not "come out" publicly and declare my apostasy, Muslim society ostracized me, together with my immediate family (wife and kids).

This ostracism was based merely on the grounds that "I became too modern." Being condemned as a modernist in traditional Muslim circles is enough to invite serious censure from the Muslim public. My "modernity" at the time was that I ditched the Islamic garb of the *kurta* and began wearing western style clothing, and I cut short my fist-length beard.

When asked by the children in the Muslim school whether they can listen to music, I responded that: "as long as it is music that does not lead to illicit sex and drinking alcohol, and other vices, then it is fine." Believe me, these kids were all into the latest pop music scene. Their school bags were decorated with names of all the pop stars of the time: Madonna, Michael Jackson, Modern Talking, etc.

They knew the names of the latest singers and bands, way better than I could ever imagine. Their parents even took them to the shows whenever these artists were on tour or at least provided them with the money to buy the CDs. Yet, I was reprimanded by the committee for "rendering *halal* that which the *shari`a* declared to be *haram* (forbidden)."

When I brought to the notice of the students and the committee, their inconsistencies, they replied that: while they "acknowledge their indulgence in such "sins," they simply make *tawba* (repent to God) after such indulgence"; that "it is better to consider something to be a sin and repent for indulging in it, than considering it to be *halal*." This I considered to be the product of a sick mentality, a neurosis, the ultimate in delusional thinking.

The main form of persecution brought to bear upon me is the denial of employment opportunities within Muslim circles. For many years, and up to this day, I am unable to secure any form of employment in Muslim circles.

The more subtle forms of discrimination towards my family and myself is that we do not get invited to weddings, etc. unless it is

Taking New Paths *Stories of Leaving Religion*

immediate family, where I am no longer asked to carry out previously normal responsibilities in officiating ceremonies.

The usual chatter at such functions is invariably situated around discussions concerning the plight of Muslims in the world today; how they are being "victimized" by the West and other non-Muslims; the onslaught against Islam in the modern world, "Islamophobia," Jihad, Osama bin Laden, and so forth.

Given the fact that I am by nature someone who cannot tolerate listening to such prattle, I always "put my two pence into the discussion," but to no avail. I end up having to stop at some point, since the discussion would ultimately lead to fundamentally questioning their basic religious and faith-based presuppositions.

That's when we, the "apostates and heretics," (I prefer to use the term "brights") have to yield to the discourses of a belief system that is based on delusion and fantasy, in order to save ourselves from being harmed and abused, if not physically, then certainly financially and socially.

If you ask me if it has all been worth it, I will respond that despite all that, I will never be able to "un-bake this cake." That is, I can never possibly go back to "being a true believer." My eyes and my mind have opened up to entirely new vistas of thinking rationally and philosophically, for which I am forever grateful. At least I am free of the shackles of religious delusions and fallacies that govern the lives of the erstwhile members of the Islamic community.

They have deprived me financially, but they will never own my mind. I will never submit to their hegemony and their apparitions. I may die as a pauper, (which fortunately I am not), but I will proudly die as an independent and free thinker.

At least I own my self and use my own mind independently of an imaginary deity, or "holy" books or prophets. I make my decisions on the basis of my own free will, according to my own deeply held convictions, the best verifiable evidence I can obtain, and by being mindful of universal values, ethics, and morals.

The price of freedom is high and great, but the price of mental and social enslavement, by wanting to "fit in," to be accepted as part of the "in-crowd,"—albeit a very essential psychological human need—is an even greater cost to the soul, and for one's conscience.

The answer to such questions in essence evolves around

issues of "what it means to be happy." Does happiness entail living a hedonistic life, where one enjoys wealth, the good material things of life, social acceptance, and the like, or does it require one to be stoical, and in touch with one's own deep-seated existential reality, despite the vicissitudes of one's derisory existence—as per Socrates and other great philosophers?

That, I guess, is the bugbear question for every human soul to deal with, be they believers or unbelievers.

I for one have chosen the latter route. Make no mistake, it is no easy route, but if it gives me ultimate and deep-seated inner satisfaction, then I believe that is what matters most. That is being "spiritual," in my book, at least.

Long live the "BRIGHTS" of this world!

Taking New Paths *Stories of Leaving Religion*

16

Out of Watchtower

Written collaboratively after interviews between

Shawna and Doug Matheson

NO ONE WILLINGLY and knowingly joins a cult. So how could Shawna, a strong intelligent independent Black woman, get involved with a high control religious group, the Jehovah's Witnesses (JWs), for over two decades?

It began with childhood indoctrination, seeping in from a world dipped in misogyny and White supremacy. Like piranhas, high control groups "see blood" and often prey upon people going through personal tragedy and desperation to attract new members, offering an ultimate solution to all their problems. Then, like any successful corporation, they rely on repeat business (i.e., the children of converts) to maintain their membership base.

It was October of 1972, and a young twenty-two-year-old Jamaican woman named Marie immigrated to Canada on a work permit with the intention of just making enough money to help her family out of poverty back home. What she didn't know then was the system was rigged against her.

Although Canada had recently relaxed its anti-Black immigration polices under the leadership of Prime Minister Pierre Trudeau, these anti-Black systems of oppression, created by Prime Minister Wilfrid Laurier, were already baked into Canadian society.

Thus, this young single Black mother of two, faced education, housing, and employment discrimination, while trying to navigate her own personal and generational trauma in a foreign land.

It was under these tumultuous circumstances—alone in a foreign country, facing hardships, and without her children—that Marie started receiving proselytizing from Jehovah's Witnesses. Marie's cousin, who was a Witness, began preaching to her about a world without pain and suffering, and convinced her there was one solution to ALL her problems.

There was only one catch—become one of Jehovah's Witnesses and devote her life to the teachings of the Watchtower Bible and Tract Society, that they positioned as synonymous with Jehovah (the name JWs call God) and the Bible. Then, one day in the imminent future…just around the corner, all her problems will be resolved when there will be a global massacre of non-JWs at Armageddon, when she will have an immortal perfect life on a paradise earth. This sounded good to her, so she converted to the religion.

After years of facing reality and coming to terms with the fact that Canada was not the "promised land," and that the slim likelihood of finding a husband in the church to support a young woman with two children in Jamaica, Marie re-ignited a love interest with a young man from back home, who was not a JW.

Before long they were engaged, he immigrated to Canada, and they were married. The marriage license ink was barely dry when the first few cells of soon-to-be Shawna were being formed. With a new marriage, baby on the way, and arranging for her children back home to relocate to Canada, there was little time for congregation meetings.

So, Marie became "inactive," a term Jehovah's Witnesses use to describe a member who has been absent from church activities for an extended period.

During this time, with her marriage and home life in disarray,

Taking New Paths *Stories of Leaving Religion*

riddled with the trauma and the tension of trying to blend her first two children with her new husband, Marie found herself desperate for help.

Rather than recognizing that her problems were a result of a perfect storm of the social environment, injustice systems of oppression, and poor decisions, Witnesses contacted her in an attempt to reactivate her in the religion, asserting to Marie that her problems were a result of not following direction from "Jehovah" (i.e., Watchtower), by missing church activities and marrying a "non-believer."

Later, and shortly after Marie escaped her abusive husband, she went straight into the "love bombing" of JWs who helped her to settle, reactivated her, and then began to indoctrinate her youngest child, Shawna.

This is where Shawna's story begins.

From early childhood, Shawna felt conflicted about what she was taught by her mother and JWs about the world around her. JWs view anyone not part of their religion in a negative light, but that was not Shawna's experience growing up in the multicultural streets of Toronto.

She saw no difference between kids who bullied her at school and the microaggressions she experienced at the Kingdom Hall. She experienced connection and community from bus drivers, neighbors, and teachers, while receiving acceptance and support from some fellow JW congregation members.

Although she was a naturally obedient child, she felt pressured to conform to her religious and societal programming, while the fire of curiosity and creativity within her conflicted with JW philosophy, through her teenage years.

She dreamed of having a singing and/or acting career, and higher education, which were all frowned upon by Watchtower doctrine. Having close friendships with children other than Jehovah's Witnesses was forbidden. Having or attending events, like birthdays and most holidays, were also against church teachings.

Shawna, at the time, didn't fully comprehend that she was

Out of Watchtower

experiencing cognitive dissonance, where her beliefs were not consistent with her reality.

In the movie, *The Truman Show*, a stage light falls from the "sky" to land in front of Truman, who begins to recognize his perfect world is out of place. The Truman Show is about a man who grew up living an ordinary life that—unbeknownst to him—takes place on a large set populated by actors for a television show.

Yet, like Truman in *The Truman Show*, it seemed everyone at the Kingdom Hall was giving the performance of their lives to ensure she remained mentally trapped and under the control of Watchtower for decades.

One of Shawna's first "falling lightbulb" moments, was at the age of twelve, when Dina, a woman her mother was attempting to convert, revealed in confidence that her husband contracted AIDS from an extra marital affair.

Shawna's mother had been conducting a progressive Bible study with Dina, meaning she was on the verge of conversion—attending congregation meetings, receiving love bombing, participating in congregation events, and speaking about getting baptized. Even though Shawna was young when she overheard the conversation, she knew not to be a snitch and to keep her mouth shut about what she had heard.

However, Marie's loyalty to Watchtower superseded Dina's privacy. Watchtower teachings encourage an atmosphere of reporting on the behaviors of others that may contradict church rules, which creates a highly charged gossip and meddling environment.

Marie rushed to the Elders (church leaders) to tell them what Dina had told her in confidence, to "protect" the congregation. By the next congregation meeting, the love bombing toward Dina stopped. Congregation members would not even shake her hand nor sit near her, supposedly in fear of contracting AIDS.

Although there was still much to learn about the virus at the time, the evidence indicated that HIV/ AIDS was contracted by blood and/or semen. Shawna nearly had whip lash from how quickly one rumor caused people to treat Dina with such inhumanity, though they claimed to be God's one true religion, which showed genuine love.

Throughout the years, there were many more examples of

Taking New Paths *Stories of Leaving Religion*

Shawna seeing family members, even, cut off their loved ones who were excommunicated from the religion.

There were many moments that caused minor doubts throughout her teenage years. In school she was an honor student and well respected by her teachers and classmates, but in the religion, she noticed that women were considered the "weaker vessel" and like a second class.

She was pressured by her mother and some members in the congregation to not take post-secondary education, as Witnesses believe in an imminent "Dooms Day." However, she rebelled by going to college, though she had to compromise, as she really wanted to go to university.

As is typical amongst Jehovah's Witnesses, Shawna married young, at the age of twenty-one. Although her husband was a Regular Pioneer and a Ministerial Servant—a prestigious combination in the community— soon after their marriage she began to recognize toxicity, incompatibility, and then abuse, necessitating calling the police. This led to her separating from her husband.

When she informed the Elders, and they found out that she had called the police, their great concern was clearly on her having reached beyond the church community to the police—not on her health and safety.

It was during that two-year separation, when she stopped attending meetings to take a break from the meddling of congregation members in her affairs, that Shawna began experiencing soft shunning from friends and relatives.

While her so-called Christian brothers and sisters were soft shunning her, non-JWs would show her compassion during her difficult time, which made her begin to seriously question her religion for the first time.

When her mother discovered Shawna was inactive, Marie said, "Whenever you wake up and decide to come back from Satan's world, get back in touch with me then." She was stunned that her own mother would choose a religion over her own child. This combination of events, questions, and developing insights, together became the straw that broke the camel's back.

Shortly afterward, all members of her family who were in the religion, namely her older half-sister, brother-in-law, three nieces and nephews, followed suit. For over a decade they continue to shun her and exclude her from family events like graduations, weddings, etc.

She knew that her close relatives, and the members of her Kingdom Hall whom she knew well, bore individual responsibility for choosing to be part of shunning her, but she also knew clearly that the whole organization—whose leaders gave talks ostensibly focused on love—required members to cut off ties, cut off all communication, with any member who was deemed to have gone wrong.

And leaving an abusive husband, and calling the police, was somehow judged to be wrong? She eventually began to do some informal comparing of religions on the practical level, and sometimes saw better constructive community involvement, even if something as practical as soup kitchens. In instances of seeing the simplest examples of decency, of humane and empathetic action, she wondered about apparent mixed motives.

For the first time, she began to wonder about God, and do some soul-searching. If Christians, who apparently do good things, do them in order to avoid the eternal punishment, or to gain a reward from an appeased God, what does that say about God, himself?

When she still tried to pray, she found herself wondering if it was just self-talk, or if she was praying to anyone or anything real, or even if she was behaving like someone temporarily suffering a mental breakdown.

She began to see religion as a well-constructed scheme to control people, to exercise power. Both the notion of religion, and of god…they could no longer be connected to any form of real evidence. Further, the ethical dilemma of the miscellaneous supposedly "answered" prayers in a world full of horrific accidents, childhood diseases, abuse, and large-scale horrors from famine to war and genocide, simply couldn't wash.

As her mother became elderly, she resumed limited contact with Shawna. Perhaps Marie recognized the religion took more than it gave. The young twenty-two-year-old who had been told "Armageddon was just around the corner" was now sixty-five. She had been pressured to shun her daughter and had lost out on precious moments… simply because her daughter had chosen a different path.

Shawna has been out for more than fifteen years now, and her

Taking New Paths *Stories of Leaving Religion*

only regret is that she took so long to make her final break. She says she is "proud that I've not only survived, I've thrived." She is grateful that she didn't allow the Watchtower's view of women to keep her from achieving the awards and accolades she gained in her profession.

As she reflected on her achievements, Shawna paused in conversation, noting sadly how many other people, especially women, have limited themselves in numerous ways to roles defined by others, and expressed her fervent hope that women, and other held-down and held-back people, will not allow any organization or others to define their capabilities, and who they are.

Recommended Reading:
Mars and Venus: Starting Over, by John Gray for those coming out of a toxic marriage/relationships.
Breaking The Chains of Psychological Slavery, by Na'im Akbar for Black people dealing with both breaking cognitive dissonance and the challenges that come with being black in a world filled with white supremacy.
Crisis of Conscience, by Raymond Franz
Leaving the Witness: Exiting a Religion and Finding a Life by Amber Scorah
The Reluctant Apostate, by Lloyd Evan

A Turbulent Journey

17
A Turbulent Journey From Judaism and Orthodoxy to Secular Humanism
Todd Kadish

I WAS BORN into a Jewish family that was very involved with Jewish and synagogue life, long before we all became Orthodox. Our family initially belonged to a synagogue affiliated with the centrist Conservative Jewish movement, religiously in between the more liberal Reform and more strict Orthodox movements, in a suburb of Hartford, Connecticut. I attended that synagogue through Bar Mitzvah, Confirmation, and participation in the Conservative movement's high school youth group.

I also became familiar with Reform Judaism after my family moved to a neighboring town with a Reform synagogue. (At the time,

Taking New Paths *Stories of Leaving Religion*

the Conservative movement was the largest Jewish denomination in the U.S.A.; subsequently, the Conservative movement shrank dramatically and Reform and Orthodox Judaism grew in their share of congregants, along with the growing number of Jews who chose not to affiliate with any religious movement.)

The Conservative movement was an attempt to meld the traditional/Orthodox belief that Jewish law is binding and its observance obligatory for all Jews with the Reform Jews belief that Jews are free to choose their ritual practices and to do so with an openness to academic viewpoints regarding human authorship of the Bible which Orthodox Jews consider heretical. In reality, Conservative rabbis, including our own, tended to be strict in their observance of Jewish law similar to Orthodox Jews, while Conservative congregants, including my family, tended to pick and choose their practices like Reform Jews. On average Conservative Jews were, and still are, somewhat more traditional than Reform Jews.

My parents, like most of those who attended suburban American Conservative synagogues, did not observe Jewish law as understood by Conservative or Orthodox rabbis. For example, they ate food which was not kosher, and did not follow rules restricting various activities on the Sabbath. Still, their level of involvement in Jewish and synagogue functions was unusually high. They were vocal supporters of Israel, and they were part of a small group of local Conservative families which got together for traditional Sabbath meals. Also, they were very concerned about Jewish assimilation and the prospects for "Jewish continuity," the survival of Judaism in light of assimilation and intermarriage.

Throughout my childhood, before my family's journey towards Orthodoxy began, my parents repeatedly expressed their disapproval of "interdating" and "intermarriage" with non-Jews. They even argued that Jews who intermarried were "finishing Hitler's job" of destroying the Jewish people, because many of their children were not Jewish.

The first person in my family to become Orthodox was my older brother, who became interested in Orthodox Judaism around the

A Turbulent Journey

age of eleven. He was inspired by the writings of extremist/militant Rabbi Meir Kahane, though my brother would later become a more religiously and politically moderate Orthodox rabbi who opposed many of Kahane's teachings.

After some initial resistance, a couple years later, my parents started becoming interested in Orthodox Judaism themselves through my brother and the Orthodox Rabbis and communities he was in contact with. My parents' move towards Orthodoxy was partially a reaction against assimilation (many of their Jewish friends and relatives intermarried), partially because they liked what they saw, and, I now realize, partially because they had many personal problems and religion offered some diversion or escape from that.

Looking back, even with all of the complicated and conflicted feelings I now have about both my family and Orthodox Judaism, I have to give my family, and particularly my brother, credit for their commitment and perseverance in becoming Orthodox Jews while living in a town where there were no other Orthodox Jews. I remember my brother bravely deciding to wear a yarmulke to a public elementary school in sixth grade. Soon thereafter, my brother became fully observant of Orthodox Jewish law and started attending Orthodox schools. My brother wished to attend services at an Orthodox synagogue when he was home for the Sabbath, as Reform and Conservative synagogues had "mixed" male and female seating, and women who led the services, which Orthodox Jewish law generally forbade; in Orthodox synagogues, men and women sit separately and only men lead the main service.

Because my brother could not use or benefit from electricity or the burning of gasoline according to Orthodox Sabbath restrictions, instead of traveling in a car, he walked approximately six miles to and from the nearest Orthodox synagogue, which was in a neighboring town. However, walking such a distance was in violation of a Talmudic restriction against traveling more than approximately one kilometer beyond the limits of one's home city on the Sabbath.

Therefore, before the Sabbath, my brother placed food on the ground in the neighboring town. Per the legal fictions of the Talmud, the food established his "home" as extending into the neighboring town, thereby allowing him to walk an extended distance and into that town on the Sabbath.

Taking New Paths *Stories of Leaving Religion*

After I graduated from high school, my parents moved away from such difficulties and to a town which had a sizable Orthodox community and multiple Orthodox synagogues in walking distance of each other. That community was welcoming to my family despite our non-Orthodox backgrounds; I recall the many invitations extended to my family for Sabbath meals. Most of that community considered itself "Modern Orthodox," meaning that they believed in combining the better parts of modern culture and an education, including secular subjects, with Orthodox belief and practice, and my family chose to identify as Modern Orthodox, as well.

I resisted becoming Orthodox myself at first; I didn't feel an attraction to it. Its myriad rules and loopholes seemed somewhat odd and irrational. My interest was finally piqued after I read and reread conservative talk show host Dennis Prager's and Orthodox ordained Rabbi Joseph Telushkin's grossly misleading book, *The Nine Questions People Ask About Judaism*. I came to believe, mainly from that book, that Judaism was eminently universalistic, rational, and ethical. That view, combined with my positive impression of the Modern Orthodox community, left me slowly drifting towards Orthodoxy.

I began college at the University of Connecticut, where I found myself becoming more concerned about Jewish assimilation. I noticed that most of my Jewish friends were "interdating," and even that most of my "brothers" in my Jewish fraternity (AEPi) had non-Jewish girlfriends. I also began reading books by Modern Orthodox Rabbis such as Rabbi Hayim Halevy Donin's *To Be a Jew*, and I came to believe in the concept of *Torah m'Sinai"* (Torah from Sinai).

Torah m'Sinai is a widespread traditional Jewish belief that became a central belief of Orthodox Judaism, differentiating it from the other denominations theologically. It is the belief that the text of what Jews now commonly refer to as "the written Torah" (the five books of Moses, also known as the Pentateuch) was conveyed to Moses and the Hebrews while they were wandering in the Sinai desert, even though the Pentateuch itself says no such thing. Many, though not all, Orthodox Jews actually believe the entire Masoretic

A Turbulent Journey

Hebrew text of the Pentateuch, the authoritative/accepted version of the Hebrew text used in Torah scrolls today, was dictated to Moses, letter for letter, on Mount Sinai.

Regardless of whether the Orthodox belief is that the text of the Pentateuch was given to Moses on Mount Sinai, in parts in the desert, and/or letter for letter, such beliefs are all in opposition to the overwhelming opinion of historians and Biblical scholars that the bulk of the Pentateuch was written at a later time by multiple authors, and compiled, edited, and redacted over an extended period.

Still, at the time I thought my decisions to adopt Orthodox beliefs and (gradually) to observe Jewish law were rational choices that were supported by the evidence. The evidence to me was mainly the "impossibility" of Jewish history without divine providence, as illustrated by the Jewish people's disproportionate impact on the world and its survival against the odds through centuries of discrimination, persecution, violence, and genocide. I also thought the "proofs" advanced by Orthodox propagandists, such as the "Kuzari hypothesis" contending that the Hebrews could not possibly just make up a story about mass revelation in the desert, were intriguing, even if not absolute "proofs."

For a time, I was the only Sabbath-observant undergraduate student at the University of Connecticut, which was difficult and lonely. As I became stricter in my observance, I could only eat kosher certified cereals, salads, and frozen kosher dinners in the school cafeteria. Because I did not use electricity on the Sabbath, I had to climb ten flights of stairs to get to my dormitory room. Because I could not "carry" on the Sabbath, which was interpreted as prohibiting the transportation of items placed in a pocket, I had to hide my dormitory room key in creative places when I went out to services on the Sabbath.

In light of these difficulties, I transferred into New York University, which had a significant undergraduate population of Modern Orthodox Jews in a city filled with Orthodox Jews of all types. NYU also had a fully kosher student cafeteria, and dormitory doormen who knew how to arrange for the Sabbath needs of Orthodox students.

Taking New Paths *Stories of Leaving Religion*

I made the many sacrifices Orthodoxy requires despite the fact that, from well before the time I started becoming Orthodox, I saw what should have been warning signs.

For example, around the time I started high school, there was a series of apparently anti-Semitic arson attacks in Connecticut; a Jewish politician's home and synagogues, including the one I would later attend, were set on fire. The arson left the Jewish community on edge and led to Jewish neighborhood lookout patrols, along with an invitation to extremist Rabbi Kahane to speak about antisemitism and Jewish self-defense.

However, when the arsonist was finally caught, he turned out to be my brother's mentally ill roommate at his *yeshiva*, the private Jewish school he was attending, and where a leading rabbi at that *yeshiva* was later convicted of sexually abusing a student there. I have wondered whether that rabbi's behaviors somehow played a role in the arson.

At the University of Connecticut, there was an organization on campus affiliated with Chabad, a Hasidic sect which conducted religious "outreach" activities aimed primarily towards non-Orthodox Jews. In order to register as a student organization, they had fraudulently claimed that various students the Chabad Rabbi knew, including myself, were its "officers," without our knowledge. We complained to the University, after we learned not only of that breach of trust, but also that the Chabad Rabbi asked Rabbi Kahane to speak on campus under our names. The Chabad Rabbi attacked me, even calling me a "*moser*," the Hebrew word meaning an informant to the gentiles who, under Jewish law, can be put to death; I did not know what the word meant when the rabbi uttered it.

A couple of years later while I was a student at NYU, a fellow student, who had been my first Orthodox friend at NYU, was deeply disturbed following Rabbi Kahane's 1990 assassination in Manhattan by a jihadist. As a result, he invited another extremist to speak on campus, a violent and mentally unstable individual who ran a fledgling militant Jewish "defense" organization. After I wrote an editorial in the school newspaper denouncing Jewish extremism and took other actions that upset the extremist, my friend conveyed to me an alleged personal death threat from the extremist.

In addition to these unfortunate experiences, I was also

A Turbulent Journey

quite disappointed with my fellow non-extreme Modern Orthodox Jews, albeit perhaps due to the unrealistic expectations I had. Because I believed that Judaism properly interpreted was eminently universalistic, I was surprised to learn that there was as much casual racism in the Modern Orthodox community as in general society. Despite the mass of traditional/Orthodox Jewish literature forbidding gossip and demanding the highest of ethical standards in interpersonal relationships, I did not find that Modern Orthodox Jews conducted themselves in exceptional ways when interacting with others.

One of my deepest disappointments came when Connecticut's most prominent Modern Orthodox Jew, state Attorney General and future Vice Presidential candidate Joseph Lieberman, successfully ran as a Democrat for the U.S. Senate seat held by a well-liked moderate Republican, Lowell Weicker (later, a governor of the state).

I was deeply conflicted at first, as I liked both candidates and their politics were similar to each other's and to my own at the time. To my shock, late in the campaign Lieberman attacked Weicker with television ads depicting the overweight Weicker as a hibernating bear sleeping through Senate votes. The ad was obnoxious and personally insulting as well as deeply dishonest; Weicker's voting attendance record was typical.

The advertisement likely led to Lieberman's narrow victory. I remember my fellow Modern Orthodox Jews debating questions such as whether Lieberman could vote in the Senate on the Sabbath or Jewish holidays, and even whether he would be able to observe the Sabbath and eat only strictly kosher food if he were ever elected President. I did not understand why nobody was asking whether it was a violation of Jewish law for an Orthodox Jew to run nasty, misleading political advertisements.

I stuck with Modern Orthodox Judaism despite unfortunate experiences with extremists and my disappointments with the mainstream community, because I believed Orthodox Judaism's claims were true. I also believed that Kahanists and other militant Orthodox Jews, as well as those ultra-Orthodox who were extreme in their religious practices, had misinterpreted Judaism.

But also through the years, I became more cognizant of the moral backwardness of much of the Hebrew Bible, the Talmud, and other traditional Jewish texts. At first, that only left me more dedicated

Taking New Paths *Stories of Leaving Religion*

to Modern Orthodoxy, as I believed it alone understood the true ethical, universalistic core of Judaism. Subconsciously, however, I was beginning to realize that the more I learned about the tradition, the more problematic the tradition became.

My harshest experience came between college and law school, when I spent time studying at a *yeshiva* in Jerusalem. That *yeshiva* advertised itself as a place where people without an intensive Jewish background could learn how to seriously study Jewish texts, and not a school, like many *yeshiva*, which pushed a particular Orthodox ideology.

To their credit, that was true. Most of the students were Modern Orthodox *"Baalei Teshuva,"* "returnees" to the faith like myself, while most of the teachers were black-hatted ultra-Orthodox Rabbis, and that dichotomy caused little tension in classrooms devoted to the serious study and understanding of the grammar, structure, and logic of the Talmud and other texts.

However, I could not just let the disturbing ethical implications of the things I was learning pass by without further questioning and analysis. I probed as deeply as I could to understand how traditional Judaism viewed non-Jews, women, and non-religious Jews by asking questions. The answers were often disturbing, and I learned that Judaism's most central texts were usually the source of the most serious problems. At one point I privately broke down in tears, because I realized I had lost something permanently....the idealized Jewish religion of books and my imagination, which I had placed at the core of my identity.

The rabbis at the *yeshiva*, and even the students, thought I went a bit overboard in my concern with issues regarding traditional Judaism and human equality. Perhaps I did. At one point, I even asked a former Chief Rabbi of Israel a question pertaining to violating the Sabbath to save the life of someone who isn't Jewish. I asked if that was done out of respect for all human life, or simply to prevent antisemitism, as the sources related to that question were, I discovered to my horror, unclear.

He provided me with sources for both answers, and then asked

A Turbulent Journey

me if I was studying to become a doctor who might have to confront that question in relation to his work. I believe he asked because he did not understand why I found my question so distressing.

I left the *yeshiva* around the time of the Purim holiday to return to the U.S.A. for my brother's wedding. I was told that the Purim *spiel*, a humorous play and a Purim tradition, the *yeshiva* had arranged was partially about me and questions I'd asked the rabbis. In the *spiel*, someone playing the character of...well, me...was walking down the street on the Sabbath, and saw a person wearing a T-Shirt that said *"akum"* a Talmudic acronym which means idol worshiper. My character sees that person get struck by lightning. The character playing me did not know what to do; could he violate the Sabbath to save the idol worshiper's life? My character mulled it over; one rabbi says such-and-such, but another rabbi says something else. By the time my conflicted character was done thinking about it, the *"akum"* had died from his wounds.

In defense of the *yeshiva*, they knew I was self-deprecating with a somewhat warped sense of humor.

But I still returned to the U.S.A. dedicated to Modern Orthodox Judaism as the antidote to all problematic traditional Jewish beliefs, not to mention the excesses of modern secular/liberal culture. I moved to the upper west side of Manhattan, with its large population of Modern Orthodox singles, while I was in law school and for a short time thereafter.

Later, while working as an official with the Anti-Defamation League, I moved to a suburban Modern Orthodox community in New Jersey that was very friendly. In fact, my social experiences with various Modern Orthodox Jewish communities were positive. I had good friends, some of whom I'm still in touch with, most of the women I dated were nice, and there was always a more liberal (religiously and politically) contingent of people within those communities I could seek out, even if they were in the minority as mainstream Modern Orthodoxy was becoming increasingly Republican and traditional.

My move away from Orthodoxy—and Judaism—did not begin until I was around thirty years old when I moved to Midwood,

Taking New Paths *Stories of Leaving Religion*

Brooklyn, with its large ultra-Orthodox community. I stayed Modern Orthodox for the first few years, and was part of a small but friendly Modern Orthodox community there. However, seeing how extreme many knowledgeable Orthodox Jews in the area were, I started questioning the foundations of my belief that, even with its flaws, Judaism correctly interpreted looked like the most progressive elements of Modern Orthodoxy.

I began to consider the possibility that a plain reading of the texts, in line with mainstream traditional Jewish thought, could lead to tribalism, sexism, homophobia, and a resistance to change and antipathy towards competing knowledge. Maybe, even if there was enough room in the tradition to interpret the texts in a more liberal way, the ugliness was too deeply entwined into the tradition to ever fully root it out.

Then I started questioning whether it was all true. I did not realize at the time that there was a growing online community of Orthodox and ex-Orthodox skeptics debating Orthodoxy's claims and "proofs," which was largely centered around the blog of my own former Modern Orthodox roommate, whose brother, an Orthodox rabbi, was publicly excommunicated for his beliefs in evolution and about other scientific matters. My ex-roommate's blog, along with web pages exposing wrongdoing in the Orthodox community, impacted thousands of Jews who left Orthodoxy, which was becoming known as "going OTD," for "Off the *Derekh*," meaning off the one true path; a term intended as an insult by the Orthodox, but proudly adopted by those striking out on their own path.

While I was late to the game in finding the online Jewish skeptic and OTD movements, research played a role in my own OTD journey. The most impactful thing for me was the realization that the central story of the Torah—of the slavery of millions of Hebrews in Egypt, their sudden escape and decades of wandering in the desert, and their rapid, violent conquest of Canaan—would have left a substantial archaeological record if historically true, while in fact there is no archaeological record of it at all.

While some Modern Orthodox Jews read portions of Genesis "allegorically," such as the days of creation, thereby allowing for a billions of years "old" universe, they still, by and large, insist on the historical truth of Biblical stories regarding their putative ancestors,

A Turbulent Journey

including Moses and his contemporaries. Personally, I could not imagine Judaism being in any significant sense "true" if those stories were untrue. Therefore, I could no longer reconcile my belief in Judaism with the evidence.

This rift between hard evidence and the beliefs I adopted left me angry...at Dennis Prager and those supposedly secular-knowledge-respecting Modern Orthodox rabbis, who didn't even think this was an important enough issue to address in their books drawing people towards tradition and Orthodoxy.

I was also a bit upset about the lack of attention paid to the findings of archaeology and Biblical scholarship in my public school education and American society at large. I now believe the vast conflicts between the extensive archaeological record of the ancient Near East and the claims of Biblical "history" are so straightforward and consequential that they should be taught in every public school in America. In fact, they should be taught to every child on Earth who is being raised in an Abrahamic faith so they can make an important life choice armed with a vastly important piece of knowledge.

Still, to this day, to some extent I'm also mad at myself, because even without access to the materials which are now easily available on the Internet, significant scholarship about archaeological findings and biblical authorship was available in libraries at the time. Like so many other young people, I should have researched further and asked more questions before deciding to become religious.

My family did not take my decision to leave Orthodoxy well. At one point my mother started asking me questions about the decision, and when I told her that there were many things in Jewish tradition I found deeply immoral, she asked "like what?" In response, I gave the example of the Jewish law requiring that a man of priestly descent (a *"Kohain"*) divorce his wife if she is raped.

A look of shock came over my mother's face; she had no idea that law existed. In fact, many "returnees" to the faith and I came to learn, even many *frum* (religious from birth) Modern Orthodox Jews, have no knowledge of much of the worst ugliness in traditional Jewish texts and law. After my discussion with my mother, she mentioned what I had told her to an Orthodox rabbi, who responded that perhaps I "know too much."

I now believe that nobody should ever become Orthodox

Taking New Paths *Stories of Leaving Religion*

without first knowing that God and Moses command and follow through with the murder of their enemies' babies in the Torah, the many disturbing laws about people of priestly descent which are still applicable today, and that there is a mountain of Jewish source material which is particularistic and anti-gentilic, and which far outweighs the universalistic sources in the tradition.

    I went OTD quietly at first, and was somewhat depressed about it. I was living in a highly Orthodox neighborhood, and most of my friends were Orthodox. When I became aware of the growing OTD community which could be found online, as well as an organization called Footsteps which assisted OTD Jews, particularly the ex-ultra-orthodox, I became very involved with them. I could probably relate to the large percentage of ex-ultra-Orthodox Jews who are in those groups more than some ex-Modern Orthodox Jews because, like many of the ex-ultra-Orthodox, I was completely estranged from my family at that point. Religion played a large role in this but there was more: I slowly came to grips with the fact that I was a survivor of child abuse, and that my family's deep problems played a role in their lifelong obsession with religion and turn to Orthodoxy.

    I wanted to give something back to the OTD community, so I started a Facebook group which has connected hundreds of ex-Fundamentalists from all backgrounds around the world, as well as a meet-up group in New York City which brought OTD Jews together with people in the area who left other fundamentalist faiths.

    It was overall a great experience, but people in the OTD community were struggling with more problems than I expected. The first OTD person to help me with the Formerly Fundamentalist meet-up group I started was an ex-Hasidic woman who tragically committed suicide by jumping off a Manhattan rooftop.

    While I sometimes feel I can't completely relate to the struggles of people who come from more culturally extreme fundamentalist backgrounds than my own, I have developed a great deal of respect for them, and particularly for the ex-ultra-Orthodox community. I have seen very young people somehow overcome tremendous challenges, including excommunication and secular educational deficits from the

A Turbulent Journey

yeshivas they attended, and accomplish amazing things. I also deeply respect people I've met from the ex-Muslim community—the bravest people you will ever meet, ex-Jehovah's Witnesses who are shunned every bit as much as ex-ultra-Orthodox Jews, and ex-Mormons who are similar to the ex-Modern Orthodox in terms of prior exposure to the outside world, but from a more centrally organized, cultish faith, albeit a less demanding one.

Unlike most ex-religious people, I identify as agnostic and not atheist because I think that the evidence against religion is far more obvious and powerful than the evidence against any type of "God" or "higher power." I find the mysteries of existence and consciousness perplexing, and I do not find myself gravitating towards beliefs that the universe is at heart mechanistic or random, or lacking any type of "higher power." Still, some atheist friends insist that I am technically an "agnostic atheist" because I do not have an affirmative belief in God. Also, unlike some OTD'ers, who call themselves ex-Jews (and I accept their self-definition), I don't mind calling myself "culturally Jewish" based upon my background.

I have maintained some friendships with Modern Orthodox Jews and religious Christians. However, in recent years, I have felt increasingly disconnected from my former community and many other religious Americans as a result of the unfortunate embrace of former President Donald Trump by so many allegedly pious Americans including most Orthodox Jews. This embrace included their failure to oppose his administration's gross corruption and its immoral, cruel, and anti-democratic policies, up to and including Trump's attempt to overthrow democracy itself with his Big Lie about the 2020 election.

I was particularly surprised to learn that conservative talk show host and moralist Dennis Prager, who played such a significant role in my embrace of Judaism, had disavowed his early opposition to Trump and become one of Trump's most vocal and disingenuous supporters. Prager turned a blind eye to his prior statements and writings about the importance of character and even endorsed Trumpist lies and conspiracy theories about Covid-19 and the 2020 election.

Videos produced under his "Prager University" moniker have

Taking New Paths *Stories of Leaving Religion*

provided misinformation to millions. He wrote disturbing articles about rape and child abuse, and joined Trump in supporting the Alabama Senatorial candidacy of Roy Moore, who was credibly accused of serially harassing and assaulting teenage girls, based upon Prager's "greatest conservative principle" of "defeating the left." On top of this, other Prager writings in recent years sound like they are playing into growing (and racist and antisemitic) white nationalist sentiments in this country. *This* is the person who convinced me to turn to religion as an ethical imperative, and to Judaism as a universalistic faith?

My shock regarding Prager led me to go back and re-read the book Prager co-wrote which most impacted my decision to become a religious Jew: *The Nine Questions People Ask About Judaism*. I discovered that, in addition to the simplistic and at times misleading claims about Judaism, the book was filled with ethnocentric material. For example, in his preface to the book, Prager writes:

> *People often ask me why I returned to Judaism. 'I saw the rest of the world,' I tell them. This answer is meant neither to denigrate other cultures or religions nor to be flippant. But the more I come to know and experience the world and its history, the more I come to venerate Judaism and the nation which it has produced. I remember walking around the exquisite Indonesian island of Bali, seeing men gathered everywhere cheering at cock fights. Watching animals scratch each other's eyes out was as entertaining to these men as a baseball game was to me—and as morally unproblematic.*

On their face, these words about bloodthirsty cock fighters in Bali cheering at animals scratching each other's eyes out sound nasty and ethnocentric, perhaps even racist, as they evoke images of non-white people thirsting for blood. I understand there were differing sensitivities at the time they were written around 1981, but even if I excuse the tone, how was the cock fighting Prager saw in Bali representative of the rest of the world to him? Cockfighting was outlawed or unpopular in much of the world, including much of Asia, well before Prager's visit. Moreover, cockfighting, which was not

A Turbulent Journey

outlawed in all of the United States until 2007 (with active illegal rings to this day), is not actually outlawed by Judaism. Additionally, Judaism has its own animal rights issues, such as ultra-Orthodox Jews who swing chickens they are readying for slaughter over their heads for atonement before the holiday of Yom Kippur.

I have also re-read some of Prager's writings about race, including a 1996 article in an issue of his magazine *The Prager Perspective*. In that article, Prager discussed his alleged encounter with an unnamed black cab driver who suggested he experienced racism when white passengers asked if he knew where a famous bookstore was, supposedly because they assumed a black man would not frequent a bookstore. The article is disturbing, as Prager appears to use straw man arguments against an anonymous black man to establish what he calls "The Assumption Of Racism Where It Probably Doesn't Exist." Tellingly, Prager's alleged foil for this argument "was a thinking, non-racist black man who, moreover, spoke eloquently."

I now recognize Prager's casual racism and ethnocentrism, in conjunction with his lack of intellectual honesty, depth, and rigor, going back decades in his writings. I wish I had understood the world, Judaism, and Dennis Prager then as I do now.

What has disturbed me the most on a personal level is realizing how strong the connection is between the very aspects of Prager's writings which most impacted my younger self's thinking, and the attitudes which are currently driving a resurgence of reactionary anger, intertwined with appeals to religion, on the political right. Prager's most convincing arguments to my younger self, and arguments he has consistently continued making to this day, involve the ideas that "objective," "meaning," and "morality" cannot exist independent of a belief in God, and therefore without belief in God, human lives would be meaningless and civilization (or at least Western civilization) will lose its moral foundation and collapse.

This line of thought goes all the way back to *The Nine Questions* book. While on a positive note, that book acknowledged that reasonable people may have doubts about God's existence, Prager and Telushkin wrote that even when struggling with such doubts, it is important to live "as if" God exists so we will have meaning in our lives and a moral code to live by. In other words, regardless of the evidence, humanity needs to stick with God.

Taking New Paths *Stories of Leaving Religion*

Prager now goes so far as to claim that "honest atheists" agree with him that life is meaningless and ethics illusory if there is no God, and his fake online "University" promotes a video arguing that atheists should actually lie to their children about their beliefs and teach them about "God."

In addition to the moral and practical problems with blatantly lying to children so they will believe in fictions, there are other problems with Prager's line of thought, beginning with the fact that Prager's underlying ideas about meaning and ethics do not appear to be aligned with even traditional Jewish sources. The majority of traditional Jewish philosophers appear to take a natural law approach to ethics, believing that reason and/or moral intuition can lead to ethical behavior, albeit with religion being the more direct and better guide, and there is certainly no consensus Jewish view about the meaning of life or it being meaningless without God.

In any event, concerning basic ethics, even putting aside the vast problems with Biblical, Jewish, and Christian ethics in light of today's sensibilities, our modern challenge is in maintaining a commitment to ethics in a world where every rational person should, at the very least, have doubts about the existence of whatever they may call "God." Because there is a massive amount of scientific and historical evidence which contradicts the Bible, because the Bible's allegedly all knowing and good God does not appear to be all knowing or good to so many modern people, and because arguments for the existence of a generic God are based upon disputable philosophical and metaphysical premises. Moreover, even a (somehow) strong belief in the existence of a good Biblical God does not, in and of itself, provide clear—or moral—guidance on many ethical questions, nor does it impart "objective meaning" to life.

In a world where there is simply no comprehensive guide to life's meaning, or convincing evidence that any type of God exists, what is most important is the exact opposite of what Prager and Telushkin called for; What is most important is finding meaning and reason to behave ethically in the reality we actually inhabit, in which God, however defined, simply does not exist or exists silently in relation to our daily lives and concerns.

This reality we live in is producing vastly increasing numbers of people identifying as atheists, agnostics, or non-believers in relation

A Turbulent Journey

to religion, and more believers than ever are being exposed to reasons to doubt and doubting. The doubters will need to find meaning and ethics in philosophies which transcend traditional religion, or else they will be provided with versions of religion and political ideologies which mislead with simplistic claims, lies, or even reactionary anger and hatred.

One largely overlooked study of Trump supporters provided, I believe, some insight into the connection between religious doubters and the rise of authoritarianism and racism in the U.S.A. According to this study, while Trump's most ardent supporters were Evangelical Christians, among the Evangelicals, his most ardent supporters were those who identified as such but did not attend church regularly per this article in the *Washington Post*: https://www.washingtonpost.com/news/monkey-cage/wp/2016/03/29/where-is-trumps-evangelical-base-not-in-church/.

I do not think this in any way exonerates Evangelicals who attend church regularly; after all, most of them voted for Trump too, even if more of them were holding their noses while doing so. But what this study suggests to me is that, where religious belief is not strong, as with the non-church attending Evangelicals whom I suspect are disproportionately doubters or people with shaky belief systems, a void will result.

When this void is not filled by a humanistic worldview—whether it comes from secular/atheistic humanism, or liberal religious or spiritual beliefs—anti-humanistic philosophies such as authoritarianism, racism, and fascism will rise. And, as in Nazi Germany, some religious traditionalists, armed with authoritarian backgrounds, texts, and beliefs, will align themselves with the authoritarians, even if they lean into racism and fascism. The alignment, though, is probably easier for "less religious" people of faith who don't have the better parts of religion—such as concerns with personal character and opposition to corruption—gnawing at their consciences or regularly presented to them in sermons at church.

Prager's adamant Trumpism fits together neatly with that of those less religious Evangelicals. I'm now looking back at Prager's personal, somewhat lax version of Judaism, as well as his obsession with what he calls "Judeo-Christian values" and even "Judeo-Christian religion," and I have to wonder what he really believes in.

Taking New Paths *Stories of Leaving Religion*

His denomination of one person, which doesn't look much like biblical Judaism, or any stream of rabbinic Judaism, has at its foundation a heap of oversimplifications and misrepresentations of Judaism. Perhaps Prager's own doubts and insecurities about his claims and beliefs, and the mountains of evidence against them, are driving his political and cultural extremism.

Turning to Orthodoxy, the greater Orthodox Jewish community has in a sense not followed the Evangelical pattern; ultra-Orthodox Jews (who certainly go to synagogue more often than Modern Orthodox Jews) appear to have supported Trump in greater proportion than Modern Orthodox Jews. However, I do see something like the Evangelical pattern mirrored within the Modern Orthodox Jewish community. Among Modern Orthodox Jews I maintained contact with some whom I considered particularly devout in their beliefs or practice, all opposed Trump or who identified themselves as nose-holding Trump voters, usually, because of his policies favoring Israel. Among Modern Orthodox Jews I knew who became part of Trump's base of strong supporters and cheerleaders, none were people I considered particularly devout.

One rather peculiar development in recent years is the degree to which Dennis Prager is admired, and even accepted as a serious thinker, by many Orthodox Jews. Prager has a large Orthodox fan base and has spoken at Orthodox synagogues and institutions, while writing columns for a politically conservative Orthodox Jewish newspaper, *The Jewish Press*. This is odd because Prager has also written and spoken publicly about his rejection of the Orthodox belief that the Torah was given at Sinai, as well as about his rejection of Jewish law as interpreted by Orthodox rabbis. From an Orthodox perspective, he should be considered at worst a public heretic, or at best an ignoramus publicly spreading heresy. Instead, he is embraced by many Orthodox Jews and condemned by few.

In addition to apparently being Orthodox Jewry's favorite non-Orthodox Jew, Dennis Prager may also be conservative Christian America's favorite Jew, though he is in competition for that title with with Modern Orthodox Jew Ben Shapiro of conservative website *The Daily Wire*, known for spreading misinformation to make Jewish views about abortion sound more like Christian views about abortion.

Considering Prager's Orthodox fans who should view Prager

A Turbulent Journey

as a dangerous spreader of heresy, along with Prager's Christian fans who, according to their religious doctrines, believe Prager will burn in hell for all eternity for not believing in Jesus and even publicly arguing against Christian doctrine, it seems as though conservative politics is as much of, if not more of, a priority for many religious Americans as their alleged theologies.

This is also evidenced by what appears to be a growing, wide ranging political alliance of Orthodox Jews and fundamentalist Christians, despite basic theological differences regarding essential issues such as abortion. Adding to that, the tensions between Biblical writings about charity and the poor and the conservative economic positions many religious Americans now adopt, it appears to me that it is an alliance specifically upholding a patriarchal social order which is at the heart of the concerns of many religious Americans today. Everything else, including consistency and politically inconvenient aspects of theology, can be set aside.

I am no longer surprised by the havoc which those who identify with traditional religions are wreaking with their social-issues-centered anger. When people of various fundamentalist faiths and outlooks embrace deeply misogynistic texts with barbaric commandments, and to varying degrees reject the findings of science, you will inevitably end up with people who embrace patriarchy, authoritarianism, and a politics of willful ignorance. As for those brave fundamentalists who have drawn on the better parts of religious tradition, bucked their communities, and stood against Trumpism including some Modern Orthodox Jews I know, they have my deepest respect as I realize how difficult their position is.

In a sense, the world now appears to me to be somewhat inverted from the perspective of my younger self. I thought that embracing my Jewish identity and Orthodoxy was taking a stand against fascism; "refusing to finish Hitler's job for him," as my mother put it. However, it now appears to me that some Jews who vociferously embrace their identity and religion are actually, ironically, contributing to the rise of political forces in the U.S.A. (and Israel) which are quite authoritarian and sometimes even fascistic.

Taking New Paths *Stories of Leaving Religion*

I thought that belief in God and religion was a rational path to a meaningful life guided by ethics. I now realize that belief in any particular God and deriving meaning and ethics from religion are all terribly problematic from various perspectives, and that in the modern world, humanity as a whole will only find meaning and behave ethically if sources of meaning and ethics can be found independent of God and religion. I used to pray for the advent of a Jewish messiah to lead humanity to peace and prosperity. Now, I strongly suspect that the decline of religion and the rise of a better humanity will be intertwined.

While certain aspects of my story are unusual, I think some of my experiences, such as being mislead by religious propaganda materials, not sufficiently researching issues regarding the historicity and authorship of the Bible, and not realizing the full extent of the moral and philosophical difficulties with religion, illustrate common mistakes. I hope that others can learn about Orthodox Judaism and its defectors from my story, and that it will raise awareness and understanding of those who leave fundamentalist belief systems.

Understanding us and the phenomenon we are part of is particularly important as I expect our numbers to increase, exponentially, in conjunction with scientific, moral, and societal progress. And with the profound dangers humanity is facing, including potential environmental and political catastrophes, it is my hope that we and other secularists, approaching the world as it is with clear minds, will play a critical role in overcoming challenges and building a better future for all.

Reading list for those considering leaving Orthodox Judaism and Fundamentalism:

1. *All Who Go Do Not Return: A Memoir*, by Shulem Deen
Several memoirs have been written by people who left Orthodox Judaism, but this book, by an ex-Hasid from an insular and extreme sect, is the most moving and, in a secular sense, the most spiritual. There are dangers and joys intertwined with every journey away from Orthodoxy, and you will share in Shulem's deeply emotional experiences.

A Turbulent Journey

2. *The Book of Separation: A Memoir*, by Tova Mirvis

While not as dramatic as Deen's book, this memoir about a woman's separation from Modern Orthodox Judaism and her religious husband serves as a compelling meditation on what it means to truly be free.

3. *Reasonable Doubts: Breaking the Kuzari*, by "Second Son"

Various misleading arguments have been used to sell Orthodox Judaism and its central theological belief that some or all of the text of the Torah was given to Moses on Mount Sinai along with the Ten Commandments, which were then brought down to millions of Israelites in the desert who had heard the voice of God. None is more popular than the argument often referred to as the "Kuzari Hypothesis," claiming that the "mass revelation" at Sinai described in the Bible could not have been fictionalized, and that it is unique among the origin stories of world religions. By methodically examining and unraveling the underlying claims the argument is built upon, this book uncovers the argument's many flaws and will allow those who were influenced by it to reconsider.

4. *How to Read the Bible: A Guide to Scripture, Then and Now*, by James Kugel

Regarding the critical question of whether the central story of the Hebrew Bible, that of mass enslavement in Egypt, exodus, and then rapid conquest of the Holy Land, actually happened, I do not have any particular work about Biblical archaeology to recommend. However, for questioning religious Jews and Christians, I would suggest beginning with the writings of religious academics who have been honest enough to recognize, to some extent, the problem.

For Christians, there are the writings of British evangelical Christian apologist, biblical scholar, and historian Kenneth Kitchen; I'd suggest reading up on Kitchen's theories as to how to reconcile the findings of archaeology with the text of the bible, and criticisms of Kitchen's theories by other academics.

For Orthodox Jews, however, I would recommend the above book by Harvard University and Bar Ilan University Professor James

Taking New Paths *Stories of Leaving Religion*

Kugel, who identifies as an Orthodox Jew. Although the book is not an in depth discussion of archaeology or arguments over historicity, Kugel's recognition of the magnitude of the problems, including regarding the exodus narrative, is clear. Kugel's attempt to reconcile the findings and theories of biblical scholarship and archaeology with traditional faith, by claiming that the rabbis who reinterpreted the text were divinely inspired to do so, is, I believe, unconvincing.

Further, it serves as a testament to what limited possibilities remain for those who wish to retain both their intellectual honesty and their commitment to traditional religion. Regardless, though, the book is also an enjoyable and worthy read for its thought provoking chapters on biblical stories and their shifting meanings through time.

5. *Changing the Immutable: How Orthodox Judaism Rewrites Its History*, by Marc Shapiro

Those with an ultra-Orthodox background are often unaware that they are living within societies which are in large part modern constructs, built upon rewriting Jewish history and censoring texts, sometimes, even ancient traditional texts. The resulting historical revisionism may serve the purpose of addressing modern challenges or concerns, or it may play a role in shielding the community from the modern world. This enlightening book will help ultra-Orthodox Jews gain a perspective on their communities and the teachings upon which they are built, and it will provide food for thought for anyone considering the relationship between religions which claim to be sources of truth, and actual facts.

6. and 7. *Nature's God,* by Matthew Stewart, and
The Swerve, by Stephen Greenblatt

I would recommend these two books of popular history, the first about the Enlightenment and particularly its impact on the founding of the United States, and the second about the origins of the earlier Renaissance. The modern Western world was to some extent shaped by these two movements following the Middle Ages, and both books highlight the ways in which allowances to question everything, even religious "truths," with evidence, paved the way for modernity and are built upon the rejection of traditional religious concepts of heresy.

A Turbulent Journey

Stewart traces the "heresies" of many of the United States's founding fathers, in their rejection of religion and embrace of Deism or Pantheism (seen by some as forms of Atheism), to the influence of earlier luminaries, particularly Jewish born Dutch philosopher Baruch Spinoza and ancient Greek philosopher Epicurus. Greenblatt is focused on the ways in which the philosophy of Epicurus, as interpreted by a Roman poet, rediscovered by a papal secretary, and introduced to Europe, inspired the Renaissance.

While some claims and details in both books have been subject to criticisms, I believe the central contentions of both books are on firm ground. Moreover, for Orthodox Jewish readers, as Epicurus served as the very model of a "heretic" for traditional Jews (the Jewish term for heretic is *"apikorus"*), and as Spinoza is the most famous Jewish "heretic" in history, these books provide a valuable counter-perspective on history to traditional Jewish understandings.

While Jewish theology became more nuanced and diverse over time, Maimonides suggested the term *apikorus* had a different origin, and some Orthodox Jews have tried to question Spinoza's heresy, the conflict between super-naturalism and scientific objectivity remains at the heart of the intellectual struggle most educated Orthodox Jews face. Further, the ideas of Epicurus and Spinoza, including those regarding ethical behavior, can help shape a post-religious worldview for those who leave, and the impact Epicurus and Spinoza had on history should serve as a source of pride for all "heretics."

Taking New Paths *Stories of Leaving Religion*

18
My Anthology of Influences and Choices Re-Affirmed
Charles H. (Chuck) Wells Jr.

I WAS BORN August 21, 1925, seven years after the armistice of World War I, five years after my mother and her sister-womenfolk of the nation got to vote, and one year after America's Indians became citizens. I have traveled over a fair piece of country, which has challenged and re-affirmed my humanistic spirituality as my vehicle for relating to and working with my fellow humans on this mega-environment called Earth during my time here.

My mother, Nana, the third child of ten, had tried to go along with her mother's commitment to Christian Science to the point of having a Christian Science Practitioner serve as a midwife when she was bearing me. Dad, in the middle of harvest on the farm, after twenty-four hours of her labor, threw the Practitioner out and called the local doctor who saved us both.

This contention with her mother over trying work with Christian Science, in the face of practical evidence, continued after Nana and my dad, Charley, left the New York farm. They left because of conflict with Charley's mother. They re-located next door to Mom's folks' place in Atherton, California. I was about fourteen months old.

My earliest memory was of riding my foot-operated wooden tricycle along with my two-year-old sister, Joanie on my grandparents' red brick walkway in front of their big house, under mother's smile and guidance. I was three.

Joanie's death from diphtheria later that year was a trauma Mom, Dad, and I shared in anguish, consciously and unconsciously for years.

Again, Nana had tried to contact a Christian Science Practitioner, who demurred because she had two little granddaughters and she understood there was a "sickness" going around with young children. Nana called a doctor friend from college days, who had two young girls. When she saw him trying to help Joanie breathe with mouth to mouth resuscitation, she was done with Christian Science.

Somehow, my mother found several constructive ways to cope with Joanie's death by helping others and she involved me in a number of them.

First, her brother, Jerry, an engineer, cast metal Popsicle molds of animals and a railroad engine. Clamped together we poured hard candy-flavored lollypops, and I got to stick in the wooden skewers. We wrapped them in cellophane tied with a bow. These we delivered to several outlets in Palo Alto. We were partners in business!

Right next to Stanford, there was a children's TB convalescent home supported by their women's association. During the year they collected toys and books that more fortunate kids were no longer interested in. The Palo Alto Fire Department repaired and repainted the toys while the ladies sewed and repaired doll clothing. All were destined to be distributed to the less fortunate. So, when it came time to put together the Christmas boxes and baskets, who better to select

Taking New Paths *Stories of Leaving Religion*

the proper large gift and stocking gifts for little boys than Nana's boy, me, known as "Sonny." I learned the joy and fun of Christmas "shopping" for a lot of unknown fellow kids!

Also during the Christmas season we would take the train up to San Francisco to visit the department store displays. It was a trip of wonder, but not hope. We were struggling in the face of the Great Depression. There were little electric boats driving around in a big tank, Model railroad displays, and a bunch of other stuff. Dad would meet us for lunch at the food merry-go-round where one could take whatever he wanted right off the endless beltway.

Then when I was six, I learned that we were going to have a baby. Mom took me into the preparations for and proper care of our new family member. So, when sister Stephanie was born, I was excited to help take care of her. It apparently worked out well in that I don't recall feeling jealousy, rather I felt so happy that I again had a sister.

Understandably, we were both overprotected, which we each resisted in our own ways. She became a tomboy, and insisted that she be called "Stevie."

My dad was a 1914 graduate of Cornell Agricultural School, and remained—in his heart and soul—a farmer. And I absorbed his love of nature and agriculture.

He had worked his way through college selling higher-end kitchenware. I was told that he was a popular fellow with a great sense of humor before the crash of '29 and the family conflict involving his hard-to-live-with mother.

His humor is what I recall of him, along with his ability to endure, which I later perceived and learned by osmosis. He was always loving, yet retained his lifelong social and class biases. They pretty well fit in with the rest of Mom's large family.

The Great Depression amplified family biases as employment and opportunity conflicted with their perceived "divine rights." Meanwhile, I was going to public school with a bunch of poor families' kids. All of which initiated an inner conflict regarding fairness in me.

Another underlying dissonance was my confusion over whether Joanie had gone to heaven or somewhere where she just floated lonely, or if she was just "dead and gone," (whatever that was). Several assurances had been made by caring extended family

My Anthology of Influences

members, but nobody knew for sure, so their explanations lacked conviction and commitment. I later realized that this ambiguity resided in me for some years. Over time Nana's and Charley's love, humor, and demonstrated agnosticism brought a kind of steadying comfort to my restiveness.

Throughout my childhood Granddad would take me along on camping trips. In 1939 we took a long one. Crossing the open steppe of Nevada, he and I took a walk while the driver took the car filled with camp gear to the top of a long steep grade, came back for the travel trailer, then for us, then re-loaded and got on to the next challenge.

While Granddad and I were gazing together over the vast expanse with wondrous awe he stopped, put his hand on my shoulder saying, "Chuck, if I could somehow put all my experience into your head right now, I would gladly lay myself down." What a gift to a twelve-year-old!

My maternal Grandmother, Marion, was the daughter of Brevet Captain Richard Henry Pratt, Tenth Cavalry (the enlisted ranks were "Buffalo Soldiers," many ex-slaves, and Civil War veterans).

She was born in 1868, at Fort Arbuckle, Indian Territory. She bore ten children, five boys and five girls. She was a constant source of love, stories, and guidance—all of it good, except for my conflict with Christian Science.

The stories were of her growing up on the "Staked Plains" that later became Oklahoma, She also told me about her life at the old Spanish Fort in Saint Augustine, Florida, where her father held Indian prisoners that the government could not try for serious crimes because they were "wards of the state," and then at the Carlyle Indian Industrial School, which her father had founded and directed for nearly two decades.

She told me what she had learned by living in close proximity to both "Indians" and "Negro" soldiers. I even met several elderly former students from Carlisle who came by to visit.

I began to become aware of the white man's domination of society and the colonial self-righteousness, which became my lifelong accentuated dissonance regarding humankind.

Taking New Paths *Stories of Leaving Religion*

As two illustrative examples, from Pratt's autobiography, *Battlefield and Classroom*, in 1867 he talks about leading a cavalry troop across the prairie and discussing the war with a fellow officer. "How can it be that we fought a war to preserve a constitution that says, 'All men are created equal' and I am leading troops who can never be officers because of their color and am in charge of Indian scouts who are committed to die for the flag of a country that they cannot be citizens of?"

He ran the Carlyle Indian Industrial School, modeled after the then-current residence schools and based on his statement of the need to "kill the Indian to save the man," which was intended to change the Indians' cultural orientation through the Industrial School programs.

Yet Pratt's tomb at Arlington states: "Brigadier General Richard Henry Pratt and his wife Laura," and at the base, "Erected in loving memory by his students and other Indians." At the military funeral for a Brigadier General, all his pallbearers were Indians. This in the context of the period wherein the two dominating thoughts were extermination of or confining the native peoples to reservations as wards of the government under forced and frequently-violated "treaties."

Then I met Charles Niederhauser, Superintendent-Principal of Las Lomitas Elementary School District, an experimental school related to Stanford University, and the teacher of my combined seventh-eighth grade class.

We became acquainted with self-responsibility and critical thinking, which communicated an unqualified trust between us. He emphasized, "If you have the ability to question, you have the right to question. And so, you have the obligation to question." He put this to effect in his curriculum design and in the mode of the interactive teaching-learning process.

He also said that you could, "do anything that you want as long as it doesn't interfere with learning. That is why we are here." Of course, one soon learned that quiet talk between two or more person's interests and intellectual explorations was about the limit.

We sat at tables that accommodated up to four students per side with a row of our textbooks down the center, which enabled and forced relationships deeper than the conventional regimented rows of individual desks all facing the classroom authority. This also

My Anthology of Influences

allowed for "Niederhauser," (his preferred form of address), to have selective individual time with students as well as being available to students informally.

In addition to quiet study periods, we pursued our own interests, which were personal avenues to ever greater explorations in learning, with some challenging questioning. We had grade and group interest lessons, discussions of civics, political issues, choir, and sports at recess. We surrounded the high-ceilinged wall with a butcher paper timeline, which somehow expanded into world history, science, and invention. The "discoveries" were pictured along with a written description of the event.

The hot lunch program during this period of the Great Depression was cooperatively handled by the Parent Teachers Association. A few students each day helped prepare, serve, and clean up while learning something about healthy cooking. The Italian mothers did an Italian lunch on Wednesdays, other cooking groups gave us other healthy tasty dishes.

So, we rarely were disappointed and numbers of classmates got at least one square meal each school day during these hard times. The kitchen was part of the school building so we could smell what was cooking. We broadened an intimate community beyond our own homes.

As Niederhauser told me years later, when I was an education major, in reference to John Dewey, the educational philosopher, "We learn by Deweying." In retrospect I realized that we were practicing what I have come to call a very "practical spiritual humanism."

Our class was preparing to go on to high school in 1939. My time in high school was clouded with and focused on the imminence of expanding world war. Shortwave radio accounts were of Japanese invasions in China and Korea, Czechoslovakia and Poland falling, Dunkirk and The Blitz, then Pearl Harbor on December 7, 1941, and our Declaration of War against Japan and the Axis powers.

Fred Blaze was my history teacher. He had been in New York's Rainbow Division in World War one serving in France. I came, over time, to realize that he became a teacher because of that experience.

After teaching, he had taken the train to San Francisco at least once a week to work on developing UNESCO—another lesson for me in dedication and endurance.

He encouraged us to read *All Quiet On The Western Front* and *The Road Back*, about German soldiers' views in the trenches and survival after the war. "You boys should learn all you can about conflict so you can become somewhat familiar about what you are getting into."

New realizations were confirmed by our high school curriculum and activities, as well as civil defense, in which I volunteered as a bicycle messenger in case of action against the San Francisco Peninsula. I joined the rifle club, and by summer I was working on a farm to supplement the manpower shortage.

That fall the local Fire Department hired me to serve a night shift, 7:00 p.m. to 8:00 a.m., six nights a week, to support the one paid captain. We responded to telephone fire and accident calls, hoping volunteers would respond to the coded fire siren.

I also participated in drills in one of which I was ordered to rappel down to the next floor and rescue an unconscious victim, then carry the victim out the window, and down three more floors to the safety net. The "victim" was my captain. This was a test of trust by my leader—the initial rite of passage, building my confidence, and setting my attraction to serve in emergencies.

Due to a persistent illness when I was ten, I'd had to repeat fifth grade. Consequently, I would be drafted at the beginning of my junior year when I became eighteen. So, the day before my birthday I chose to enlist in the Coast Guard, which became an arm of the navy in time of war.

I joined in the hope of serving on a smaller vessel in some form of action and with its own traditions in peace and war. I fancied it would be better than being lost in the "giant" navy.

During my three years of service, I kept trying to "go to sea" by going to landing boat school, then to radar operator school, and air-sea rescue coordination experiments, which finally got me to a commissioning crew on a new cutter destined for the invasion of Japan.

The atom bomb ended the war and I transferred to an old cutter that was ending its life's service on International Ice patrol, operating out of Argentia, Newfoundland, on the North Atlantic.

My Anthology of Influences

I finally became a real sailor, my more adult rite of passage. It was an expanded cultural and social experience of mankind's range of purposes and behaviors. It also developed my love and respect for the sea, all of which helped form my humanistic and ecological values.

Although I did not see action beyond training for several aspects of it and seeing the results of it—both in my part of post-war American society, daily life with colleague veterans, and two summer voyages as a merchant seaman to Japan, Chinwangtao, and Shanghai, China, Hong Kong, and the Philippines—I was primarily focused on trying to integrate these experiences with college studies and to determine a professional commitment of worth.

Most of my life I had focused on medicine, probably from earlier experiences, and to pursue scientific knowledge and service. But, education kept presenting itself as the broader essential interest and need.

During this six-year period I married. The birth of our two sons during my third and fourth years at San Jose State College necessitated my working full time while taking a reduced academic workload. The "P.M. Shift" in the hospital surgery and accident room (ER) allowed me to try to do both and to help during the night for two years.

At that point it became clear that I had to drop out of college and both of us had to work. Marie was in depression, conflicted over the demands of babies, and her marriage, which was in serious jeopardy. We moved to San Francisco, assuming that work opportunities would be better, and she would be in her familiar hometown. The result was that she needed to be away from me and the boys and to work in an office as a secretary on her own for a period of time.

Again, I took the children, worked driving ambulance from 8 a.m. to 6 p.m. The salary was poor, but we boys could just survive on it after paying rent, household costs, and childcare. During this period, my love and joy being with them was amplified, which eased the strain. I realized that we could live this way and I began to plan to do so.

However, after eight months Marie felt that she had resolved

Taking New Paths *Stories of Leaving Religion*

her desire to be free and wanted to take the boys. She had found a rental and lined up childcare. If it worked out during a period, she would want to get back together again and see what we could resolve or work out. Within our limited circumstances, I thought that this was the next step to whatever would evolve.

In about two months she was willing to try working things out, and so was I. We agreed that I should get my teaching degree and certification at San Francisco State; we were able to get student housing in a combined community college and SFSC and we were able to move on.

She wanted to and needed to work. I graduated mid-year upon completion of student teaching in the Chinese segregated public school and got a job in Marin County. We stayed together—with an underlying tension of irreconcilable differences—for twenty-one and a half years, until the boys were on their own. Or, as my eldest son said, "I didn't think you'd either have the guts to split."

So, with an Associate degree in 1949, a Bachelor's degree, a minor in Sociology, and academic work in speech and hearing therapy I began a teaching career in elementary education mid-year 1955. It led to part-time work teaching San Quentin inmates, grades one through community college, the educable mentally retarded, and junior high school.

I became involved in organized labor, beginning with the American Federation of Teachers, the House Un-American Activities Committee (HUAC) on behalf of a local union member, and the county central labor council.

Also during this period, I became deeply involved in Unitarian Universalism, which accommodated my spirituality and offered fellowship with generally like-minded folks.

My wife was offered a job as secretary to the president of the Star King Unitarian School of the Ministry in Berkeley, which provided me the opportunity to pursue a graduate degree at the University of California. As a result of my union and HUAC experience, I tried Boalt Law School for a term, but decided that I didn't want to be a lawyer.

I came to realize that I was in the midst of "a midlife crisis" when I applied to Starr King School of the Ministry and received admission counseling, best summarized by a Unitarian minister:

My Anthology of Influences

"At best, Chuck, we have one life." Recognizing that I couldn't be a universal man in the earlier sense of the term, I settled on a master's program in Adult Education, which provided more scope of interest and opportunity, including organizational training and development.

During my course of study, I worked as a research assistant to the University-wide Academic Senate Committee On Extension over three years. While earning my MA I also obtained state required certificates to teach and administer at any level requiring certification. I was offered a position as a program coordinator in University Extension for four years, developing and administrative programs and certificate programs for the general public.

Following that I was a contract consultant to the California State Training Department, designing and conducting specific programs for various state departments, which provided the opportunity to learn a good bit as to how state level government was operating during a time of unprecedented growth. I turned down a permanent position in preference to being a private consultant, which turned out to be a mistake in an economic downturn.

I accepted a three-year contract position with the National Iranian Oil Company (NIOC) to implement a series of month-long intensive seminars for Iranian middle managers in Abadan, Southern Iran. Employee participants ranged in education from "Twelfth Class" to graduate engineers, accountants, MBAs, and administrators. They represented all tribal areas of Persia /Iran and included Armenians and some religious sects permitted at that time by the Shah.

The oil industry was comprised of British, Dutch, French, and American oil companies, each with a separate organizational culture and style of operation. The participants reflected their employer's orientations and National Iranian Oil Company's and Iranian cultures, which often produced a bit of a circus in discussion and more frequently a lot of humor.

There was a lot of material to work with, and little obvious religious conflict. Working together ten hours a day (8:30 a.m. to 10: 00 p.m.), we pretty comfortably developed a temporal brotherhood despite my several cultural toe stubings.

I also became enamored of the calls to prayer as part of my spiritual acculturation. I perceived, again, and yet again, in my present and future cultural immersions, the universal human yearning

Taking New Paths *Stories of Leaving Religion*

for spiritual wonderment and exploration, despite the local cloaks of options presented by organized religion.

Recognizing this desire as a psychological component, I sought to share non-secular opportunities with respect to the management and interpersonal aspects of program delivery. Fortunately, in Iranian life there is great respect for their long tradition of poetry and literature, which some participants would often recall. It also helped in encouraging management to draw on the varied tribal values and presumed qualities of their workers.

Two of my first program participants were assigned to observe my "Introduction and Handover" to my successor as program director. We did so. At dinner they said that he should start his own presence alone in the evening's secession; we would retire to their room, read poetry, and drink vodka. I thought it a classic style of saying farewell, especially when they said, "This last one is for you, Chuck. Oh God, protect him who travels with a caravan of our hearts."

Back home in Menlo Park, California my wife, Marie, and I agreed to a divorce on the basis of irreconcilable differences.

I was hired to start up and manage a Training Division for Blue Cross of Northern California. Midway, during this fulfilling journey, I found my companion and constantly re-affirming Source, Sally.

A second marriage for both of us has provided a continuing journey of love, work, social and environmental commitments, gratitude, and compassion for over fifty years.

We lived and worked overseas in Libya, Sumatra, and Jakarta (Indonesia), over about ten years. Coming home we searched and found an abandoned forty-acre ranch near the traditional Klamath Tribes town of Chiloquin, Oregon.

There, and here in Klamath Falls, Oregon, we have been active in community development and support activities: Volunteer emergency services (fire and ambulance); creation and operation over twenty-five years of an environmental organization; organization of a community nonprofit and construction of a community center; passage of a county library service tax district; organizing a Friends

My Anthology of Influences

group for Crater Lake National Park; support for a local Community Health nonprofit; member of the county Public Safety Coordinating Committee. And continuing participation in the Unitarian Universalist Fellowship of Klamath County, sharing our spiritual journeys in liberal association.

    So, this has been a summary of the influences and choices that I have come to realize set my lifelong orientation of compassion, joy, and commitment to action and endurance in conflict with the traditional confines of cultural "colonialism," Humankind's "consensual reality" of the dominant culture.

    Many other experiences along the way have affirmed my "Humanistic Spirituality" as I have inquisitively "yondered," ever reaching not just wandering, through a life that has re-enforced my understanding of the vicissitudes of existentiality.

    Since all that we can prove, to the best of our knowledge, is that we have but one life, as do our companions here on earth, how can it be, then, that we denigrate our companions with such avoidance, subjugation, and consequent cruelty, robbing them of their time and lives?

    Since I began this effort, a primary question has developed. Despite the temptation for many, there is the inescapable dynamic that we humans will not experience either the local-regional-national nor World situation of going back to the way it was.

    Nor can we, the people, accurately project or determine how things will progress, or what degree of control we might have in shaping a refined series of consensual realities relative to the economic and societal orders that may form.

    Will it generally be a re-run of the dynamics in our history of The Silk Roads, or will a more democratically regulated series of governments emerge? I hope to see some of the events our collection of "sentient beings" may evolve.

Taking New Paths *Stories of Leaving Religion*

Afterword

ASSOCIATED WITH THIS BOOK is the Facebook page **Taking New Paths**, and the website **TakingNewPaths.org**. Although the primary purpose of these is to provide a place of community and support for individuals who are struggling with the potential confusion and loneliness of the deep and personal re-evaluation process, the Facebook page can provide a venue for discussion. It is hoped, and at this point trusted, that the discussions will be sincere, but not dogmatic or aggressively evangelistic. Still, the challenging of ideas of all kinds will be central, with this challenging being respectful to the people involved, while not expecting that all ideas merit respect.

In addition to the many supplemental recommended readings from the chapter authors, for those who wish to explore more of the research in this field, my recent dissertation is available at:

https://dougmatheson.medium.com/a-social-anthropology-dissertation-on-the-religionexiting-experience-4b41cb901403.

Using the bibliography can help further one's exploration.

Afterword

One general resource which may well be helpful to many in this process is Recovering from Religion; recoveringfromreligion.org. May all enjoy and grow.

You can contact Doug Matheson at
dougmatheson@takingnewpaths.org

Taking New Paths *Stories of Leaving Religion*

Acknowledgments

FIRST AND FOREMOST I wish to acknowledge the courage of each of the authors who shared thoughts, experiences, and feelings, which many people keep hidden in the deep recesses of their minds, too often in their subconsciouses. These contributors have knowingly and willingly taken risks, and re-experienced pain, all in order to help others who might be dealing with similar difficulties.

Further, it is likely that I can't even consciously identify all the individuals in my life who may have contributed to me being inclined to question, to try to understand complex things, and when I've seen an uncomfortable and even unwelcome insight developing, to have the honesty and courage to delve more deeply into it, and to bring it to the attention of others for their scrutiny. I'm grateful for those influences.

Among relatively recent influences on my continually evolving thinking and understanding of the human experience and circumstance, I single out: Pascal Boyer, Charles Lindholm, and E. O. Wilson. I thank them for the deep food-for-thought they've offered to me, and to all of us.

Acknowledgments

    I also want to thank Jo Johnston for her careful, thoughtful, and precise editing and proofreading, and her patience in dealing with me in some of the more subjective decisions to be made.

    Lastly, and personally, I have been the fortunate recipient of a few decades of excellent and broad-ranging reading recommendations from one of my brothers. I'm grateful for the broadened horizons.

Taking New Paths *Stories of Leaving Religion*

www.ingramcontent.com/pod-product-compliance
Lightning Source LLC
Chambersburg PA
CBHW050549160426
43199CB00015B/2586